BREAKING EVEN

BREAKING
EVEN

Financial Management
in
Human Service Organizations

ROGER A. LOHMANN

Temple University Press
Philadelphia

Temple University Press
© 1980 by Temple University. All rights reserved
Published 1980
Printed in the United States of America

Library of Congress Cataloging in Publication Data

Lohmann, Roger A   1942–
Breaking even.

Includes bibliographies and index.
1. Social service—Finance.   2. Social work
administration.   I. Title.
HV41.L63   658.1'5932   79-23692
ISBN 0-87722-166-9

CONTENTS

Figures   vii
Preface   ix

Part I. Basic Perspectives   **1**

1. Theory and Practice of Financial Management
   in Human Services   5
2. Accounting in the Human Services   22

Part II. Fund-raising   **51**

3. Grants in Human Service Financing   57
4. Fees and Client Charges   80
5. Fund-raising Campaigns from an Agency Perspective   98

Part III. Allocations   **115**

6. Budget-making in the Human Services   119
7. Budget Documentation   148
8. Programming and Budget Implementation   177

Part IV. Control and Planning Issues   **193**

9. Fiscal Control Issues   195
10. Financial Planning Issues   214
11. Evaluation Issues   237
12. Conclusion: Beyond Accountability to Management   257

Appendixes   **263**

A Programming Checklist   265
Notes   269
Glossary of Terms   285
Additional References   301
Index   309

FIGURES

1. Information Flow in an Accounting Information System
with Multiple Journals   29
2. Payroll Journal Page   30
3. Travel Journal Page   31
4. Accounts Receivable Entries   32
5. Posted Ledger Entry   33
6. Trial Balance   34
7. Audit Statement Favored by AICPA   35
8. Middle Paragraph of Qualified Opinion   36
9. A Typology of Fund-Raising   54
10. A Range Approach for Estimating Fee Revenues   92
11. An Indifference Curve: Day Care Fees per Week   93
12. Statement of Support, Revenues, and Expenses and
Changes in Fund Balances   121
13. Budget Format Elements in Sub-Fund Budgets   151
14. Line-Item Entries   153
15. Project Budget   153
16. Revenue/Expenditure Budget   154
17. Project Budget: Personnel   154
18. Line-Item/Program Matrix Budget   156
19. Departmental Expenditures   157

20. Sources of Revenue Table   158
21. Accounts Receivable Budget   159
22. Quarterly Administrative Cost Budget   160
23. Accounts Payable Budget   160
24. Capital Improvement Budget   161
25. Unit Costs Budget   163
26. Direct Labor Budget   165
27. Production Budget   166
28. Fund-Raising Budget   167
29. Supplies Budget   168
30. Costs of Debt Budget   169
31. Professional and Paraprofessional Services Budget   170
32. Old Year/New Year Table (Dollars)   171
33. Old Year/New Year Table (Standardized)   171
34. Affirmative Action Budget   172
35. Desk-Top Budget Reference   174
36. Salary Schedule   198
37. Time Line of the Work Week   223
38. Gantt Chart of the Length of Coffee Breaks   223
39. Progress in Staff Conferences   224
40. PERT Chart of Interview Process   225
41. Monthly Cash Flow Projection with Fixed Expenses   229
42. Quarterly Cash Flow Projection with Variable Revenues and Expenditures   229
43. Cash Disbursements   233
44. A System of Financial Ratios for Business   252
45. A System of Ratios for the Human Services   253

PREFACE

A number of years ago when the shape and form of this book first began to emerge, it was commonplace for professionals to attribute most of the problems of the world to "lack of communication." The true import of the loss of national unity resulting from Vietnam, the urban crisis, and the other disruptions of that period was not yet clear except to a few, and the apparent disorder and chaos of the time at first appeared to many to be the result of a simple failure to communicate. Since that time, the popularity of this idea as an all-purpose explanation has diminished. Unfortunately, "lack of communication" is still a very real problem in the human services, where some seem to speak the "dialect" of service and others the "dialect" of administration.

On the one hand, personnel selection and promotion practices mean that management personnel in most human service organizations do not come from a cadre of trained administrators comparable to the British "senior service," but are promoted "up through the ranks." Whatever additional implications this practice may have, its effect on developing the kinds of sophisticated managerial capacities found in business and government has been generally negative. Each new generation of managers must learn "on the job" and rediscover ways of doing things well known to their predecessors and to managers in other fields.

At the same time, the increasingly sophisticated contributions of business and public administration to financial management practices are often bypassed in the personal services, not only because of their patterns of selecting managers, but also because of their difficulties with adapting these techniques to the peculiarities of their needs.

The following "exchange" between a question once put to me by a friend and a statement I ran across at about the same time in a text on budgeting characterizes the nature of the problem.

Questions. "I am a professionally trained and licensed psychologist. What do I know about expenditure control and cash flow? My staff includes two M.S.W. social workers, a psychiatric nurse, four B.A.-level counselors and a dozen volunteers. We are supposed to run a mental health program delivering services to released mental patients. Among us, we don't know enough about accounting and budgeting to fill your hat, but we have nobody else to do all this stuff, so we have to do it. If we lose our grant, that's it. What can you tell us?"

And answers. "Budget inputs become the appropriation requests made by various agencies. The conversion process is the techniques and procedures used by the central staff review as it receives those requests, appraises them and decides which to include in the document. Feedback information passes between the central staff and the requesting agency in the process of making allocation decisions."

The very idea of communication is premised on a common terminology that is far too often missing in the contemporary dialogue between the "administrative sciences" and those schooled in the language and world-views of the helping professions. Thus, while public administration and urban planning, on the one hand, and psychology and social work, on the other, may trace their common origins to the urban crises of the Progressive Era, speakers of the contemporary dialects of utility theory and the various "needs" theories of helping professions have great trouble understanding one another.

To be sure, these differences cannot be dissolved away entirely by a common vocabulary. Presumably, professional therapists are what they are by choice, and they believe in what they do. The same may be assumed of planners, budget analysts, and executive directors with a background in administrative sciences. An idyllic harmony of viewpoints, however, is not a prerequisite to the successful operation of a modern human service organization. A modicum of mutual understanding, awareness, and sensitivity to the problems "on the other side of the hall" will usually suffice.

It is not necessary that "practice theories" of casework, crisis intervention, or counseling be integrated with "practice theories" of administrative science. A more satisfactory resolution is likely to be achieved simply by identifying the major problems of each perspective, how they relate to the broadest outlines of the other, and what, in detail, is known about the subject at hand. That is the approach taken here.

A minimum integration of financial management knowledge with theories of human service practice is sought. After all, the operation of a family service agency, or a children's home or senior citizens' center, is fundamentally different from the operation of an oil refinery, a bakery, or a filling station, and these differences may have as much to do with the outlook and training of the staff as with the nature of the work. (Bakeries and insurance agencies, it may be noted, also "work with people," albeit under different circumstances and for quite different reasons.)

Recognition of the uniqueness of human services, however, is not tantamount to the acceptance of the need to derive administrative science theories for the personal services from practice theories. Human development dynamics may be essential to a sophisticated professional understanding of the troubled juvenile or adult client. They may also have interesting applications to administrative behavior. However, there is a great danger of Kaplan's famous "law of the instrument" taking over: give a boy a hammer, he said, and he will find things that need pounding. Granted, all kinds of "rigidity," "identity problems," and "undiagnosed depression" may be found in administrative practice—at least by some observers. The critical insight, however, is that unless such behavior is "dysfunctional" in a major way such observations are simply irrelevant. Their irrelevance stems less from the insensitivity, immaturity, or intransigence of the administrative classes (many of whom have their professional training in helping skills, as noted above) than from the difficult, anxiety-laden, and, at times, morally compromising context of administrative issues. Under those conditions, a quicky diagnosis that the business manager shows "definite neurotic tendencies" (don't we all!) is less than helpful. It is, in the common parlance, "a cheap shot."

More important, there is little evidence to suggest that the resolution of the personal troubles of a human service administrator affects the pattern of resource distribution within an agency. Do emotionally stable administrators make better budgets? Who knows (or cares)?

The best we can expect in terms of knowledge integration in financial management occurs at a lower level. Two courses of action seem possible. On the one hand, we can deal with the subject matter using examples directly from the human services, so that the weary reader will not have to attempt to fathom on his own the relationship between a paper box factory and a planned parenthood clinic. On the other, we can attempt some slight softening of the Enlightenment rationalism of economics, business finance, and operations research, when these seem unnecessarily inconsistent with the behavioral approaches of contemporary human service practice. These inconsistencies are dealt with mainly in Chapter 1, although relevant examples are scattered throughout the book. Integration of this type is, it must be acknowledged, a marriage of convenience (or opportunity!) rather than a full union of kindred spirits.

Purpose of this book

One of the principal barriers to the integration of ends and means, however, is the diffuse nature of the bits and pieces of financial management knowledge. At present, an agency administrator would have to be a scholar conversant with aspects of at least a half-dozen social science disciplines in order to make effective use of all that is presently available. This book attempts an initial synthesis of knowledge. Fragments of the book were accumulated ten years ago, when I was an agency administrator faced with many of the problems presently included in this work, and work on the book has continued more or less uninterrupted since that time through years of graduate school and teaching.

In the past, the human service manager seeking assistance in financial management was forced to resort to one of three types of sources: (1) original monographs on the subject, which are often either theoretical (and dull) or unduly narrow in focus; (2) anthologies bringing together many different points of view but with little synthesis or integration; (3) technical materials from different fields that can be rendered useful only by considerable effort in interpretation (e.g., business administration and accounting). This book works toward a fourth possibility: a gathering together of the most important and relevant materials of the literature bearing on human service finance, interpreted from a single point of view, and presented in a straightforward style in a single volume.

To my knowledge, there has been no synthesis of this type in the past thirty years, since Street brought together the available information in a section of the *Handbook of Social Agency Administration* in 1947. All published treatments of the subject since that time have been fragmentary. Practice perspectives, however, have expanded considerably since that time. For Street, the subject was three-fold: budgets, executive-board relations, and fund drives. Major developments in third-party funding, program budgeting, cost analysis and accounting, program evaluation, and many additional topics have occurred since that time, but have not been systematically integrated into our perspectives.

This work is intended to serve the needs of a number of audiences at the same time. Students of human service administration in programs of social work, hospital administration, nursing home administration, business administration, social planning, public administration, and related fields currently must rely on journal literature and primary sources (which often prove wonderously elusive) to a grasp of financial management. Further, the lack of integration of these materials places the burden of meaningful synthesis entirely on the instructor. This book strives to relieve some of that burden, as well as standardize the treatment of these subjects in professional education programs in the human services.

The second major audience for whom the book is intended are those human service administrators who have "come up through the ranks" without any specialized training in administration. It is still true in many agencies that promotion and career ladders lead directly from service delivery jobs, for which workers have been trained, into managerial jobs, for which they have not. For these workers, the existing patterns of disseminating knowledge of the subjects treated here are almost wholly ineffectual.

Third, this work is seen—somewhat arrogantly perhaps—as useful to those highly skilled and trained administrators already familiar with a considerable number of the details of this book. I hope to provide these veterans with a single framework whose consistent point of view may suggest linkages and relationships of which they were previously unaware. I have also sought to bring into this book perspectives and techniques (primarily from business administration) that are not presently part of the standard vocabulary of most of the agency administrators I have known. Whether such techniques as cost accounting, break-even analysis, or cash-flow analysis will become standard features of human service administration in the future is still an open question. Perhaps this book will make it possible to approach this question more openly and realistically. In addition, the book may prove useful as a desk-top reference for those seeking to implement its detailed techniques.

The fourth audience to whom this work is directed are those researchers and scholars in various fields who have in the past few years created the technology that makes this book possible. Certainly, it is unlikely that these people will learn anything new about their own specialties here. However, the integration of all these diverse pieces may serve to give them a clearer view of the present "state of the art" and a basis for establishing priorities for future effort.

An overview of chapters

The chapters of this book are organized to present a sequence of discussions of the elements of a model of the financial management process in human service organizations, addressing both technical and substantive aspects of financial decision-making. The text is divided into five parts: two introductory chapters, three chapters on fund-raising, three chapters on budget-making, three chapters on control, planning, and evaluation issues, and a concluding chapter.

In the first chapter a number of important conceptual and historical issues are set forth, including the nature of financial management, the nature of human services, and the nature of the financial management process in human services. Attention is drawn to the significance of the "break-even point" where revenues and expenditures meet. Breaking even, it is suggested, can be a concept that unites planning, fund-raising, budget allocations, expenditure control, and evaluation into a single management process, which, in turn, links financial management to the goal-oriented activities of service delivery.

In Chapter 2 the fundamentals of accrual accounting are interpreted in a human services context. The recent development of audit standards for non-profit agencies by the American Institute of Certified Public Accountants is reviewed, together with the terminology of fund accounting and the basic features of non-profit financial statements. Near the end of the chapter, a number of important issues are raised, including whether accounting in human services can evolve beyond its orientation toward control into a more flexible management tool useful in financial planning. Also examined are the issues of whether accounting procedures consistent with the "program budgeting" discussed in other chapters are possible, and whether standard cost data for components of human services are possible. The question of the role and purpose of annual reports in human services is also explored briefly. The focus in this section is on the larger issue of whether accounting technology can truly be integrated into the management of human services.

Following a brief review of the development of the present public grant-in-aid economy in human services, the third chapter focuses upon the essential similarity of grantsmanship, budget negotiations, and fund-raising among large donors, including private foundations, despite the traditional view of them as separate activities. Essential similarities, such as the role of constituency support, and differences, such as the circumstances of presentations, are discussed.

The fourth chapter discusses a distinctly different form of fund-raising. Fees and charges to clients for service, it is suggested, are increasingly significant and difficult management problems in many agencies. In some human service settings, fee collections are the only form of revenue. In a far larger number of cases, however, fees from clients or third-party funding sources may be combined with block funding from public, voluntary, federated, or foundation sources. The principal types of fees—participation and membership fees, fixed service fees, sliding scale fees, and fair-share-of-cost allocations—are discussed, along with brief comments about purchase of service and insurance schemes. Management problems with fees, it is suggested, include control problems, such as recording and collecting fees, and planning problems, such as predicting revenues from fees and the problem of free goods.

The fifth chapter is devoted to yet another form of fund-raising, the organized solicitation campaign. The author suggests that this form of fund-raising, now widely used for a variety of good works projects throughout the world, is largely an invention of the American human service system. In most accounts knowledge of fund-raising campaigns is treated as a separate subject, unrelated to agency management. The link between the two is seldom made, despite the fact that the conduct of such campaigns by specific agencies is a common (although not universal) occurrence. The essence of traditional fund-raising knowledge may be represented by two topics: the social psychology of giving and the social organization of campaigns.

In Part III, three chapters are devoted to the various aspects of allocating revenues collected by the fund-raising techniques already discussed. Chapter 6 reviews the essential elements of the budget-making process. Four types of budget systems are discussed: public allocations; public distributions; voluntary, federated systems; and fee-based systems. The aspects of allocations decisions in each of these settings are explored. Budget systems are also classified by their approaches to decision-making. In the area of incremental and program budgeting principal attention is given to programming-planning-budgeting systems (PPBS) and zero-based budgeting systems (ZBBS).

Chapter 7 treats budget-making as an information processing problem, and presents a variety of formats for collecting and disseminating information. These formats are grouped into four categories related to the levels of allocations decisions: fund decisions, sub-fund decisions, supra-fund decisions (of particular significance in multi-funded agencies), and departmental decisions.

Most studies of human service budgeting treat it as a special occasion separate from the other events and activities in the daily life of the agency. Little explicit effort has been devoted to fitting budget-making into the larger agency picture. Chapter 8, however, attempts to identify the programming necessary to implement budget decisions in the period following successful adoption of a budget. Two distinct types of situations are discussed: programming for new ventures directed at the legal and organizing tasks necessary to initiate a new program (often called "program development"), and re-programming of on-going operations through the use of post-budget conferences, procedures and policies reviews, and other techniques. The assumption here is that once such tasks are attended to, administrative attention can be shifted to routine operations.

Part IV follows up a number of implications of the operational phase. Chapter 9 is concerned with control issues, Chapter 10 with financial planning, and Chapter 11 with evaluation issues.

The topics of Chapter 9 include the distribution and dissemination of reports and information control, purchasing and inventory control, cost-control policies and procedures, and supervision.

Chapter 10 focuses on such planning topics as feasibility studies, projections, project scheduling, capital budgeting, debt management, accounts payable management, accounts receivable management, cash flow management, and agency mergers.

Finally, Chapter 11 is concerned with evaluating agency programs and performance. In contrast to most approaches to this subject today, which regard evaluation as primarily a research concern, an effort is made here to link evaluation issues to management. A general program indicator, the problem-free interval, is examined from a management perspective. Also discussed are cost benefit analysis, cost analysis, and ratio analysis.

The brief final chapter attempts to pull together several threads from the preceding chapters.

Acknowledgments

As most authors do, I have accumulated a greater number of debts in writing this book than I can possibly acknowledge: The dozens of students who struggled with these ideas in my classes. The dozen or more secretaries who typed one or more versions of the manuscript. The anonymous readers and referees assigned to read and comment on the outline and various chapter drafts, and the editorial staff at Temple for many improvements on the manuscript.

There are also several people whose contributions must be acknowledged by name: Ken Badal, against whose administrative sense I checked many details; David Bartlett, Director of Temple University Press, who first gave me a sympathetic ear for a vague idea, and later offered many, many suggestions and supportive comments; Dianne Ames, my copy editor; and finally, my wife and colleague, Nancy, whose personal support and collegial advice were important to the completion of this project.

Part I

Basic Perspectives

The two chapters that together compose Part I of this book are devoted to the basic perspectives essential to an understanding of the financial management process in non-profit human service agencies. Because the initial suggestion that financial management in human service organizations is an integrated, inter-related set of activities is, itself, a somewhat novel one, attention is also devoted to the arguments in support of this view.

The underlying problem that has stalled theoretical and practical development on the subject of non-profit financing and has prevented our accurate assessment of many useful innovations is the set

1

of interrelated issues clustered around the quest for a substitute for the profit motive. In business and commercial settings, technical financial concerns and substantive goal-oriented concerns, along with certain standard assumptions about managerial and employee motivations, converge around the question of profits. At that point, the whole thing makes sense. However, the recognition that most human service organizations, by definition, are generally indifferent to questions of "profit" and "gain" except in the loosest and most metaphoric sense has never been successfully followed up by identification of a criterion that might serve a comparable purpose in the non-profit sector. If profit is not the underlying motive in non-profit organizations, then what are the purposes that can be ascribed to those activities? And, how can these purposes be systematically linked to financial decision-making? (Or, are financial and substantive concerns in non-profit settings wholly unrelated issues, as some have suggested?) If profit-seeking is not assumed to be the relevant motive of employees and management in non-profit organizations, then one is also pressed into seeking an alternative psychology to account for individual and group behavior as it relates to financial decisions. And there is always the need for an appropriate perspective that allows interpretation and understanding of financial technology while protecting the user from being overwhelmed by the seeming complexities and subtleties of the arguments involved.

The viewpoint of this book is that full systematic elaboration of these and related issues is a greater possibility in our time than it has ever been, owing to a number of interrelated historical, theoretical, and managerial developments, which are set forth in Chapter 1. Full-scale theoretical development, however, is not the purpose of this book. The treatment of issues presented here is more topical than theoretical— more an effort to explore the potentials for practice than an effort to extend management theory.

All of the concerns dealt with in this book come together in two closely woven strands, both of which are dealt with in Chapter 1. The diverse contents presented in the various chapters of this book are ordered by means of a model of the financial management process encompassing five basic periods or phases: fund-raising, allocation, control, planning, and evaluation. Furthermore, it is argued in Chapter 1 that some of the deficiencies in theory and practice related to the absence of a profit motive can be compensated for by presuming a "non-profit" motive—or desire on the part of management to break-even by finding and securing revenues to compensate for anticipated or planned costs.

The longest standing piece of financial management technology, or "know-how," consistent with this interpretation is the system of fund accounting, with its substitution of "fund balances" for "capital" and the like. Fund accounting is introduced briefly as it has emerged in the last decade through the efforts of such organizations as United Way of America, the National Social Welfare Assembly, and the American Institute of Certified Public Accountants. It is safe to assume, I believe, both that agency and program directors eventually develop a working knowledge of the financial statements emanating from their own fund accounting systems, and that many high school and college students acquire a detailed awareness of the operations of bookkeeping. For both groups, however, the underlying rationales, as well as the logical elegance of accounting, may not be clear. Chapter 2 seeks to introduce the topic of fund-accounting to complete beginners, provide a fairly complete overview of the subject for those whose knowledge may not have been systematically acquired, and introduce certain new topics (such as the AICPA Standards) to those whose perspectives may have been developed some time ago.

Little effort is made in this section, or throughout the book, to self-consciously proclaim the innovativeness or originality of these perspectives. It is my firm conviction that we are on the brink of a genuine managerial revolution in respect to the handling of non-profit financial management. However, it will be a revolution securely grounded in the solid, continuous accumulation of planning, management, and research methodologies already developed during recent decades. Thus, the intent here is more to survey the present state of the art than to suggest any radical new directions. It can be said that, in the area of non-profit financial management, we are on the right track, and I hope the contents of this work will support the view that we are also well down the line, and moving along nicely.

CHAPTER 1

THEORY AND PRACTICE
OF
FINANCIAL MANAGEMENT
IN HUMAN SERVICES

What is financial management?

The term "financial management" means different things to different people and in different settings. In the family, financial management is ordinarily most concerned with making the best uses of family income, a task principally involving planning and decision-making. In commercial organizations financial management is often most concerned with one aspect of the capitalization process—the funding of debt. In the public sector, financial management is seldom a distinct entity. It is divided instead into the separate tasks of revenue generation (tax collection), allocation (public budgeting), and expenditure.

There is a role for financial management in the contemporary human service organization as well. This book examines the nature of that role and its relationship to professional service delivery, which is the principal purpose of human service agencies and programs. Because of the multi-dimensional character of the contemporary human service organization, financial planning, fund-raising, the handling of debt, budget-making, expenditure control procedures, and dozens of other related topics are matters of daily concern to administrators.

As often as not, however, the world of numbers and dollars, of work-sheets and financial statements is isolated from the world of human service delivery. Most human service organizations operate as though they had two completely independent sets of goals and accountability patterns: one concerned primarily with the substantive goals of service, clients and professional practice, and the other devoted exclusively to money. To the casual observer this dichotomization of agencies at first glance may appear to be entirely natural. To those familiar with the line-staff division of labor made famous in classic management literature, it may appear as an artificial division of labor into "program" and "support" staff.[1]

Whatever the reason, however, the distinction is basic to human services. The lack of a common objective comparable to that provided by profit in business too often means that managers as well as staff members see little or no direct relationship between financial practices and the central thrusts of agency programs. Until quite recently professional organizations and educational practices did little to discourage this view.

It is possible, indeed essential, to take a quite different approach to the financial aspects of human services. Financial management is not necessarily concerned with a separate set of ends and management processes. It is, rather, a unique language for talking about and analyzing the relationship between ends and means, and for determining the best means of goal attainment, once the ends of service have been established. Properly understood, for example, "efficiency" and "productivity" are not simply esoteric concepts having no bearing on human services. They are, instead, practical ways of stating the relationships between any given end (including the goals of service programs, such as personal adjustments of clients or the provision of independent living situations) and the "best" means to that end. For example, the social worker who adjusts his schedule to make better use of his time or to make himself more available to his clients is engaged in an effort to improve productivity, whether or not that term is used.

Standard financial considerations of efficiency, effectiveness, productivity, and cost are seldom the only, or even the primary, considerations in human service management. Nor should they be. In fact, in many agencies it is at least as likely that financial considerations will be left out entirely as it is that they will overwhelm other considerations.

This book is not written primarily for agencies with highly skilled, specialized financial managers, nor for professionals with extensive training and experience in this area. Rather, it is intended principally for application to the distinctive problems of medium-sized and small agencies. Similarly, it is not intended for public, governmental, or private for-profit agencies. It is directed at the private non-profit (or if you prefer clumsy legalisms, not-for-profit) corporation, and the distinctive problems faced in managing the financial resources of such entities. Furthermore, the book is not intended for human service settings like hospitals or nursing homes, where specialized management practices have already been devised and widely disseminated. What is left over after all these caveats have been attached is a conceptually vague, somewhat disorderly aggregate of non-profit human services that share a number of common management problems, and these the book addresses.[2]

In the human services, financial management has generally to do with the control and planned use of money and other scarce resources in a manner designed to further organizational goals, and be consistent with the law, professional ethics, and community standards. Viewed as a system of ends, human service finance is a narrow, technical, and subsidiary matter concerned with budgets, grant applications, payrolls, tax forms, and journal entries. At the same time, as a system of means, financial management has broad implications for the primary work of human service organizations.

The challenge of financial management in the human services is not merely to keep the various technical processes from interfering with service delivery. The true challenge is for budgets, cost analyses, and the other paraphernalia of finance to become working instruments for furthering agency purposes. Until quite recently such an objective would have been little more than a pipe dream. However, the slow, steady accumulation of techniques and practical experience in the distinctive problems of non-profit human services makes this an attainable objective at present, and one that will be increasingly so in the near future.

This book is an effort to collect, within a single set of covers, a broad range of materials related to the question of financial management in human service agencies. It also attempts to take the initial steps toward a more coherent, far-reaching management theory through the interpretation of the literature in terms of a consistent framework appropriate to a managerial point of view.

There are three basic assumptions involved:

1. Financial management is one of the principal constituents of the management process in human service organizations. The problems of obtaining, allocating, and controlling scarce re-

sources are the *sine qua non* of human service administration—
the crucible in which the success or failure of management is
tested. While numerous published accounts and private opinions in the field attribute much importance to a single aspect of
financial management—budget-making—it is also important
to note the essential roles of record-keeping, reporting, analysis, planning, and fund-raising. In other words, individual
aspects of the financial process of social agencies are less important, in the last analysis, than the overall process.

2. Financial management comprises a set of concerns distinguishable from other managerial issues, such as personnel
questions, community relations, and long-range planning.
Financial management also encompasses a distinct set of
skill and knowledge areas, including accounting, decision-
making, and economic analysis, without being entirely subor-
dinated to any of them. Consequently, it is a serious mistake to
assume that the financial problems of the contemporary
human service agency can be automatically resolved by hiring
technical specialists in the skill areas, and leaving them to the
practice of their diverse crafts. Instead, one should expect a
continuing role for the general manager, who is dependent on
experts to some degree, but can also interpret their work.

3. Finally, financial management is considered from an "action"
frame of reference. That is, less attention is devoted to the
environmental context and structural arrangements of financial
processes, and more attention is given to the daily decisions
and dilemmas faced by managers. The central model for the
book is an ideal-typical ordering of the sequence of critical
decisions faced in a non-profit human service agency.

What are the human services?

Much has been written, and even more spoken, on the question of
what to call the principal activities of non-profit agencies. One of
the more recent labels for this aggregate of services is the term "human
services," but like such predecessors as "social services" it suffers
from the lack of a widely publicized and accepted definition. The
earliest drafts of this volume used the term "personal services," in
keeping with a fairly explicit concept offered by Kahn.[3] However, one
reader of a draft chapter objected, noting that a standard industrial
classification he consulted included valeting, grooming, and tonsorial

services under "personal services"! Not wishing to contribute further to the confusion, I have dusted off "human services" and used it throughout. Even so, I include Kahn's definition of personal services, since it serves to define the context of these services. The services we are most concerned with are those which: (1) contribute to the socialization and personal development of persons; (2) provide social care for the aged, handicapped, mentally ill, developmentally disabled and others incapable of full personal autonomy; (3) provide counseling and guidance to persons and families in crisis situations; (4) support the self-help efforts of persons and the mutual aid activities of kinship, friendship, and other social networks; (5) disseminate information about access or entitlement to any of the above services; and (6) carry out the planning, organizing, financing, and evaluating of these services.[4]

What are agencies?

It is also necessary to introduce a note on a topic that may appear to most readers to be self-evident. One of the meanings of the term "agency," and its correlate, "agent," has to do with acting in the interest of, or for, someone else. This connotation is not unrelated to human service agencies, since these are typically organizations of persons who seek to provide service to clients, advocate for the rights and interests of clients or the community, and in other ways assume responsibilities in the first sense above.

Agencies engaged in the delivery of human services come in all sizes, shapes, and complexions: public bureaucracies, private bureaucracies, private profit-making companies, group practices, partnerships, solo practices, and non-profit corporations. While relevant to the financial situation of all these service agencies, this book is particularly concerned with non-profit corporations.

Although statutes governing incorporation vary from state to state, there are certain universal characteristics to the non-profit agency:

1. Non-profit corporations are created (or chartered) by a group of incorporators to serve some facet of the common good.
2. Non-profit corporations are legally under the control of a board of directors whose members are empowered to act collectively on behalf of the corporation.
3. Non-profit corporations are "non-profit" because they are explicitly forbidden by law to distribute their assets to board members and shareholders as profits, capital gains, or dividends.

4. Non-profit service corporations are restricted by the Internal Revenue Service and many state statutes from participation in partisan political activities.
5. Non-profit corporations are expected to hold annual meetings to elect board members and corporation officers and to show they are publicly accountable for their actions.
6. Non-profit corporations are specifically empowered to hire employees to conduct their business and engage in fund-raising to support their service activities.

Despite the amazing growth of the non-profit service agency in the past few decades, relatively little additional information is available.[5] This book is, in part, an effort to fill some of the void and to stimulate more work on the subject.

The financial management process

In the on-going non-profit human service agency the various activities linked to the matching of revenues and expenditures can be divided into several categories on the basis of the purposes they serve. Five principal types of activities can be identified. *Financial planning* is concerned with determining the financial implications of program planning, examining expected income under various contingencies, and matching the expectations of cost and income. *Fund-raising* refers to the financial management process of identifying, soliciting, and obtaining income, whether through contributory campaigns, fund drives, grantsmanship, fee collections, or other means. *Allocation* is a general term used for decision-making, dividing available resources, and assigning them to various purposes. In many human service agencies, the planning, fund-raising, and allocation activities converge in the budgetary process. Financial management, however, continues after funds have been secured. Concern for adequate *expenditure control* through employee supervision, accounting records, and other management processes is an integral aspect of management in every human service agency. Finally, recent enthusiasm for "accountability" has accentuated what has always been a major element of financial management. *Evaluation* is, in this context, the retrospective assessment of the worthwhileness of activities. It is also the antecedent of planning, as the cycle begins anew.

There is considerable overlapping and interplay among the various elements in the financial management process, and each has its own linkages to the substantive concerns of service delivery. However, it is most useful to conceive of the entire financial management process of an agency roughly in terms of the cycle presented above: planning leads to fund-raising, which leads to budget-making, which leads to expenditure control, which leads to evaluation.

Breaking even

It should not be difficult for most readers with experience in human service settings to identify with several of the elements of the financial management process. It may be somewhat more difficult for readers to perceive the integration that links the various elements, or that separates them as a group from other aspects of management. In attempting to identify this common theme we are ultimately raising a question of theoretical significance: are the topics of financial management casually tossed together because they all have some identification with money, or do they have some semblance of conceptual unity?

Recent work suggests that unity can be found. One way to approach this integration is to use the criterion of "breaking even" as the central fiscal objective of human service finance, as well as the key to the linkage between the financial management process and the goals, objectives, and operations of service delivery. Breaking even is simply the balancing of variable revenues with equally variable expenditures to avoid either a major deficit or a surplus. In the remainder of this chapter we shall examine this concept in light of current practical developments and recurrent theoretical concerns.

The improving state of the art

A highly popular device for presenting material on the status of practical skills in many fields has been the "state of the art" report. Such reports, in general, attempt to ascertain the present level of technical capability as well as suggest new directions for work in the immediate future. This format will be followed here.

One need not venture too far into the subject before it becomes clear that it is only quite recently that the financial practices of non-profit entities have come to be regarded as aspects of a single art. For one thing, there is one distinguishable organizational form, rather than many. Nor has it always been clear that consistent financial practices exist in human service agencies. In the past there were, in fact, enormous variations in terms, practices, and just about everything else. Since the 1960s, however, it has become increasingly possible to speak in general terms about uniform national practices and potentials with the expectation that in most instances the similarities will outweigh the differences.

Inevitably, there are still great variations in the emerging language of non-profit finance, and these will be reflected both directly and indirectly in what follows here. While appearing abstruse to some, they will appear impossibly naive and simplistic to others. Similarly, the practices suggested may seem old hat to some readers, while others may find them impossibly demanding of skill, time, and energy. While the range and diversity of practices are still large, they are considerably narrower in many respects than they were previously. And counterbalanced against the inevitable variations is the growing significance of a uniform perspective—a financial management perspective—which this work seeks to identify and document.

Before we begin the task, a few more words must be said about this developing perspective. Why, after a century of voluntary human service activity, have many of the characteristic problems suddenly become manageable? What beneficial changes accompany the financial management perspective? First of all, the emergence of this perspective has by no means been sudden. Rather, like the techniques of financing themselves, it has been built up bit-by-bit over several decades. A spate of recent developments, however, appears to have accelerated our knowledge and sophistication.

Of great importance has been the growth of public expenditures for human services since World War II. Even recent cutbacks in federal funding have not yet returned the human services to their pre-war levels, nor even come close. With the increased scale of funding have come increased experimentation, innovation, ad hoc problem-solving, and, as a result, the accumulation of new ideas and practices. For example, a great many human service agencies owe their present accounting capabilities entirely to the federally imposed requirements of grant funding.

A second factor in the growth of financial management technology in the human services has been the increased integration of national service delivery systems. Such "vertical" linkages, superimposed upon traditional "horizontal" community linkages, have created vast information networks along which information about "bright ideas" and innovations has passed widely and quickly.

An innovation today in Omaha may be duplicated in Seattle or Montpelier within the year!

Yet another implication of the profound changes being wrought by financial management in the human services has been the development of new management knowledge and skills. Foremost among these have been the so-called "grantsmanship" skills. One gets the distinct impression from some discussions on the subject that the ideal grantsman must be a blend of guru, confidence man, and ward heeler! For the non-profit agency, however, the effective grantsman appears to be an extension of the traditional voluntary fund-raiser and the public budget-officer into the bureaucratic environment of categorical discretionary grants. Many other new skills in the planning, control, and evaluation of agency finances are also becoming more widely practiced.

The increasingly clear delineation of program management and supervisory roles within human service agencies is yet another development with implications for our growing collective capabilities in financial management. As in the past, when management personnel are largely promoted up from the ranks rather than being specifically trained for the task, it is not at all surprising that little cumulative knowledge is built up. Under such conditions, each generation of administrators must learn for itself—by trial and error—the necessary knowledge and skills. Furthermore, operations are becoming increasingly complex because agencies are becoming "multi-functional" and multi-funded. This increases the necessity for management skilled in integrating diverse activities, and also, incidentally, expands the need for generalized, as opposed to program-specific, knowledge of financial practices.

Also important in an agency's changing financial perspective has been the proliferation of new services, new client populations, and new service delivery strategies, and other innovations, real or imagined. The introduction of such novelties into the human services frequently has proven to be an occasion for rethinking traditional assumptions, and financial management has been among the beneficiaries of such rethinking. To take but a single example, unit-cost measurement techniques worked out in the emergent day-care area could have vast implications over the long run, for cost measurement in other areas.[6] Cost-measurement strategies appear to be partly a direct outgrowth of the allocational problems faced by the fledgling Office of Economic Opportunity in financing the highly popular Head Start programs.

A trend that has been noted time and again during the 1970s is the growing concern with "accountability," a term that seems intended to cover everything from program effectiveness to the assignment of managerial responsibility, the provision of opportunities for client "feedback," and a wealth of related issues. Equally significant has been the proliferation of interest in management science techniques among human service administrators and educators. Once concerned only with the human relations aspects of the management task, these professionals have become increasingly aware of and interested in PPBS, PERT, MBO, and other weapons in the management science armamentarium.

One trend that has had enormous impact upon the field but a minimal one on traditional financial concerns is the growth of interest in consumer, client, and citizen participation. When such participatory claims are extended into the financial arena, it is to be expected that the financial statements and reporting practices of non-profit agencies will take on new and added significance.

Furthermore, the federally inspired proliferation of human service planning systems in aging, health and mental health, criminal justice, and other fields has accentuated the need for financial planning in the agency context. Such planning systems have, in many cases, systematized the competition for scarce public funding, thereby creating formidable incentives for increasing agency management and planning competency.

There are several other trends that may have significant impact on the future design of the financial management of human services, even though their impact to the present has been minimal. One of these is the general movement in the direction of the automatic data processing (ADP) of information and records. A second is the general lack of movement in the direction of cost accounting. The third is the underdevelopment of financial management training in comparison with training in other management topics in human service professional education programs in social work, nursing, public administration, and other areas.

Finally, it would be difficult to overestimate the theoretical significance of behaviorally oriented studies of human service organizations to financial management theory.[7] Once it was widely believed that the altruism thought to be characteristic of human services and the self-interest thought to be characteristic of economic man were polar opposites of human conduct. Consequently, no satisfactory substitute for the business world's profit motive—and the standard of authority and accountability that pertain to it—was thought to be available to the human services and other public and non-profit enterprises. For several decades, this lacuna has been a major stumbling block, in both a practical and theoretical sense for non-profit human services.

Practical and theoretical problems

A number of the practical problems faced by agency administrators can be traced directly to the absence of an analog to the profit motive. In many agencies a gap exists between purely "fiscal" issues and the "substantive" issues of program and purpose. The gap has also created major problems in measuring and defining the results or "products" of service activities, as well as in establishing criteria for assessing employee performance.

One authority on the question has noted:

> In a large business firm, authority to make decisions can be safely delegated on a broad scale to subordinate officials more or less to the degree that their performance can be appraised in terms of its effect on the goal of the firm, which is primarily profit. But in a large organization that does not sell its output and does not have to compete in the capital market for equity funds, extensive delegation of authority is more hazardous, since there is no single measure resembling profits by which performance can be appraised.[8]

While it is certainly true that non-profit corporations, by definition, are deprived of the theoretical and practical advantages of the profit motive, it is also true that profit alone is not the essence of the issue. Profit, as used in business finance, is a central concept and measurement tool within a vast network of clearly formulated and interdependent definitions, concepts, and measurement techniques. The challenge for the human services, by comparison, is not simply to find our "profit motive" and adopt what has already been formulated. That has been tried many times without notable success. Rather, the task is to build up a similar edifice of theory and technique. Each reader must judge the matter for himself, of course, but for the author, the materials reported in the following chapters make a convincing case that we have already come a long way in this direction.

Two propositions, examined in the remainder of this chapter, appear to the author to have considerable power to bring together and unite these diverse materials. They are measurement multi-dimensionality and the "break-even motive."

Multi-dimensionality

The concepts of profit, gain, and achievement are so engrained in our culture that most of us seldom give much thought to them, preferring to accept them as natural phenomena. This has worked to the detriment of the set of issues inherent in human services financial questions, in which "the profit motive" has been dealt with mostly as a cliché. In the contemporary world of "the corporation man," private bureaucracy, insurance pension benefits, personnel departments, leisure time, and service industries, it is simplistic nonsense to suggest that every employee in the private sector is rationally governed by the motive and calculus of profit, while public and non-profit decision-makers, lacking a similar standard, wander aimlessly and in an irrational wilderness. Such nonsense makes for impassioned political speeches, but bears little resemblance to reality. Yet, in human service finance, we have still to locate all the pieces of the rational edifice we need.

Solution to part of the problem can be found in a recognition of the role of money measurement in business. First, it cannot truly be said that money is the sole measure, even in business. It is far more accurate to see it as the central measure—related in certain standardized ways to such measures as time, physical units of input (tons of coal and steel), and units of output. It is from the theoretical explicitness of these relationships and their practical acceptance by business people that the usefulness of money measurement is derived. Also important is the "anchoring" that is brought to the whole scheme of things by the fact that money measurement has a "zero point." Indeed, in well-managed corporations the integration of various measurement dimensions with money measurement is so well understood that virtually all major aspects of planning and goal setting, achievement and accomplishment, can be compared and considered in light of one another, and ultimately on the universal scale of dollars. It is imperative that those who are inclined to follow this example be very clear about the fact that this edifice of ratios, tests, procedures, and practices is not the inevitable consequence of the profit motive but a methodically created system of interdependent and experience-tested techniques.

This task is complicated by the nature of service activity. Questions like what is and is not a service, when services start and end, and whether all similar services are really similar have proven to be highly complex and troublesome. However, some progress has been made along these lines, and there is reason for optimism. Recent advances in the measurement of attitudes, social activity, and similar matters have been widely applied to evaluation research problems bearing on the questions of service output and outcome.[9] Relatively little effort has been expended in the human services, however, to link these measures to money and other financial measurement scales.

At the same time, the organizational studies mentioned above make it increasingly apparent that the absence of profit cannot be entirely equated with the absence of goal-oriented, rational behavior. Rational behavior, however, often appears to follow two quite distinct "tracks" in human service settings. On the one hand, there are the purely financial goals of locating and expending funds, and on the other, the purely substantive goals of service. Expenditures in many non-profit agencies may rise and fall, for example, without noticeable effect upon the output of services produced or delivered.

For some limited purposes, such as calculating, planning, or predicting revenue and expenditure patterns, there is an analog to the profit motive: the break-even motive. Furthermore, in some limited senses, the goal of breaking even may serve part of the motivational role attributed to the profit motive. To understand these possibilities, we must examine more carefully the relation between problems, goals, revenues and expenditures. We can identify at least the major scenarios in the funding of agencies.

Three general problems

Type A. The most fundamental situation, and the historical starting point for many human services, is the situation in which a set of problems or needs is identified and a decision is made to pursue a collective solution. Under such conditions, some form of fund-raising activity is likely to be a natural consequence of "getting organized." Standard practice in this case would involve "costing out" the solution and locating adequate funding (or, more likely, scaling down the original estimate to match available funds).

Type B. In an organized on-going human service venture the need for funding to continue operations may be a periodic (annual) or continuous concern. In either case one of the fatal weaknesses of the non-profit form of financing is that, unlike the sales function in business, there is no way to scale a continuous source of income to fluctuations in the level of activity. Fee collections come closest to meeting this weakness, but many forms of human service (public welfare services, public health, and mental health education) have inconsistent fee formats, and even agencies that depend on fees seldom generate all their income from them. In this situation, as in "Type A," the most basic financial management problem is matching income with anticipated activity (and expenditure). The agency must deal with the problem of demonstrated performance. In such cases, concern for how well the agency used the resources at its command becomes central.

Type C. Not infrequently, the problem-solution equation is stood on its head: agencies may recognize a problem, and have adequate funding, but have little idea of what to do. Creating a programmatic solution within the terms of the available funding is the immediate management problem. The issue, then, is one of what to do with the money. "Type A" and "Type B" are simply variants on standard, recognizable business situations. In the first, the entrepreneur defines a potential market and takes steps to capture it, in a manner analogous to the service agency (although for wholly different reasons). In the second, the principal distinction between the on-going agency and the on-going business is to be found in the profit margin. To succeed, the business must generate sales income in excess of expenses, but the non-profit agency need only break even. With "Type C," however, one encounters phenomena seldom, if ever, faced in business. Under these topsy-turvy circumstances, the human service agency will be under considerable pressure to spend its funds—even on projects of dubious worth—for failure to do so can be interpreted as evidence of a callous disregard for those suffering from the problem, or the agency may be accused of "bureaucratic rigidity," "lack of imagination," or worse.

The three situations, when taken together, illustrate the double-edged quality of the fundamental financial management problem. There is, ordinarily, the expectation that agencies will solicit only as much money as they need. Requesting too little will necessitate, at some point, layoffs of staff, cutbacks in services, and other undesirable results. However, requesting too much can also leave the agency open to criticism. While surplus left over after expenditures constitutes profit and is a hallmark of success in business, with the size of the surplus measuring the degree of successful operation, it has quite the opposite effect in the human services. Surpluses are not profit, they are just unused resources. Far from being signs of success, they are often viewed as signs of failure, with the size of the surplus directly related to the degree of mismanagement. While slight surpluses (say a fraction of a percent of total income) may be negligible, a surplus of 50–70 percent of total revenues is usually cause for concern, whether or not any direct sanctions result.

The point here is simple: the matching of revenues and expenditures is the central financial management process in human service ventures, to which all other financial operations can be directly related. And this matching process is necessarily a two-directional one. In other words, the expectation is neither that human service agencies will make profits (even slight ones), nor that they will engage in deficit spending. The assumption is that agencies will "break even" (income matching expenditures) or come quite close to it. Creating the circumstances that enable the agency to break even is the principal financial obligation of the agency manager.

Theoretically, this concept of breaking even also informs each of the phases of the financial management process, creating in skeletal form a network of linkages between the technical, financial aspects and the goal-oriented, substantive aspects of service.

From this standpoint, the most critical aspect of the agency financial planning process is the determination of the projected costs of planned activities. This task ordinarily involves assigning likely expenditure outlays to various cost elements. One is hard-pressed to discover or develop "cost principles" appropriate to human service settings in the absence of detailed information about the particular service in question. In this case, substantive knowledge of client needs and service activities goes hand in hand with technical skill in pricing cost elements and projecting changes. Only when both the technical skill and the substantive knowledge are present is there a real likelihood of success in planning. Furthermore, one can seldom engage in such analysis without raising the companion issue of finding sources of income to offset these new costs.

Likewise, fund-raising is usually interpreted as an effort to achieve the largest feasible addition to agency assets in return for the smallest outlay. Funds are not raised on general principle or for the mere sake of fund-raising itself, but for specific "causes"—projects, programs, or activities. One seeks to wipe out certain diseases, build a new wing for the children's hospital, start a day care center, and so forth. From the outset, consequently, there is a matching of fiscal and program objectives in most human service settings, even though the accounting, reporting, and control technologies that exploit this relationship are not necessarily well developed. However fund-raising approaches the problem, success is ordinarily measured in a break-even manner, either in direct comparison with needed expenditures or against a set campaign goal.

The linkages between fiscal and program concerns have probably been the most completely developed at the level of budget-making. The use of program and project budgets in federal and state categorical grants and in many federated campaign allocation schemes has had one overarching positive result: although the level of sophistication in practice often falls short of the potentials discussed in the budget literature, most of the funding disbursed within the human services system today is handled through what might be termed "program budgeting" approaches. That is, funding decisions are made on the basis of proposals for program packages and certain assumptions specified in a budget statement of the expected costs of those proposals. The fact that program budgeting in this sense is not simultaneously used as a fiscal control or accounting device, and in other ways falls short of the ideal, should not be allowed to obscure the essential insight: we have come a very long way in the direction of distributing funds by purposeful planning, and the basic financial frameworks which result are quite sound. What is wrong, in most instances, is not the design of our decision systems, but the choices that we make (or, as frequently, do not make). The essence of the budget problem, in other words, is moral and political, not structural.

Just as budget-making proves to be the area of greatest integration of the fiscal and the substantive, so it is also reasonably clear that these linkages are weakest in the area of fiscal control of expenditure. This is true not only in human services, but also in virtually all non-profit settings (including public or governmental ones). In business settings, departmentalization, the assignment of cost-accounting centers, and a variety of other interrelated devices insure not only the minimal fiscal control afforded by adequate accounting, but a measure of "program control" as well. When sales are off, or inventory must be reduced, or a certain department is contributing a disproportionate share to the final cost of items sold, such integration allows reasonably exact measurement of the problem in dollar terms. Although a number of techniques and concepts appropriate to increasing the level of fiscal control in human service agencies are discussed throughout this work, control continues to be a major problem.

To the extent that gains of the type outlined above are made in the fiscal control of human services through the linking of fiscal and substantive goal systems, similar results are to be expected with respect to questions of accountability. In the absence of these linkages, talking about efficiency, effectiveness, and productivity in the human services setting is purely metaphorical. As in the case of control, however, to the extent that fiscal and substantive goal systems are linked in decisions through the budgetary process, and revenue-inputs and expenditure-outputs are linked with service-outputs through fiscal controls, the existing technology for the assessment of efficient production is being brought to bear on human service problems. While one should not over-stress the level of accomplishment to date, neither is it appropriate to engage in breast-beating, on the assumption that nothing has or can be done.

Conclusion

The basic themes to be laid out in the following chapters should now be clear; what follows is organized following the financial management process outlined so far. The chapters on fund-raising are presented first, followed by the chapters on budget-making. Because of its com-plexity, the chapter on planning is set far back in the book, between the discussions of control and evaluation. The primary emphasis of the discussions in each case is on reviewing what is currently available and suggesting how this may be understood and applied in the case of human service organizations. Running throughout, however, is a concern with the broader theoretical issues raised in this chapter: discovery of the means of integrated measurement of financial and sub-stantive concerns, and utilization of breaking even as the starting point of financial management.

CHAPTER 2

ACCOUNTING
IN
THE HUMAN SERVICES

Stereotypes and cosmopolitanism

Those who are, or seek to be, managers of human service agencies have a fundamental need to understand the proper role and scope of modern accounting. As a body of knowledge, accounting provides the inner logic of all contemporary efforts at "accountability" for resources used in human service activities. It is also directly involved, as a profession, in management decision-making in many of the larger human service operations today, and, through the performance of periodic audits of agency and program financial records, has an indirect impact upon the parameters of service delivery, which most human service practitioners are only vaguely aware of.

If one were to place much faith in the stereotypes of accountants and social workers, it would not be at all difficult to foresee difficulties. In the conventional wisdom, the accountant is male, tense, macho, task-oriented, pale and drawn, while the social worker is female (or at least effeminate!), intense, process-oriented, and engaging but not too clearly focussed. Surely the two types would totally avoid one another, were it not for their mutual need in the agency context. This is because few, if any, social workers receive enough training in accounting to handle even routine financial reporting tasks, while accountants think of the average social agency as a "piece of cake."

Fortunately, the stereotypes of accountants and social workers are no more accurate than other occupational stereotypes. Well-trained accountants are, and will continue to be, valuable members of the "management team" in contemporary human services—whether as members of the staff, outside consultants, or auditors hired to examine agency records.

In this chapter some of the most fundamental concepts of contemporary accounting theory and practice will be laid out as they relate to human service concerns. It should be noted at the outset that the presentation here is topical. Accountants present the same materials within a highly rigorous, logico-deductive theoretical format. Such an approach is principally useful to those concerned with the legitimacy of accounting, or with the detailed examination of esoteric arguments and issues. Such matters are beyond our concern. Accounting is assumed to be both necessary and highly useful in the context of managing human services. (Those who cannot accept this premise will have to seek elsewhere for enlightenment!) Meanwhile, this approach will enable us to outline the basics of accounting.

This chapter approaches accounting from a management perspective, rather than an accounting one. That is, accounting is seen as a technical resource useful at various points in the management process in human service agencies.

Management by exception

Consistent with this approach is what may well be the single most useful "management principle" for human service administrators who deal with the maintenance and preparation of agency financial records (that is, the accounting task): this is the principle of "management by exception." Stated briefly, it holds that most financial practices should be routinized into rules and procedures, and that administrators should only have to become directly involved in financial record-keeping when exceptions to these rules and procedures arise. Exceptions include the occasions when new employees must be hired and trained for bookkeeping or accounting tasks; when questionable transac- are discovered, or unintelligible reports are presented; or when breaches of agency policy are observed or suspected. Ideally, the accounting system should yield data on the performance and current position of the agency and its programs whenever such data is needed, in the form needed, with a maxium of accuracy and a minimum of fuss and bother for the management. Furthermore, such data should have been collected in as nondisruptive a manner as possible. *Yes, indeed. That is how it should be.*

In truth, few human service agencies today are blessed with such an ideal accounting system, and it is by no means clear that agencies desiring a system to meet such specifications could obtain it. For one thing, the "technology" of accounting as it has developed for non-profit and service enterprises lags behind developments in business (especially manufacturing, where cost-accounting techniques are most advanced), and there are real limits on the kind of data that can be produced (especially data relating expenditures to performance criteria). Nevertheless, this chapter presents a basic overview of accounting concepts as they relate to the human services. For those interested, but completely unfamiliar with the subject, the chapter may serve as a stimulus to more reading. (See the Additional Readings at the back of the book for this—and each—chapter.)

Accounting defined

Because it is an occupation with official professional spokesmen, as well as a discipline and technology, accounting has a fully authoritative and widely accepted definition, set forth by the American Institute of Certified Public Accountants: "Accounting is the art of recording, classifying, and summarizing in a significant manner and in terms of money, transactions, and events which are, in part at least, of a financial character and interpreting the results thereof."[1]

The preparation of accurate, standardized financial statements is the key link between accounting and the human services. Accounting may be viewed as the know-how (principles and practices) underlying the financial record-keeping system that currently is the only complete and integrated information system available in most human service agencies.

Management uses of accountancy

Generally, there are three levels of use for the outputs or products of the Accounting Management Information System (AMIS) of a personal service agency. The most basic of these is fiscal *control*, the minimum condition of service delivery. It simply would not do for the executive director and the bookkeeper to fly off to Accra or Buenos Aires for weekends at agency expense, simply because there was no way to prevent them. Consequently, most agencies have elaborated complex sets of fiscal controls—policies, procedures, reports, vouchers, and the like. At the very heart of the operation of fiscal controls is the accounting system, which provides a means for integrating the various elements of policy, and so forth, and also a routine feedback scheme by which the agency administrator, funding source, board members, or others may assess the performance of the fiscal controls.

Second, with the advent of "performance budgeting," "program budgeting," "cost analysis," and other techniques, it is becoming increasingly clear that the accounting systems of human service agencies must also serve a *planning* function.[2] It is desirable, however, to break the notion of planning, as it relates to accounting, into two parts. On the one hand, there is the matter of the day-to-day tactical resource allocation questions tied to the accounting system. When will present inventories in the day nursery program be exhausted? What are the costs of short-term shifts in personnel between programs? Such issues are often referred to as managerial planning, tactical, or *programming* questions. We shall use the third of these terms in this work. By contrast, on certain occasions financial information supporting a longer (or broader) view will be necessary. What are the costs of services per unit of service delivered? How have these costs changed in recent years? How can we estimate most accurately the costs of delivering a new type of service or program? What are the tradeoffs among cost and quality of service, justice, and so forth? We shall call these program development, *policy-planning* questions.

Presently, the level of accounting knowledge applied to the human services makes its use in fiscal control far more feasible than in either programming or policy planning. Even in those cases where accounting practices and principles have not really been developed or tried, however, the "language" of accounting—the terms, concepts, and basic relationships—tend to be employed. The term "social accounting," for example, has been applied to everything from expanded cost-accounting systems, in which "social costs" are included as items on a firm's balance sheet, to efforts to develop social indicators.[3] And, who has not referred metaphorically to a weak program as a liability, and a strong staff member as an asset?

Developing patterns

Interestingly enough, accounting is a development of the Italian Renaissance. Paciolo, a fifteenth-century Italian, is credited with the invention of the "double-entry" system of recording offsetting debits and credits that made contemporary accounting systems possible. As a system of integrated financial records accounting came into its own in the mercantile and capitalist revolutions that swept over the Western world. The maintenance of financial accounts was a basic consideration of all business practice by the time of the Charity Organization movement, and today business practice would be unthinkable without the records and the reports they yield. Although the point is less widely recognized in the service setting, the same can probably be said for social services.

Today accounting concepts for human service organizations are reflected not only in agency record-keeping, but also in non-profit corporation requirements, Internal Revenue Service regulations, state and local tax collection policies, and a range of other institutional practices. Many states use the disposition of assets as a key indicator of non-profit status. For example, they exempt non-profit health and welfare agencies from sales, property, and other local taxes on this basis. The Internal Revenue Service, likewise, relies upon certain accounting practices to determine the taxable status of organizations. The growth of such special provisions, however, has not been an entirely unmixed blessing.

Even the smallest and newest of organizations can readily become involved in maintaining minimal systems of financial accountability as a legal requirement. Clubs, groups, social action organizations, and a wide variety of voluntary associations may all hold certain "assets" collectively (in a "pot," "kitty," or "treasury," for example) and designate one or more of their members to supervise these funds and make the necessary state, local, and IRS reports. In general, however, the difference between the demands of accountability in truly voluntary organizations and those of the more highly organized social service agency brings us to one of the most basic distinctions among systems of accountability.

Types of accountability

Forms of voluntary association, operating solely with funds provided by its members, will ordinarily be concerned only with *internal accountability,* that is, the treasurer's responsibility to the other members for the appropriate use of their shared resources. Another example of such internal accountability is the responsibility of the director to subordinates for the fair administration of expenditure policies. In addition, however, the origin of financial resources outside an agency itself leads to at least two additional forms of accountability to which agency administrators must be sensitive. First, there is *fiscal accountability*, which is the direct legal obligation an agency may assume upon receipt of outside funds. Second, there is *community accountability*, which is direct, immediate, and legally enforceable. For example, acceptance of a program grant by an agency is predicated on the assumption that expenditures will be related only to the purposes of that program—and administrators can be called to account in a variety of ways for failure to abide by grant guidelines. The concept of community accountability is much more difficult to recognize or measure, but very influential, nonetheless, as any administrator whose community has undergone a scandal over social service funding will readily attest.

Ultimately, community accountability concerns must focus on the legitimacy and effectiveness of the agency and program, which is, it appears, the agency viewpoint on the general issue of accountability. More will be said about each type of accountability later in this chapter.

Social welfare agencies have gradually come to depend on the knowledge and skills of trained accountants. In the earliest days of Charity Organization Societies (and State Boards of Charities) operational information about income, expenditures, and remaining assets and outstanding liabilities was not much of an issue. Eventually, however, an awareness of the value of accounting data for management and planning purposes set in, and bookkeeping became the province of accountants—or, at the very least, a Certified Public Accountant or Licensed Public Accountant was retained for consultation and auditing purposes. Even today, it seems likely that the employment of bookkeepers and accountants varies widely from the part-time housewife who took a commercial course in high school to a B.A.-level accountant or business manager. Even so, in the absence of hard data, it seems unlikely that more than a relatively small proportion of social agencies employs fully trained personnel in these positions.

Several trends, however, point toward the increased use of trained manpower. National certification bodies and the federal government, for example, have only set forth performance standards in this area within the past decade.[4] Also, the growing use of federal and other public monies in the voluntary sector points toward a continuing and increasing need for trained accounting personnel. Finally, the dramatic upsurge of interest in management science techniques and systems such as MBO, PPB, and cost analysis requires a level of accounting sophistication beyond that found in the field today.

In summary, it appears that the pattern in human service organizations increasingly is for agencies to employ trained accountants as "business managers," that is, as part of the "management team." This trend has already been visible for some time in hospitals, nursing homes, and certain classes of human service organizations.

Principal accounting responsibilities

Whether or not a business manager occupies a formal position on the management team of a human services organization, there are four principal accounting activities for which management must assume responsibility: recording transactions, summarizing transactions, preparing and circulating periodic reports, and "hosting" and following up audits. Let us examine each of these.

Recording transactions

For accounting purposes, a transaction may be defined as an action that increases or decreases the assets owned or held by an agency. Generally speaking, income transactions add to assets while expenditure transactions decrease assets. (Liabilities and other special cases of deferred income or expenditure "lags" are discussed under accrual accounting.)

The initiation of any accounting system begins with the recording of transactions in various "journals" (also called "books of original entry"). As an absolute minimum, an accounting system will have a "general journal" with ruled columns for entering the date, description, and amount of a transaction, and the type of action involved (income, expenditure), as in Figure 1. The number of journals used in an accounting system is partly a function of agency size (measured by the number of transactions in a given accounting period) and the types of transactions. Agencies with large numbers of specialized types of transactions will usually have specialized journals designed to match the peculiar recording needs of those transactions. Thus, social agencies whose primary transactions are for personnel costs (salaries, fringe benefits, etc.) will usually have a separate "payroll journal" (Figure 2) and perhaps a separate "travel journal" as well (Figure 3). Likewise, agencies that collect fees from clients may require an "Accounts Receivable," "Fee Collections," or comparably named journal in which to record these entries (Figure 4).

As a matter of course, journal entries are recorded as they occur

FIGURE 1

*Information Flow in an Accounting Information System
with Multiple Journals*

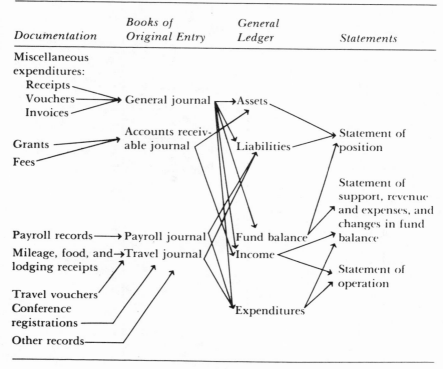

(or at least daily), and adequate provision must be made for the secure storage and retrieval of journals and supporting documents (receipts, bills of lading, vouchers, and the like). The principal concern of the financial manager in a social service agency, however, is less with the details of recording than with the supervision of recording work. In addition to the usual connotations, the supervision of bookkeeping involves some additional responsibilities, including the training of new workers in "agency procedure," the supervision of workers to see that procedures are followed, and the periodical review of their performance. (Or, when such tasks are delegated to a business manager or office manager, the supervisor periodically insures that the performance is acceptable.) It should be emphasized that in few

FIGURE 2
Payroll Journal Page (with Allocation of Effort)

Human Services, Inc.
Payroll Record
Week Ending January 16, 19—

Employee	Total Hours Worked — Regular time	Over-time	Allocation of Effort (hrs.) — Coun-seling	Day Care	Manage-ment	Fund-raising	Hourly Rate	Regular Pay	Over-time	Gross Pay	Deductions — FICA	With-holding	Insur-ance	Credit Union	United Way	Total	Net Pay	Check No.
Johnson, S.	40	0	10	10	10	10	$3.00	$120.00	0	$120.00	$ 6.84	$ 15.60	$ 1.50			$ 23.94	$ 96.06	101
Earl. B.	40	8	10	18	10	10	2.80	112.00	22.40	134.40	7.66	17.47	1.50			26.63	107.77	102
Rabin. J.	40			35	5			230.76		230.76	13.15	50.76	4.00	$20.00	$5.00	92.91	137.85	103
Bearden, C.	40		40					192.30		192.30	10.96	40.38	4.00			55.34	136.96	104
Prentil, F.	40				35	5		211.54		211.54	12.06	46.54	4.00	50.00	1.00	113.60	97.94	105
Weekly totals	200	8	60	63	60	25		$866.60	22.40	$889.00	$50.67	$170.75	$15.00	$70.00	$6.00	$312.42	$576.58	
% of effort			28.85	30.29	28.85	12.01												

*A problem which emerges is that payroll data must be aggregated for both individual employees for *all* pay periods in the year and the total agency for *each* pay period. Most agencies probably keep both individual and pay period records. For an example of an individual record, see United Way's *Accounting and Financial Reporting* (Alexandria, Va: United Way, 1974), pp. 144, 156.

FIGURE 3

Travel Journal Page

Human Services, Inc.
January, 19—

Name	Voucher No., etc.	Mileage	Rate	Mileage Charge	Meals	Lodging	Conference Registration	Airfare	Cabs, etc.	Total Paid	Check No.
Rabin, J.	T-1147	400	$.12	$ 48.00						$ 48.00	106
Bearden, C.	OT-128				$18.00	$47.00	$80.00	$271.00	$12.00	428.00	107
Bearden, C.	T-1148	180	.12	21.60						21.60	107
Prentil, F.	T-1149	600	.12	72.00	27.00					99.00	108
Monthly totals		1180		$141.60	$45.00	$47.00	$80.00	$217.00	$12.00	$596.60	

FIGURE 4
Accounts Receivable Ledger Entries

Account No.: F-142

Name of Account: Accounts Receivable—Fees
Peter Client
4117 Main St.

Date	Description	Post Reference	Debits	Credits	Balance Debits	Credits
1/1	Balance carried forward				$180	
1/15	Office visit		$25			
1/28	Payment received— client			$ 10		
2/1	Balance				195	
2/8	Payment received— Blue Cross			200		$5
2/10	Office visit		25			
3/1	Balance				20	

areas of social agency management are "work norms" as precise and specific as in the case of bookkeeping. The management styles used in supervising other employees may be only partially satisfactory in this case. There is, it should be apparent, no margin for error in recording.

Summarizing transactions

All accounting systems are designed to include periodic "closing" procedures, in which sequences of journal transactions are terminated and totalled, and these totals are "posted to" ledger accounts (see Figure 5). Finally, all account totals are listed in a "trial balance" (see Figure 6) in which the debit (left) and credit (right) columns are expected to agree, or balance. In a related action, many accounting systems also specify, as part of the closing process, the "reconciliation" of checking accounts with the "Cash in Bank" entry on the trial balance. Such closing operations in most social service agencies are usually performed on a monthly basis, primarily due to the number of transactions involved and the frequency of needed financial statements.

FIGURE 5

Posted Ledger Entry

Account No.: <u>18</u>

Name of Account: <u>Staff Travel</u>

Date	Debit	Post Reference	Credit
1/30	$596.60		

This closing process satisfies all three of the accountability questions noted above. From an internal standpoint, the process of entering "posting" entries in the general ledger and the trial balance is a means of checking the accuracy and appropriateness of transactions. Management review of the trial balance serves the concerns called internal accountability. Has the process of recording produced the desired result? Has the agency overspent in any expenditure category? Is income being received as expected? Are there any outrageous or obvious errors in recording?

Preparation of reports

By lending itself to the preparation of necessary and optional reports, the trial balance also serves as the basis for the separate needs of fiscal and community accountability. Reports to funding sources, as well as monthly reports to boards and committees, will probably originate with the account balances shown on the trial balance (particularly the income and expenditure items). In cases where standardized reporting forms are required, therefore, it is essential that there be maximum "fit" between the agency's account headings and the items required on the report. When such consistency is not apparent, an accounting consultant should be brought in to examine the question. This is a frequent occurrence in multi-funded agencies in which several different funding agencies, each with its own reporting requirements, may be involved. It may not be possible to fully reconcile such differences, but it can mean real savings in staff confusion, as well as greater clarity in presenting information to the community.

The culmination of fiscal and community accountability processes,

FIGURE 6
Trial Balance Entries

Non-Profit Services, Inc.
Trial Balance
June, 19—

Account No.	Title	Debits	Credits
	Assets, liabilities, and fund balances		
101	Cash in bank	$ 49,718.71	
102	Petty cash	150.00	
103	Pledges receivable	8,650.00	
104	Allowances for uncollectable pledges		$ 865.00
105	Accounts receivable–client fees	47,112.71	
106	Allowances for uncollectable fees		4,712.00
107	Inventories	6,141.19	
108	Prepaid expenses	4,142.32	
201	Accounts payable		4,781.17
202	Payroll withholdings		6,118.79
203	Accrued expenses		917.42
301	Fund balance		95,172.23
	Revenue and support		
401	Unrestricted contributions		78,219.54
402	Allocations from local United Way		98,674.78
403	Fees from public welfare (Title XX)		57,241.43
404	Grant income		43,717.48
405	Program service fees		91,366.19
	Expenditures		
501	Salaries	261,487.41	
502	Hospitalization and insurance	7,844.61	
503	Employees share—FICA	22,749.36	
504	Professional fees	31,393.31	
505	Supplies	6,275.68	
506	Telephone and telegraph	12,551.37	
507	Postage and shipping	2,562.57	
508	Occupancy	9,924.00	
509	Printing	187.50	
510	Local travel	10,895.29	
	Total	$481,786.03	$481,786.03

in most agencies, is the construction of an audited statement of *financial position* (or balance sheet) and a statement of *financial performance* as part of an Annual Report.[5] Usually, the annual closing process signals a readiness for auditing to begin.

Audits

Auditing may involve only a single auditor or a whole team, depending again on the scale of the operations. In any case, however, the financial manager should keep in mind the basic purposes being served. The principal concern of a financial audit is with the accuracy of financial records and their fidelity to standard recording practices, which in the case of social agencies usually includes the issue of whether expenditures conform to grant or contract requirements. The results of this process are likely to be of two types. One is a routine statement of the type shown in Figure 7, indicating that the agency meets minimum expectations, along with a set of "authoritative" financial statements. If, on the other hand, there are difficulties, the

FIGURE 7
Audit Statement Favored by AICPA*

We have examined the balance sheet of Human Services, Inc., as of December 31, 19—, and the related statements of support, revenue, and expenses and changes in fund balances and of functional expenditures for the year then ended. Our examination was made in accordance with generally accepted auditing standards, and accordingly included such tests of the accounting records and such other auditing procedures as we considered necessary in the circumstances.

In our opinion, the aforementioned financial statements fairly present the financial position of Human Services, Inc., as of December 31, 19—, and the results of its operations and changes in fund balances for the year then ended, in conformity with generally accepted principles applied on a basis consistent with that of the preceding year.

Smith and Jones,
Certified Public Accountants

**The statement shown is for an unqualified statement and includes a "scope" and an "opinion" paragraph. A qualified opinion would also include a middle paragraph detailing concerns (see Figure 10). AICPA also recommends several other opinion formats. See American Institute of Certified Public Accountants, *Audits of Voluntary Health and Welfare Organizations* (New York: The Institute, 1974), pp. 35-39, and United Way of America, *Accounting and Financial Reporting* (Alexandria, Va.: United Way, 1974), pp. 46-48.*

audit may produce a financial statement at great variance with that obtainable from the year-end closing trial balance, and perhaps even a list of "audit exceptions," which are practices of the agency singled out by the auditors as not in conformity with accepted accounting practice. (See Figure 8 for a sample.) Since in the nature of things audit reports are usually required by granting agencies, additional consequences may stem from such a list.

The agency administrator has a definite but subdued role to play in "hosting" a financial audit. The occasion may provoke unjustified anxiety on the part of personnel, particularly in small agencies or among inexperienced workers. Some soothing and patient listening may be required. By all means, however, administrators should avoid crass (and stupid) efforts to impress auditors, like withholding information, explaining every detail, or interfering with the conduct of the audit. The role of the administrator during an audit should simply be to provide auditors with a good working environment, full access to information, and other essentials necessary to the completion of their task. By the time the auditing team arrives the time to worry about whether everything is right has already passed.

It should be noted that in addition to regular annual audits, paid for by the agency, in some cases, federal auditors—from a program agency, the Internal Revenue Service, or the General Accounting Office—may also visit an agency. The same ground rules apply. In sum, the administrator should recognize that auditing is a routine task for those who engage in it, and that it is in the best interests of the agency and program.

Although there are important, if somewhat incidental, tasks to be

FIGURE 8
Middle Paragraph of Qualified Opinion

Human Services, Inc., exercises insufficient control over door-to-door cash collections prior to the initial entry of the contributions in the accounting records. Accordingly, it was impracticable to extend our examination beyond the receipts recorded.*

*If such departures from standard or acceptable practice are not considered very serious, they may sinply be noted in the opinion. More serious breaches may bring either a disclaimer of the auditor's ability to render a judgment, or an adverse opinion. In cases where an agency employs a cash accounting system, AICPA recommends a special format for the audit statement. See American Institute of Certified Public Accountants, *Audits of Voluntary Health and Welfare Organizations* (New York: The Institute, 1974), p. 39.

performed by the administrator in facilitating an agency audit, the most important management role emerges in the post-audit period. At that time, three actions may be necessary: the dissemination of information, corrective action within the agency, and, in extreme cases, negotiation and advocacy.

The first task required by the audit is likely to be the dissemination of the audit report, including the audited financial statements, to the necessary parties—governing boards, funding sources, and state agencies. If the timing can be worked out, it is highly desirable to include an audited copy of financial statements in the agency's annual report as well—as an additional measure of community accountability.

Second, in some instances, the necessity of remedial action may be revealed by the audit report. The agency's procedures for recording accounts receivable collected from clients may be too haphazard. The responsibility for opening mail, counting cash, and depositing funds may be vested in a single employee, with no adequate assurance that all the incoming cash is being deposited. In such cases, it would be up to the agency management to find ways of dealing with this problem and oversee their implementation. (This is, in effect, an example of the "management by exception" principle.)

Finally, in some instances an audit report or specific exceptions may contain recommendations with substantial policy implications for the agency. For example, a change in cash disbursement policies intended to bring them into line with accepted accounting practice may have important ramifications for low-income paraprofessionals working in the agency. In such cases, the agency may be faced with a choice between actions dictated by its goals and actions dictated by the demands of its accounting system. The agency administrator may need to negotiate with funding sources, the paraprofessionals involved, and the CPA who performed the audit to seek an acceptable solution.

Basic accounting concepts

We have now identified the major aspects of the relationship between management and accounting in the administrative processes of an agency, but we have not yet discussed in any detail the organized body of concepts that constitutes accounting theory.

The accounting concept most relevant to our purposes is that of fiscal "entity." In accounting terms, an entity may be a program, an agency, a group of programs, or even several agencies. The basic criterion of an entity is fiscal, rather than substantive, integrity or unity. The critical question in the determination of an accounting entity is not the empirical activities involved, but rather the existence of a "fund," which is defined by the American Institute of Certified Public Accountants as "an asset or group of assets, together with associated accountabilities (liabilities and equities), which are related as to activity or purpose and maintained as an accounting entity."[6]

Assets, in this case, can be defined simply as the resources that are owned or held by the agency. The assets of most human service agencies are primarily money, although property, stocks, bonds, and other securities may also be involved. Thus, a given fund includes the value of those assets less the liabilities (or obligations against them, such as unpaid bills, mortgages, and the like). In both non-profit agency and governmental accounting, such groupings of assets and their associated accountabilities (liabilities and equities—simply the difference between assets and liabilities), which together are termed "funds," represent the most fundamental financial entities. This is in contrast to business operations, in which the "firm" is the basic entity. The inconsistency between organization theory—in which the agency is the basic unit—and the accounting theory of the fund has many practical consequences for human services.

"Fund accounting," then, is the practice of using the fund, rather than the program, agency, or some other basis, as the basic entity. It is common practice in both governmental and non-profit accounting systems. For our purposes, the doctrine of fund-as-entity has great practical significance for several reasons. First, it determines the "boundaries" of certain allied financial practices. Second, the definition of a fund is often related to the demands and constraints of external funding arrangements. Third, an insight into the relationship between funds-entities and other management concepts, such as agency and program, is basic to a full understanding of the possibilities of program budgeting, cost-benefit analysis, and other management and planning technologies.

The use of funds as accounting entities, for example, determines the handling of the financial reports that are ordinarily prepared for each fund, regardless of how many there may be. Thus, an agency with twenty separate grants and twenty corresponding funds would be expected to produce twenty sets of financial statements each month.[7] Likewise, since the assets in a given fund are regarded as an accounting entity possessing a certain logical, legal, and practical unity, it is very likely that they will be handled by a single checking account, and that the journals and ledgers for each fund will also be handled separately.

The use of funds as accounting entities also has considerable practical significance in supporting and enforcing the concept of fiscal accountability outlined above. If an agency were to maintain only a single set of accounts (one fund), grants and other blocks of revenues received from various funding sources would simply disappear into the general financial records. As a result, funding sources would be totally unable to determine whether or not the funds had been used for their designated purposes, apart from the total agency effort. This would, in effect, nullify the possibility of fiscal accountability to funding sources. When a program grant is maintained as an accounting entity, however, complete fiscal accountability to the grantor becomes possible. In fact, this might be viewed as the principal purpose of the accounting enterprise in that fund. Whether in government or the voluntary sector, such fiscal accountability to grantors, legislative bodies, and the public has constituted the principal rationale of fund accounting as practiced in the human services today.

Fiscal accountability currently is not the only rationale for the use of funds as entities. When funds are granted to an agency for programmatic purposes, so that an agency has a separate accounting entity for each major program area, a major hurdle in the struggle to institute direct links between fiscal and program objectives has been passed. Unfortunately, in many instances the fiscal demands of granting agencies, together with failure to adequately recognize the existing potential for program budgeting and related technologies, have meant that many agencies have only partially implemented or variable relationships between programmatic and accounting entities. Thus, an agency with eight major programs may have only six funds—one funding source supporting three of these programs with a single grant, therefore requiring only one fund. Even in such instances, however, the possible uses of modified program planning practices should not be underestimated. The budget format worksheet (Figure 35) discussed in Chapter 7, for example, offers a relatively simple means of converting data from such multi-program funds into programmatic terms.

Basic transactions

Once the basic concept of a fund-entity is understood, it becomes possible to see certain additional relationships more clearly. For example, we have already indicated that assets are, essentially, those things of value held by the fund. In the case of human services, such valuables are most notably cash, with property, investments, and other forms of assets ranking considerably lower in importance. Liabilities are claims against the assets of a fund, such as credit purchases, mortgage payments, and salaries "accrued" but not paid. By definition each fund must always be in a state of balance, according to the following formula:

$$\text{Assets} = \text{Liabilities} + \text{Fund Balance}$$

In this equation the fund balance is simply what it says—the balance of remaining assets after liabilities have been allowed for. In business, this figure is ordinarily termed "equity" or "capital" and represents the amount to which the owners of the firm hold clear claim (their collective "net worth" in the firm, as it were). However, since no one truly owns either public or non-profit entities, the meaning of this fund-balance is considerably less clear in the case of non-profit human services. One can view the fund balance as the assets remaining for possible allocation and use during the given fiscal period. (More will be said on this point under the discussion of the problems of surplus revenues and break-even analysis in Chapter 10.)

Other commonly used terms can also be systematically connected with the concept of fund entities. The terms *revenue* and *income* are both used in human service contexts to signify additions to assets, and a variety of terms (disbursement, expenditure, outlay) are used to signify reductions in assets. One of the more difficult concepts for beginners to grasp is the distinction between cash and accrual accounting systems. Until quite recently, cash systems were the order of the day in many human service accounting arrangements. This simply meant that transactions were not recorded until payments were made. Thus, a grant approval would not be recorded as an asset until the actual check was received and deposited, and an expenditure would not be recorded until a check was written out. The principal disadvantage of cash accounting systems is that they misstate an agency's financial position by not taking into account those transactions which have been made ("accrued") but not paid. In small simple systems it may be possible to keep track by other means of accrued expenditures and income, but when the number of transactions is large, failure to systematically incorporate them into the system can be very risky. Conceivably, an agency or program official could spend several times the total assets of a fund in charged purchases, and be unaware of their impact until the bills were actually paid.

Most accounting authorities today endorse the use of accrual, rather than cash accounting systems, in human services. The principal practical difference between cash and accrual systems can readily be seen on the trial balance (Figure 6). If the system shown were a cash system, the accounts marked "Accounts Receivable" and "Accounts Payable" would not be included. Fee collections, in particular, would be virtually unmanageable on a strictly cash basis.

In some instances, however, a fully accrual-based accounting system would be too rigorous and demanding for the benefits involved, and therefore, accountants have also devised what is termed a "modified accrual basis." The American Institute of Certified Public Accountants 1974 *Audit Guide* defines this as follows:

> Under this method such items as receivables, inventories and payables may be accounted for on an accrual basis, while other items such as income from investments, insurance, rent, salaries, etc. may be accounted for on a cash basis.[8]

The key to understanding a modified accrual basis is grasping the consistency with which some items are handled on a cash basis and others are accrued.

Other accounting concepts

Certain additional accounting concepts are basic to a full understanding of accounting systems: those of function and consistency, and the principles of conservatism, materiality, disclosure, simplicity, accuracy, and flexibility. Let us examine each of these briefly. According to the United Way's *Accounting and Financial Reporting:*

> The functional basis of accounting is a method of accounting which requires that the year end financial reports segregate the organization's expenditures into two broad categories: Program Services and Supporting Services. . . . The theory behind the functional basis concept of accounting is that the organization's management, as well as its *donor constituency,* need to know what portion of the available financial and other resources is expended on so-called program services and what portion is expended on so-called *support* services.[9]

In the terminology employed here the functional basis of expenditure classifications is an operationalization of the concept of fiscal accountability. This concept of function is also recognized in the 1974 *Audits of Voluntary Health and Welfare Organizations* issued by the American Institute of Certified Public Accountants.[10] In its authoritative volume, the AICPA acknowledges three functional classifications of expenditures: service or "program" expenditures, administrative expenditures, and fund-raising expenditures. (The last two types are both examples of what the United Way publication calls support services.) Program expenditures are not actually defined by AICPA's *Audit Guidelines*. The guide notes that "program services will vary from one organization to another depending upon the services rendered." Thus, the authoritative conception of program expenditures at present is residual— they *are* what administrative costs and fund-raising costs *are not*.

By contrast, administrative costs are, according to AICPA:

> those which are incurred for: the overall direction of the organization, general record-keeping, business management, budgeting, general board activities, and related purposes. [Direct supervision of social services, of public information and education and of fund raising should be charged to those functions.] "Overall direction" will usually include the salaries and expenses of the chief officer of the organization and his secretary. If he spends a portion of his time directly supervising fund-raising or social service activities, those salaries and expenses should be prorated to those functions.

> Expenses incurred in keeping a charitable organization's name before the public, while it is not properly classified as a social service or as a fund-raising expense, can be classified as an administrative expense. The cost of dissemination of information of this nature should be so classified because they inform the public of the organization's stewardship of contributed funds through publication of appointments, the annual report, etc.[11]

Clearly, then, administrative costs are related to both fiscal and community accountability.

Finally, fund-raising expenditures are defined as follows by AICPA:

> The fund-raising function encompasses more than the requesting of donations. Various expenses related to fund solicitation and collection, which should normally also be charged to this function, are: costs of transmitting appeals to the public, including postage, addressing and maintenance of mailing lists and files; record-keeping; the issuance of receipts; the deposit of cash and the salaries of personnel connected with the [fund-raising] campaign. Salaries of personnel connected with fund raising should include those of regular staff members who devote the major part of their time to the processing of contribution income, whether during the campaign period or not. Fund-raising services and materials received from affiliates should also be charged to this function.[12]

It should be noted that all the above considerations relate specifically and directly to fund-raising through fund drives, donations, and solicitations. The status of the costs of collecting accounts receivables in agencies using fees is not mentioned in the above quotation, and usually would be handled as an administrative expense instead. By contrast, in agencies dealing directly with the federal government in the grants arena, the real costs of grant preparation and solicitation are most emphatically not handled in this manner. Instead of being classified explicitly as fund-raising costs, the costs of staff time, duplication of materials, and other costs incidental to preparing and submitting grant applications ordinarily are "hidden" in the regular program and administrative costs of the agency—and woe to any agency that attempts to do otherwise![13]

Another concept basic to the adequate operation of accounting systems is consistency. United Way quotes Kohler's *Dictionary of Accounting* on this point: "Continued uniformity, from one period to another, in methods of accounting, mainly in valuation bases and methods of accrual, as reflected in the financial statements of a business enterprise or other accounting or economic unit."[14]

For accounting data to be of maximum use, the operational definitions employed must be consistent. If, at the end of one month, the item for "accrued salaries" includes the amount of paychecks to be issued the following day, presumably the same procedure should apply to the preceding and following months. Otherwise, this seemingly simple inconsistency may indicate that the agency has no personnel costs some months and twice (or even three times) the actual rate in other months. Without basic consistency in reporting procedures and practices, financial reports are quickly reduced to meaningless numbers.

The concept of conservatism in accountancy has nothing to do with the political affiliations of accountants or social workers. Instead, it refers to an extension of the concept of consistency in the handling of the classification to those discretionary items that periodically arise, particularly with regard to income items. In the words of the United Way guidebook: "Where a choice exists between understating and overstating income and equity, the concept of conservatism favors understatement."[15]

Indeed, "modesty" would be an equally applicable term for this concept. Perhaps the most interesting, and at times frustrating, applications of the concept of conservatism in human services lie in the handling of "in-kind contributions," a form of "income" unique to the agency receiving grants with matching requirements. Thorough application of the concept of conservatism in recording in-kind contributions would tend to act as a check upon the "generous" (and even creative) practices sometimes observed in this area. When a mandatory percentage of matching funds in the form of local in-kind contributions are required, it is particularly likely for abuse of the conservatism principle to result.

In the early sixties, for example, it was not unheard of for run-down buildings donated for use with various federal "anti-poverty programs" to be valued for in-kind contribution purposes at rates comparable to the cost of office space in new buildings.

Finally, there are the concepts of materiality, disclosure, simplicity, accuracy, and flexibility, about which the United Way guidebook says the following:

> A statement, fact, or item is material, if giving full consideration to the surrounding circumstances, as they exist at the time, it is of such a nature that its disclosure, or the method of treating it, would be likely to influence or to "make a difference" in the judgement and conduct of a reasonable person reading the financial statements.

> Disclosure must be full and fair. Full disclosure requires the presentation of all relevant information regarding the organization's financial position and operations.

> An accounting system should be as simple as is consistent with the principles of good management.

> [It] should be set up in a way that there is no question as to the accuracy of the event or transaction that is recorded and subsequently reported.

> Since it is difficult to predict with accuracy the nature and volume of financial events and transactions an organization may have to handle from time to time, it is essential that the accounting system used be flexible enough to accommodate the various contingencies and eventualities.[16]

Financial statements

The critical step in the accounting cycle of a human service organization is the preparation and dissemination of financial statements. Indeed, from the professional accountant's standpoint, the production and distribution of such statements is the veritable consummation of the accountancy effort—its prize product. Unfortunately, due to unfamiliarity, faulty design, and a host of other reasons, human service administrators fail to recognize the management potential in such statements. In this section I shall attempt to sketch briefly some of the basic concepts underlying the types of financial statements used in human services today, and some of their potential uses.[17]

Because of the divergent reporting requirements of literally hundreds of federal agencies, foundations, state and local agencies, private donors, and the like the financial statements prepared and distributed in the field today are a true testament to the diversity of the human kind. Unfortunately, the diversity of terms used in headings, layout techniques, the level of detail included, and many other minute variations also means that comparability is often difficult. This is so not only with reasonably sophisticated items, like the handling of accrued expenditures or unearned income, but also in "meat-and-potatoes" matters like the amount the agency took in in income and the amount paid out in expenditures.

Fortunately, there is a relatively small number of principles that tend to clarify considerably these goings-on. Perhaps the most basic consideration in financial statements is that they tend to be of two types: *statements of operations* and *statements of condition*. The first of these is akin to the social worker's concept of process and reports on financial resources flowing into and out of the fund in question. To make sense of such statements of process, one reports them for a given period of time. Thus, time is ordinarily a key to the identification of statements of operations. If a financial statement carries a title line indicating "for the period from . . . to . . ." or "for the fiscal (or annual, or program) year ending . . . ," chances are it is a statement of operations. If, on the other hand, the time line in the title indicates a specific date (December 31, 1976), chances are you are dealing, instead, with a statement of condition, for statements of condition are cross-sectional assessments of the total financial picture (the total assets, the claims against them, and the difference between the two).

Other tip-offs to the types of statements are the section titles or column headings. When reporting "inputs" and "outputs," statements of operations are prone to display terms like "income," "expenditures," "revenues," and "disbursements," while statements of condition typically report assets, liabilities, and fund balances or equity. Because of the historical confusions in human services, there is also the ever-present possibility of encountering a creative agency that has somehow combined its statements of opertions and condition into a single statement, or fractured them into six, eight, or more.

A further difficulty is introduced by the concept of reporting by fund rather than by agency. Unless the statement is explicitly labeled as an agency-wide or consolidated report, there is simply no convenient way to determine when all of the statements for the various funds of a multi-fund agency are in hand. Consequently, in those instances where determination of the full financial picture of operations and conditions of an entire agency is necessary, some prudence may be necessary in this respect. Furthermore, there is a good deal to be said in favor of agencies producing the type of consolidated financial statement discussed in Chapter 7 for use in community accountability. With the use of the kind of conversion matrix discussed in Chapter 7, the procedures for doing so can be relatively straightforward.

Cost accounting

The types of accounting concepts and artifacts discussed in this chapter represent the minimum essential to produce valid, reliable information about the financial transactions of a human service agency. Unfortunately, like its analog in the budgeting area, line-item budgets, the kind of functional accounting system described here has one great weakness from a management perspective: the data on financial condition and operations that are produced have no direct or consistent relationship to program operations or conditions in the agency. As a result, while a program may be fiscally sound, programmatically things are going badly, or vice versa. Although financial indicators produced in functional accounting speak directly to the financial condition of a program or agency, they reflect nothing consistent or meaningful about program conditions.

By contrast, in modern business operations the bridge between the fiscal and the substantive goals of the enterprise has been made. Part of the reason for this is the much-heralded concept of profit, which is usually seen as simultaneously a fiscal and substantive goal. A major share of the credit, however, is also due to modern cost-accounting techniques, which operationalize these basic concepts and make accurate the matching of the production costs of specific units of the firm with income generated by the sale of products from the unit. Indeed, if one dismisses the ideology involved, and assumes that the human service agency is a kind of firm in which the concept of breaking even is itself a kind of designated "profit point" (in essence, a zero-profit margin in which the income equals the cost of production), it seems clear that application of cost accounting to human services is a very real possibility. (See Chapter 1.) In this way, cost analysis and accounting for human services may be scaled down from theoretical to technical problems.

Although to my knowledge there has never been a direct, head-on assult of the problem of applying cost-accounting techniques to the human services, it is clear that much of the groundwork has already been laid. In addition to the concepts of program, administrative, and fund-raising costs outlined above, the various efforts proceeding from the ground-breaking Philadelphia cost studies, completed over two decades ago, are basic in this respect.[18] This is because the essence of cost accounting in the human services is the development of practical procedures for classifying costs by "costs centers" related to the meaningful (programmatic) activities of the agency, not functional areas. At the same time, systematic program classification schemes, like the UWASIS II system produced by the United Way, are essential, since cost accounting also requires the systematic relation of revenue to costs.[19] In truth, the trend toward program funding encouraged by the present system of federal grants, foundation grants, and the United Way may be the biggest practical impetus toward the development of cost-accounting procedures.

Some significant impediments to the meaningful implementation of cost-accounting procedures remain. Most notable is the question of the handling of internal subsidies. Must every programmatic "cost center" carry its own weight and break even financially, or is it permissible for some cost centers to subsidize others without undesirable consequences (like resentment among staff and resistance from funding agencies)? While it can be argued that such subsidizing already occurs, and cost accounting would merely make the reporting of it explicit, we will need to face serious and profound questions about handling our hypocrisies in this area.

Principal issues

Whether such issues are squarely faced, addressed obliquely, or ignored completely, it is quite clear that the principal thrust of the technical developments outlined in this chapter—from the AICPA audit guidelines to the UWASIS II and the generation of cost-analysis studies—is toward the recognition that cost accounting is becoming possible in the human services to a degree never before thought possible. During the coming decade the issue may become increasingly less a matter of academic interest and increasingly more a management concern.

The state of the art in accounting raises five issues that affect the dynamic partnership between accountants and managers in human service programs and agencies.

  1. Can accounting transcend fiscal control?

2. Can purposive accounting systems, linking programs, and finance be devised?
3. Can accounting be fully integrated into human service management?
4. Are industry standard costs possible?
5. To whom is the human service agency accountable?

The concluding discussion of this chapter will briefly explore each of these issues.

Transcending control

Indeed, the question of whether accounting in human service organizations can transcend its present fiscal control orientation can be asked in other ways. We might, for example, ask whether the accounting system can become an integrated part of the "accountability system" in human service organizations. (This is, of course, a highly complex and controversial question. For additional comments on the subject, see Chapter 11.) At this point, we may simply note that movement in the direction of converting accrual-accounting systems into cost-accounting systems appears to be a major step in the right direction.

Purposive accounting systems

The issue of cost accounting is clearly related to contemporary efforts in the direction of program budgeting, which originate largely in the public sector. In both instances, the emphasis is on categorizing expenditures by integrated sets of activities ("programs"), rather than by the so-called "line item" or "functional" categories. It would appear, therefore, that break-throughs in either of these areas would contribute to developments in the other area. For example, the agency that develops an effective program-budgeting scheme will, in the process, also go a long way toward the creation of an adequate cost-accounting scheme.

The integration of accounting and management

Both of the above steps are also closely related to the question of the relationship between financial data generated through the accounting system and agency decision-making arrangements. It would not be unreasonable to suggest that compared with contemporary business practice, most agency accounting systems generate data of relatively little value in agency decision-making. (The reasons for this are detailed elsewhere.) It is very likely, however, that the integration of accounting data into management decision-making is the natural outgrowth of either of the steps mentioned immediately above.

"Industry standard" costs

A related outgrowth of developments in program budgeting and cost accounting for human service organizations is, in all likelihood, the articulation of "industry standard" costs on a broad scale. For example, it may soon be possible for individual agency administrators to compare the costs of their programs (in terms of producing units of service) with the costs of similar programs in communities across the country. Such comparisons would resemble the sorts of "costs-of-production" data readily available in most businesses and industries today.[20] It should be noted that some efforts along this line are already possible. For example, since its origins in the mid-1960s, Head Start and its successors and off-shoots have been accumulating data (and preparing budgets) on the basis of "cost-per-child-per-month" calculations. The increasing acceptance of uniform classification systems for program expenditures (such as UWASIS) make such comparisons a very real possibility in the foreseeable future.

Annual reports

A related issue involves the handling of annual reports. Most non-profit organizations are required by state law to submit an annual report to their governing board. In large sections of the human service system, however, such reporting practices are often carried out reluctantly, if at all. Part of the reason for this is that, under existing conditions, financial data are often difficult to relate to program activities, virtually impossible to interpret meaningfully, and in a host of other ways, susceptible to misinterpretation or direct partisan use against the agency itself. Consequently, as accounting and reporting procedures become more complex and sophisticated, it seems likely that agencies will be able to increase their use of such information in dealing with their constituencies and supporting groups. The day may come, for example, when data on agency and program performances are routinely distributed among boards of directors, advisory groups, staff members, local media, funding sources, and interested public officials. Although such widespread dissemination may occasionally occur today, it is far from standard practice.

Conclusions

An attempt has been made in this chapter to place the profession and practices of accounting within a broader financial management perspective. Several general observations should perhaps be reiterated. First, the transition from cash to accrual accounting is very much a part of the recent history of large sections of the contemporary human service system. Moreover, an additional transition to program budgeting, cost accounting, and similar accounting formats in which revenues and expenditures are classified in ways systematically related to production outcomes lies within the foreseeable future.

Second, the recent efforts of federal agencies, the American Institute of Certified Public Accountants, and the "house of accountability" of United Way of America have together made tremendous advances in the accounting technology available to human service organizations.

Third, and above all else, managers of human service must learn to respect and relate to the professional competence of accountants in the same way that they relate to one another in service delivery contexts. The average human service administrator is not, and never will be, a professionally trained accountant. Consequently, substituting his judgment in the establishment of new accounting procedures for the advice of trained accounting professionals is a highly risky business.

Part II

Fund-raising

In Part I the stage was set for a detailed consideration of the specific tasks involved in managing the finances of a human service agency. From a management perspective, this effort consisted of five major components: planning, fund-raising, allocation/distribution (budget-making), the management of on-going operations, and accountability. Since all other discussions are premised on the existence, or promise, of adequate funding, it makes sense to consider fund-raising first. However, it is important to keep in mind that financial management is an agency responsibility that is never-ending. In fact, while planning and the design of accounting systems or controls may precede consideration of funding in specific instances, the logical precedence of fund-raising gives us a handy point at which to enter the cycle.

First, a couple of comments are in order on the use of the term "fund-raising." Anyone requiring a general term for the revenue-seeking activities of human service agencies quickly becomes aware that none is currently in widespread use. In some respects, the term "capitalization," as used in the for-profit sector, fits the bill. However, in using this term one is constantly reminded that the vast majority of public and voluntary human service agencies do not have capital in any strict sense of the term, because they are not owned by anyone. The term "fund-raising" is to be used instead, even though it is not without some problems. For example, this term is commonly used in the narrower, more limited sense of seeking contributions from benefactors and the public. Here this usage is not violated, but rather expanded into a general focus on the processes of gathering together funds, or critical masses of human and financial resources, in order to make possible the initiation and conduct of a set of activities, or program. In recent years many in the human services have chosen terms such as "resource allocation" or "resource generation" to fit these circumstances. That usage is avoided here, because most definitions of "resources" cover a substantially broader set of circumstances than is intended here. We shall not be concerned with generating such resources as adequate staff, political support, or favorable public opinion, but rather with raising money.

Fund-raising seems the most appropriate term for raising money. First, it is already in use in a somewhat narrower sense. Second, the technical precision of several of its connotations is useful. A fund, as discussed in Chapter 2, is technically a group of assets and their associated liabilities. Fund-raising, then, is the act of contributing to or increasing such funds.

Perhaps it is well to comment briefly on fund-raising as a management responsibility. Traditionally, responsibility for fund-raising in the voluntary sector of human services has been assumed by a board of directors or governing body. It is increasingly clear, however, that a "managerial revolution" has occurred in human services, and the responsibility for securing financing is now recognized as a major responsibility of the director or principal administrative official of an agency. Today one is likely to find such administrators either working along with board members to organize and coordinate fund-raising drives, or assuming direct responsibility for raising funds through grants and contracts. Likewise, when fees are the principal source of revenue, fund-raising may become essentially a matter of administrative routines—albeit under the direct supervision of the administration.

As a consequence of this important transition, fund-raising has gone from being a topic associated with community organization, volunteers, and the like, to being the very heart of administrative concerns. In the complex division of labor in the contemporary human service agency, fund-raising has become one of the most important—perhaps *the* most important—of management responsibilities. Furthermore, with the single exception of fee collections, the on-going nature of fund-raising operations has generally not resulted in the reduction of fund-raising to a series of rules, discrete tasks, and routines that can be assigned to subordinates. Instead, in public and private agencies alike, a major portion of the time and energy of the highest officials must be devoted to this task.

The proliferation of human services has brought with it a great deal of diversity in the fund-raising patterns and practices of contemporary agencies. Three patterns are especially worthy of note. First is the "multi-funded" agency, which receives revenues in a number of different forms and from a number of different sources, and must consequently operate in response to several sets of demands and expectations simultaneously. At the opposite extreme are the relatively fewer "single-source" agencies, which ordinarily respond to a far narrower range of demands and expectations, but are more at the mercy of their donors. Many agencies today fit a kind of "hybrid" pattern, in which either numerous sources of funding may be sought, but only a few actually eventuate at any given time, or there may be many sources of funds, but only one or two account for the greatest amount of revenue and, consequently, receive the greatest attention.

The principal sources of fund-raising utilized in human services can be divided into five categories—two of which will receive only limited attention here. Ultimately the preponderance of human service funds today come from tax revenues, as discussed below. Generally, however, human service agencies seldom become directly involved in the issues of levying and collecting taxes. As a result, this topic is beyond the scope of a management study. The other sources of funds to be considered include fees, grants, organized fund-drives, and unsolicited contributions. The first three will be the subject of a separate chapter, while solicited and unsolicited contributions will be discussed in both the fees and fund drives chapters.

A typology of fund-raising

The three chapters in this unit are based on a typology of the relationships among those who provide funding ("givers"), those who use funds to provide benefits and services ("agencies"), and those who benefit ("clients"). If we display the possible relationships among these three in a three-by-three table, we can readily attach common labels to several of the resultant cells, as shown in Figure 9.

Rather than engaging in extensive justifications of these terms, let us simply employ them as operational definitions. ("Contributions occur when agencies give money directly to agencies.") In any event, from our management point of view, we are principally concerned with the middle row and column. When funds are received directly from (unorganized) givers, we shall identify them as "contributions." When received from organized agencies—such as HEW and United Way—we shall call them grants. And when funds are collected from clients, usually on a *quid pro quo* basis in exchange for services, we shall call them "fees." As far as possible, the use of these terms in the following chapters will be consistent with this typology.

A note on taxes

Central to all facets of human service fund-raising, but not directly a management concern, is the relationship of taxes to human services. A number of important human service ventures, such as public welfare, public health, and many state and local mental health programs, are operated with direct tax appropriations from public bodies. Most other human service ventures are indirectly affected by public taxes and tax policy. For example, the tax-exempt status of voluntary agencies and tax

FIGURE 9

A Typology of Fund-raising

		TO: Givers	Agencies	Clients
FROM:	*Givers*	Mutual aid	Contributions	Charity
	Agencies	Control?	Grants	Service
	Clients	Gratitude?	Fees	Mutual aid

deductions allowed for contributions to such agencies form their fiscal backdrop. Likewise, the allocation of tax revenues to the many federal and state grant-in-aid programs has become a central facet of the human service economy. The fund-raising practices of human service agencies are built upon the superstructure of public tax systems. Consequently, the reader should keep in mind that questions of taxing policy and procedure are seldom far from the surface of all aspects of fund-raising in human services.

CHAPTER 3

GRANTS IN
HUMAN SERVICE
FINANCING

"He'd rule the world if he
could get a government grant."
—Second mad scientist,
Help

In general, grants are unilateral transfers of funds from one person or organization (the fundor) to another (the recipient). In human services, such transfers are often made for the pursuit of a specific set of objectives (program grants). Such grants are, for many, the paramount necessity in human service financing. Careers are made and broken on the success of grant-getting efforts. Grants are seen by many as the only hope of coming close to meeting human needs in the community. On the negative side, others see grants as the keystone of non-accountability and wastefulness, the tools of elitist domination, or the agents of debauchery in the voluntary sector. Despite all the interest in this subject, or perhaps because of it, grants have not received anywhere near adequate attention in the human service management literature until quite recently.[1] Much of what has been written on the subject is little more than anecdotal accounts of the experience of grant-seeking, and a good deal of what is published is written from a "macro-economic" perspective principally concerned with the economic impact of grants as a form of income redistribution.

Obviously, therefore, a single chapter devoted to this subject should not be expected to produce definitive pronouncements. In this chapter we shall concentrate on two principal points instead. First, an outline of terms and concepts necessary to a basic understanding of grants is presented. Second, the major portion of the chapter is devoted to a discussion of "grantsmanship" as it relates to fund-raising behavior in the human services. Certain parallels between "grantsmanship" and other forms of fund-raising—particularly budget negotiation and solicitation of funds from large donors—will be identified and discussed.

Background and theory of grants

Grants are associated with large blocks of money allocated to agencies by various funding sources (most typically federal and state governments, or large foundations) for pursuit of agreed-upon purposes ("programs"). From an economic standpoint, such grants are not unique, but rather comprise one aspect of the larger topic of unilateral, or one-way, transfers of funds within the public sector, between levels of government, or between the public sector and other levels of society. In addition to grants as used in the human services, such transfers might also include welfare payments and other subsidies and allowances. Conceivably, one might even wish to include political favors and patronage as somewhat illegitimate transfer payments.

The reasons for making such transfer payments are as numerous as the multiple purposes of modern government. Boulding's recent work on the subject, however, reduces such purposes to two basic motivations—altruism and tribute (or, love and fear). While most of us would like to believe that the economics of love prevails in the human services, evidence to the contrary is abundant.

For agencies, grants have two important and interesting characteristics. They are often large—considerably simplifying the task of locating revenue sources. At the same time, however, stipulations and requirements (so-called "strings") for the use of grant funds may considerably complicate agency administration, and even re-direct agency goals and objectives.

During the colonial period in the Americas, European monarchs dispensed grants to supporters, in the form of large tracts of land. Although for private use, such land grants occasionally served public purposes, too. Georgia, for example, was founded as a colony for relocating the "street people" of London. With the emergence of the American federal system of governments, grants became a vehicle suited to the redistribution of funds within a pluralistic public economy. The Northwest Ordinance of 1789 and the Morrill Act of 1864 allowed the federal government to indirectly subsidize a number of state government enterprises in human services and other areas, by deeding to the states large tracts of land for resale. Such land grants allowed the establishment of state universities in many states. Beginning with the vocational rehabilitation legislation of 1920, direct cash transfers from federal to state government were initiated—a pattern later incorporated into the public assistance titles of the Social Security Act. Until the post-war period, however, such grants were viewed as strictly internal transactions between governments. Only later, in the flood of Great Society and New Frontier social legislation, was the principle of grants to voluntary, and even for-profit, enterprises developed.

The great reversal

Very few of us who worked in the grants environment of recent years are truly capable of understanding the great chasm in ideology concerning the nature of American federalism, which was bridged in order to make that system possible. The states' rights interpretation of federalism was sufficiently strong at the enactment of the Social Security Act to shape the system not as a national system of income assistance, but as a federal program of fiscal assistance to the various states. Even today public welfare operates on, and is constrained by, the useful fiction that the federal purposes in this area are purely fiscal— economic support for purposes that are the sole prerogative of the states.

While this useful fiction is maintained in the formal language of much social legislation, the realities of bureaucratic guidelines, as well as the economics involved, have tended to drastically undercut this pluralistic conception. Moreover, in broadening the role of federal aid to include agencies in the voluntary and private sectors, the fiscal role of the federal government in social policy was further modified. After all, a substantial case in political philosophy can be made for the states of California, Tennessee, and Montana being allowed to define the public purpose of grants, unconstrained by anything except federal constitutional oversight. It is less clear, however, that the private consulting firms, research organizations, and service enterprises receiving federal grants should be granted similar prerogatives.

The enormous expansion of federal aid for the human services has brought a continual erosion of the emphasis on the purely fiscal role of the federal government in social policy, and brought a plethora of federal social mandates pursued by states, localities, voluntary agencies, and private companies assigned aspects of the public works and reimbursed for their efforts. This "great reversal" in the historic pattern of revenue-sharing in the United States has yet to be completed or fully recognized. Its management implications, however, are widely seen: less administrative autonomy, in which the director of an agency is accountable only to a board of community representatives, and a commensurate expansion of "management broker" roles, in which administrators are intermediaries who must satisfy both board and grant source, but whose hand in both cases is strengthened by the very ambiguity of the role. There is, in fact, quite often an opportunity for agency executives to play off their grant source and board against one another. This opportunity further reinforces the tendencies noted elsewhere toward management's control of fund-raising in human service enterprises.

Typology of grants

In discussing the role of the federal government, it is possible to identify five major types of grants used to distribute funds for human services: categorical grants, program grants, limited categorical grants, revenue-sharing grants, and performance contracts. The five types are listed in approximately their historical order.

Prior to the development of categorical grants to the states—first for vocational rehabilitation, later for public assistance, unemployment compensation, and medical assistance—human services were viewed as the sole concern of the states, localities, and voluntary sector. In 1854, President Pierce even vetoed legislation intended to provide land grants to the states for mental hospitals, citing federal separation of powers as the reason. Thus, it is not difficult to understand why categorical grant programs developed the way they did: the purpose was said to be purely fiscal assistance for state initiatives. Federal programmatic guidelines were, and are, minimal (many argue too minimal). Distribution of funds is a more or less continuous process, often based on a population or income formula.

From an agency standpoint, then, two important dynamics are displayed by categorical grants (but not by other forms of grants). First, the distribution is regular, recurrent, and as a consequence, dependable. The state of Colorado can go about its business with relatively little concern about whether federal public assistance priorities will shift in the next few months, forcing it to alter or eliminate its public assistance operations. Second, funds are distributed to the whole universe of those eligible: no state need be concerned with being eliminated from the competition. Finally, because the distribution formulas are established and publically available, the state discretionary role is maximized. In short, the matching money appropriated by state legislatures, not the federal government, becomes the real determinant of expenditure patterns in categorical aid programs.

However, the administrative advantages have proven to be social policy liabilities in many instances. As a consequence, the future of at least some categorical aid programs is genuinely in doubt at present. Three major public assistance programs were federalized, that is, placed under direct federal administration, in 1972, and it seems only a matter of time before the same happens to AFDC. In addition, the 1975 amendments to the Social Security Act placed expenditure ceilings on the previous provisions for unlimited social service expenditures, thus creating what are called "limited categorical grants."

Widespread dissatisfaction with the seeming structural limits of social policy premised on federal, decentralized initiatives has brought about interest in several new approaches to the business of granting. Limited categorical grants, for example, continue the fiction of the federal fiscal role, while mandating expenditure ceilings and "priority areas" of service. While some states have implemented the limited categorical approach at the state level, others have "passed through" the actual choices of the services to be funded at the local level—in effect creating a local system of funding similar to the program grants discussed below.

Strictly in terms of the numbers of different granting operations, the most significant category of human service grants are those termed "program grants." All together, the federal establishment contains several hundred organizational entities with granting discretion and money available to them. Three characteristics serve to set such program grants apart from categorical grants. First, they are both legally and operationally "one-shot" funding, with all the risks to agencies that that implies. While formal or informal arrangements for continuation can often be devised—at least in the short run—there are definite limitations built into the program grant system as a means for on-going support of social service programs. Second, such grants are increasingly seen as direct expressions of federal social policy initiatives. From this view, then, the purpose of the grant is not the provision of fiscal support, but rather the creation of incentives for grantees to respond to and pursue federally initiated policy objectives. One does not have to be politically conservative in order to see the very real potential of loss of control and autonomy for agencies in this type of funding. Finally, the fiscal and social costs borne by agencies in this form of funding are often substantial. Unlike categorical grants, most program grants operate in a positive environment in which they are able to pick and choose among applicants for funding.

Such selectivity is, from the agency standpoint, quite costly, not only in terms of the number of proposals and reports that must be prepared, but also in terms of the risk of not being funded. This fact alone has certain telling implications for human service agencies that face continuous expenditures and, therefore, require continuous funding. Second, such grants are increasingly seen as outgrowths of definite federal policy objectives. The purpose of the grant is now not fiscal support, but rather the creation of incentives for states and localities, voluntary agencies, and private companies to pursue federally initiated policy objectives. Third, applicant-eligibility is defined in such a way that large numbers of potential recipients may apply. The net effect of this arrangement is the creation of "quasi-market" conditions and excess demand around each grant program. Such conditions are only quasi-market in character because, while federal "buyers" of proposals may have a wide selection to choose from, agency "sellers" of proposals frequently must tailor their "product" to a single seller. Thus, the essential market condition of a crowd of sellers and a crowd of buyers is only partially fulfilled. Instead, program grants are usually a buyers market!

In recent years, dissatisfaction with the categorical and program grant concepts has been pushing federal agencies in several new directions. We have already seen one of these, the limited categorical grant program. Two other forms of fiscal distribution mechanisms have also been proposed and tried in recent years, while another form—the voucher system—has been proposed, but remains essentially untried in a service delivery context. The food stamp program is an example of human service voucher system. However, the problems of distributing commodities like food stuffs are relatively different from (and simpler than) the problems of distributing services. It remains to be seen whether services can be distributed in this way on a large scale.

Revenue-sharing has had a checkered past. Originally proposed by liberal economist Walter Heller during the Kennedy Administration as an antidote to the "structured inequalities" of tax revenues in the American federal system, it was later implemented on a limited basis by the conservative Nixon Administration. Based on that experience, many in the human services have come to see revenue-sharing as a threat of a return to the pre–human services era in federal-state relations.

Most of the money distributed so far has been spent by states and localities on roadwork, capital construction, and other expenditures outside the human services. It is not at all difficult to see that replacement of categorical and program grants with revenue-sharing on any scale at all would be tantamount to major cutbacks in human services expenditures. Such a shift would have major implications for agency financing.

A more likely approach, implemented in programs of the Manpower Administration and other areas, is the substitution of performance contracts for program grants. The essential difference is that such contracts spell out more clearly and in greater detail the requirements of the program of work to be conducted under the grant. While a grant might call for "a demonstration of the effectiveness of casework in public housing," a comparable performance contract might specify the delivery of 1,000 hours of casework to 250 clients during a ninety-day period. Thus, the performance contract represents virtual abandonment of the principles implicit in the categorical grant, in favor of the direct control of grantee activity.

The future of both revenue-sharing and performance contracting in human service financing is unclear. If revenue-sharing is, as some have suggested, the wave of the future in American fiscal federalism, a drastic realignment of the structure of the fund-raising organization is inevitable. If, on the other hand, revenue-sharing continues at approximately the present levels, its principal implication for human services is a pluralistic one: the probability of getting funding from state and local governments for human services is in direct proportion to the amount of such money that is uncommitted.

The future of performance contracting appears to be directly tied to the accountability movement, for the feasibility of performance contracting as a method of distributing funds is directly tied to the ability to identify specific, measurable performance objectives. At present, some areas of human services, such as training and technical assistance, appear to be much more amenable to such arrangements than other areas. In cases where performance objectives are unclear, or unrealistic, numerous difficulties and complications for funder and recipient alike can arise.

The art of grantsmanship

That grantsmanship is an art form rather than an exact science there can be little doubt. Questions about the exact form of the grant-getting art, however, are not susceptible to easy answers. One can ask whether the character of the grantsman closely resembles any of the stock characters of the social sciences. Are grantsmen like Aristotle's rhetoricians, good persons speaking from an ethical basis? Or like Plato's rulers, essentially amoral for a higher purpose? Is their role advisory like that of Machiavelli's advisor to the Prince? Or, are grantsmen entrepreneurs, á la Adam Smith, or con men, á la Erving Goffman? The answer seems to be that most grantsmen are at times all of these and more: they also combine some aspects of Weber's rational bureaucrat, Merton's bureaupathic personality, and even at times Mannheim's planner-intellectual, consciously and intentionally stepping outside the constraints of narrow interest. There is, in fact, much that is contradictory in the grantsman role as it is portrayed in human service folklore. Furthermore, many of the contradictions of the role arise out of its explicitly boundary position, intermediary to two organizations, operating in one while representing the interests of another.

Despite the contradictions, ambiguities, and outright conflicts, "grantsmanship" is a recognizable reality in human service financing. Every human service organization could benefit from someone who performs this role—an agent of the organization capable of identifying, developing, writing, negotiating, and following-up grant proposal possibilities.

The division of grantsmanship labor varies widely. Sometimes the task falls to the director or chief executive officer of the agency. At other times the task is the responsibility of a designated staff person, who typically reflects those traits that are identified by the agency as most closely associated with success in the grants game. There is, overall, a surprising diversity of views on what constitutes successful grantsmanship. Some agencies prefer "hustlers," and others go for "experts." Some prefer "charming" types and others want "hardnose" types. The aggressive pursuit of funding is seen by some as a virtue and by others as a defect. These divergent views point to this rule of thumb: agencies seeking to be successful in grant-getting activities should seek out a successful formula and stick with it. Analysis of the *why* and *how* of successful grant-getting is a task best left to cocktail party chatter and serious research analysis.

Amidst all the apparent contradictions, one thing stands out clearly: the realities of financing human services today mean that only a handful of agencies—the smallest, the most securely funded, and the least successful—can steer away entirely from the realities of grant financing and its attendant grantsmanship activities. For all the rest, grants are an integral part of the capitalization process.

The present perspective

The position taken in this book is simply that grantsmanship activities are a part of the reality of the situation for agencies today: an important subject and deserving of attention, but a set of tasks hardly deserving of the mystique sometimes attached to them. Indeed, the very term "grantsmanship" is often used to connote some mysterious set of skills not otherwise found in the world of the human service administrator. The number of books, pamphlets, conferences, and short courses promoted by private and corporate consultants on this topic is truly amazing. During one three-month period, I received more than a dozen pieces of junk mail promising to increase my skill in this area—always for a healthy fee. It is clear that the idea of grantsmanship as an occult art represents a "grubstake" for many who could hardly be expected to advertise their skills as conventional wisdom. And yet when closely examined, a good deal of grantsmanship is precisely that. Can we not assume, for example, that most "corridor-wise" administrators are aware that, when seeking money, everything possible should be done to create a favorable impression—including neat, well-typed proposals and presentors who are prepared to answer most questions that arise and willing to follow up their formal presentation with additional information? Far from being an occult set of skills, when closely examined, grantsmanship is good, sound administrative practice.

The position taken in this chapter is that grantsmanship is not a unique form of administrative behavior, but rather has much in common with other forms of fund-raising that involve relatively large blocks of money from single sources. The skills of the grantsman are equally applicable to negotiating grants, negotiating appropriations, and "putting the touch" on large donors (particularly institutional ones) in fund drives. Because of these commonalities, all three forms of fund-raising activity will be covered together, and in light of one another, in the remainder of the chapter.

In all three instances one is seeking to get the largest amount of money possible in order to provide support for previously determined purposes. The representative of the agency (hereafter referred to as the agent) must decide how far he is willing to go to get funds, do whatever is necessary within those limits, and not lose sight of the original purposes. This is no small accomplishment. Furthermore, only rarely will the fund-raising agent encounter a funding source (whether a government agency, a foundation, or the union-management contributions committee of a large factory) not already experienced in giving and possessed of a relatively clear set of expectations. Often, therefore, the single most important task facing the agent is the identification of those expectations and the efforts needed to meet them. It is in this area that the skills of the fund-raiser are really tested.

The skills of the fund-raising agent

There are a number of practical guides and "how-to-do-it" manuals on the market today in each of the three areas of fund-raising. Most of them offer a distillation of the wisdom of someone who has actually engaged in the business of raising funds. The purpose of our discussion, however, is not simply to offer one more guide on "what to do next." Instead, our focus will be on identifying the common strategies of the fund-raising agent, based on a review of certain standard works in each of the three areas. Those works singled out for review here are Wildavsky's *The Politics of the Budgetary Process*, which contains an excellent discussion of the strategies employed by the agents of federal agencies appearing before congressional budget committees; Seymour's *Designs for Fund Raising* and Warner's *The Art of Fund Raising*, which discuss large donors; and MacIntyre's *How to Write a Proposal*, which deals not only with the title subject but also with preceding and follow-up negotiations.[2]

Together these works present a profile of the basics of successful agency fund-raising. To restate the point succinctly: the literature that discusses the ostensibly separate topics of budget negotiation, grantsmanship, and fund-raising from large donors can be considered from the management perspective to be complementary and interrelated.

The keys to recognizing the commonalities that link the divergent topics are to be found in the concepts of "base" and "increment" and the three action principles uncovered by Wildavsky in research on the federal officials responsible for budget negotiations with the Congress.[3] "Base" refers to those funds that are relatively secure or taken for granted as belonging to an agency on the basis of past practice. An "increment" is the amount of increase (or decrease) requested, expected, or anticipated in current action. If one makes the simple "entity" assumption that an agency is an on-going enterprise, the need or demand for a base is self-evident: on-going agencies need continuing revenues ("a base") to survive. If the agency is relatively sure of the continuity of its base, as in the case of public agencies, which receive legislative appropriations, the increment will simply be the amount of increase (or decrease) in appropriations. From an agency management perspective, similar funding base assumptions can be made with income from fees, in which case the base becomes the normal amount of fee-income expected.

In the case of human service agencies, however, unmet needs and external circumstances have combined in many instances to offer agencies additional opportunities to actively pursue budget increments in quite different contexts, like public grants and fund drives. In both instances the management dynamics involved are identical to the pursuit of increments in appropriations, as discussed by Wildavsky. Such agencies are seeking to simultaneously pursue all three of the basic strategies: (1) defending the base of present revenues against cuts in existing programs, (2) increasing the size of the base by expanding old programs, (3) expanding the base by adding new programs.

Of the three avenues—appropriations, grants, and fund drives—it should be clear that the soundest strategy is to pursue the first, although this is often the most difficult. Consequently, agencies seeking to increase the size of their base with either new or old programs may turn to grants or fund drives. Both options are not without drawbacks. Grants, like appropriations, must be renegotiated periodically, with the further difficulty that funding may be "zero-based" (that is, not assured for more than a year at a time), guidelines may be revised, or the demonstration or initiative nature of the federal mandate may require a limit on the number of years for which funding may be received. Likewise, fund drives are complex to manage organizationally, and only a relative handful of human service agencies have been able to mount recurrent fund drives successfully. Consequently, fund drives are often reserved for special-purpose and one-time-only budget increments, such as capital construction or endowment campaigns.

The juxtaposition of budget appropriations, grants, and fund drives in this manner highlights the fundamental management decisions regularly faced by all human service administrators: (1) defining the base of the agency and assessing its stability and potential for expansion; (2) identifying new avenues of agency budget increments, particularly in the context of grants and fund-raising campaigns; (3) determining the feasibility of particular options; (4) working out a detailed strategy for the pursuit of those options.

With the advent of primary management responsibility for fund-raising in contemporary human services, it is likely that no single set of decisions has more importance to the continued successful operations of the agency than the working out of detailed answers to these four questions. Furthermore, in the modern agency, such questions cannot be answered once and for all, but must be resolved as opportunities present themselves throughout the life of the agency. The juxtaposition of concepts from grantsmanship, appropriations politics, and fund-raising below is intended to support the importance of this topic in financial management and also to underscore the complimentary nature of these topics, as asserted above.

Proposal writing

One position claims that the essential skills involved in grantsmanship are those concerned with developing and writing a proposal. MacIntyre elaborates this position in a slim volume entitled *How to Write a Proposal*.[4] MacIntyre goes beyond the usual notions of rhetorical skill, for his model involves not only a formal written proposal, but formal presentation in hearings or interviews, and follow-up activities as well. MacIntyre states:

> No agency or group should consider writing a proposal for program funding unless the funding source allows for a formal presentation of the proposed material. There is simply no way to write out all of the various aspects of a program in a one-shot written proposal. Sometimes it will certainly be necessary to do without a presentation; however, this is grossly unfair to both the program agency and the funding agency. The funding agency cannot help but have questions about the program and the program agency should most assuredly be put "on the line" to answer these questions.[5]

MacIntyre suggests five points to be covered in presentations: (1) introducing the agency staff, (2) introducing the agency, (3) stating the need, (4) proposing the program for dealing with the need, and (5) answering questions. In making the presentation, he argues, appearances are important. Presenters should be well-prepared and well-rehearsed. They should not appear threatening to reviewers. They should know the audience of reviewers—their likes and dislikes—in advance, not appear superior or insincere, and avoid angry replies to questions. Handouts should be well-prepared, timely, and to the point.[6]

Following the presentation, MacIntyre believes, there are certain essential follow-up steps the authors of funding proposals should engage in. He defines follow-up as "the practice of using politics (i.e., exercising influence) to monitor the attitude of the decision-making process."[7] Furthermore, he offers a simple maxim: "If you don't do follow-up, you won't get funded." This is, perhaps, overly simplistic:

if you don't do follow-up, you may never *know* whether you were funded or not.

> This "action" should be carefully planned, programmed and executed. Additionally, a system of monitoring these actions should be implemented. Follow-up action is always ethereal. So much so that many, if not most, are frightened away from this tool because of the characteristic of intangibleness. Yet very tangible results often result from proper use of follow-up action tools.[8]

The "proper use" of follow-up, he goes on to say, involves three simple rules:

1. Never by-pass a decision-making authority.
2. Never "step on toes."
3. Never initiate an action that is not justified.

In more conventional English, one may say that proponents of funding proposals should take care that negotiations, influence, and hard bargaining are limited to the period before the decision, and to the proper decision authorities. Although his reasons are not clearly stated, McIntyre feels strongly that funding decisions should not be appealed to higher authorities. Second, he recommends care in not offending potentially valuable allies or destroying potentially favorable relations during the follow-up process. The third rule, he argues, involves careful strategy and skillful execution, while avoiding departures from "the plan."[9]

Budget strategies

Success in budget-making (and by inference, in the other two areas of fund-raising) is, according to Wildavsky's informants, principally a matter of strategy—that is how well you play the game: "It's not what's in your estimates but how good a politician you are that matters."[10]

> Being a good politician, these officials say, requires essentially three things: cultivation of an active clientele, the development of confidence among other governmental officials, and skill in following strategies that exploit one's opportunities to the maximum. Doing good work is viewed as part of being a good politician.[11]

In *Politics of the Budgetary Process*, Wildavsky identifies several dozen strategies pursued successfully by federal agencies, many of which are equally applicable to agency situations and other non-budget fund-raising contexts. The major entries are laid out in brief in the following sections.

Using constituencies

The term "clientele" as used by Wildavsky refers principally to the individuals and organizations able and willing to give support to an agency or program. This usage, which is common in political, organizational, and planning literature, overlaps substantially with that of "clients," said to be those served in the human services. To avoid confusion, therefore, the term "constituency" will be used in place of clientele to identify existing and potential supporters, and clientele, and client, will be used to signify the beneficiaries of services— who may or may not also be constituents.

Wildavsky argues, understandably enough, that the first major strategy should be to identify a satisfactory constituency.[12] Not all groups will do for fund-raising purposes, and the public perceptions of many deviant populations make this task particularly difficult in the human services. Parents of abused, abandoned, or neglected children, alcoholics, mental patients, juvenile delinquents and their parents, are hardly ideal constituencies for gaining the ear of legislators and others in a position to grant or withhold funding! Regardless of how we in the human services may feel about it, the tradition of the unworthy poor has resulted in the stigmatizing of many of the groups served by human services, and such stigmas are facts of life for fund-raisers. In many cases, however, this problem can be dealt with by the formation of constituency support groups of the "friends-of-the-unworthy" type— particularly if care is used in selecting the leaders and spokespersons of the groups.

Once the constituency has been identified, efforts must be made to *serve* them, or, in the case of non-client interest groups, to keep the constituency informed of service to clients. As Wildavsky says, "Informing one's clientele of the full extent of the benefits they receive may increase the intensity with which they support the agency's request."[13] There simply is no substitute for a large group of satisfied clients and constituents to fall back on at fund-raising time. This fact cannot be overstated. Identification of a constituency, however, need not be a one-shot effort. Once the constituents have been identified, and courted, there is always room to expand the constituency and increase its significance. Furthermore, among large agency followings, there may be some value in identifying specific constituent groups and directing special attention to them. Finally, one should always attend to "feedback" from constituent groups. Many agencies maintain special files of "letters of support" and "testimonials," and include these in grant proposals or with budget documents. It is certainly not unreasonable to request such letters from those who already may have offered their verbal support.

Often among novice administrators the question of how to approach constituencies for their support arises. "I can't just beg them to help me, can I?" many a recent graduate has been heard to plead. Indeed not, and the careful working out of an approach is one of the elements cited by Wildavsky's sources as important in the Congressional context.[14] Certainly, an approach is equally important in the community.

One such strategy is termed "Divided we stand" and involves the structuring of administrative units to obtain greater constituency support.[15] Wildavsky cites NIH as an example of this pattern at the federal level. It has separate constituencies interested in heart research, cancer research, mental health, aging, and numerous other areas. In other situations, a strategy he calls "United we fall" may be more appropriate. In recent years, for example, there have been a number of instances where "holding back" constituencies supporting issues of high current interest, such as child abuse, cancer cures, and behavior therapy, in the interest of fairness to all constituencies, would simply have been undercutting one's funding potential.

Perhaps one of the least recognized strategies in many communities is the use of advisory committees to expand the funding base—in Wildavsky's words, "Advisory committees always ask for more." "Get a group of people together who are professionally interested in a subject, no matter how conservative or frugal they might otherwise be, and they are certain to find additional ways in which money could be spent.[16]

In negotiating with funding sources, it is bad form to admit giving in to pressure from constituencies, but if funders press you on the point, hit them for more money! Wildavsky quotes one official appearing before a Congressional committee as saying,

> I cannot think of any local service case in which we have not had at least 15, 20 or 25 members of Congress each one urging an extension of the local service to the communities in his constituency as being needed in the public interest. . . . We felt that they, if anyone, knew what the public interest required . . . as to local service . . . with full knowledge that this would require additional subsidy.[17]

The same gambit may be employed on agency officials negotiating grants and on "fat cats."

Finally, the agency working with constituencies should avoid being "captured" by them.[18] Since the point of using constituencies is to provide clout to back up agency initiatives, it hardly needs to be pointed out that the tail wagging the dog is not part of the strategy!

It also should be noted that constituencies are not always external to the funding source. Sympathetic budget reviewers, foundation directors, and United Way budget committee board members can be as valuable, and in some instances, more valuable, than interest groups, citizens' advisory committees, and other "outside" constituencies. In fact, the very idea of constituent *groups* may be somewhat misleading. Successful fund-raising is dependent on what businessmen call "good will," and the wider one is able to spread a favorable impression of the agency, the more valuable it is likely to be at fund-raising time. Perhaps no point is more fundamental to successful fund-raising than this: one simply cannot expect to get large sums of money for the operation of human service programs from enemies, opponents, and those indifferent to the agency and its purposes. What, after all, are friends for if not to help when needed?

The cultivation of constituencies, however, should not be interpreted as a "touchstone," or magic wand, that can be expected to produce results in a flash. Fund-raising is an art, not an exact science. Human relations are, after all, too indeterminate for such expectations. There are several exigencies that can be expected to intervene from time to time with the operation of even the best-organized fund-raising operation. One of these is the influence of "fads," "trends," or "moods" on funding sources. During the days of the Nixon attack on human services, for example, no amount of constituency support appeared adequate to overcome strategically placed opposition in the administration.[19] Such trends also occur at the local level, and about all the prudent agency can do is weather the storm as well as possible. Whether the slogan is "balancing the budget," "cutting back lavish expenditures," or "becoming more efficient," the point is the same, and discretion may well be the better part of valor.[20]

Developing community confidence

Translated out of the congressional context, Wildavsky's second point might best be interpreted as "developing community confidence":

The sheer complexity of budgetary matters means that some people need to trust others because they can check up on them only a fraction of the time. . . . If we add to this the idea of budgeting by increments, where large areas of the budget are not subject to serious questions each year, committee members will treat an agency much better if they feel that its officials will not deceive them.[21]

Again, the essential points of transactions—the "incremental" (partial and sequential) examination of requests and the consequent need for trust—appear to apply equally well to all three contexts. The large donor interested in poring over detailed financial records and making a detailed study of an agency prior to making a bequest is about as rare as the legislative committee willing or able to do so. It appears that the social work principle of "building relationships" based on trust, mutual respect, and confidence is a central element of fund-raising success.[22] In particular, the fund-raising agent must be very skillful at selecting and distributing information that informs and persuades without overwhelming.

Wildavsky cites a number of strategies that can be employed to build confidence and trust in the fund-raising context. The first of these he entitles "Be What They Think They Are:"

Confidence is achieved by gearing one's behavior to fit in with the expectations of [funding sources]. Essentially [in the Congressional context], the desired qualities appear to be projections of the committee members, images of themselves. Bureaucrats are expected to be masters of detail, hard-working, concise, frank, self-effacing fellows who are devoted to their work, tight with taxpayer's money, recognize a political necessity when they see one, and keep the Congressmen informed. . . . To be considered aboveboard, a fair and square shooter, a frank man is highly desirable.[23]

Closely related to this is Wildavsky's advice to "Play it Straight." Lies, misstatements, and deceptions are not only morally reprehensible, but in the context of fund-raising they are usually poor strategy. Wildavsky states that "if a [Congressional] committee feels that it has been misled, there is no limit to the punitory actions it can take."[24] The same might be said to apply, perhaps to a lesser extent, to other funding sources. Playing it straight with funding sources should, over a period of time, result in the development of a trusting relationship between fundor and fundee, one that will substantially enhance the bargaining position of the fundee, and render the task of negotiations simpler for all concerned.

Organized fund-raising

It may be less controversial for some readers to compare budget-making and grantsmanship than it is to include a third category, fund-raising from large donors, in the same context. It is relatively easy, however, to demonstrate the essential similarities involved, despite differences in terminology. Addition of this third element to the profile of an agency fund-raising agent further refines and clarifies the requirements of this role. In this section, some standard treatments of this subject will be reviewed for their contributions to the skills of fund-raising agents.

First, it is necessary to do a brief profile of fund-raising as that topic has traditionally been treated in the literature. Although the term may be extended to cover all aspects of the problem of generating revenues and be applied not only to individual agencies, but to the traditional federation of cooperating agencies as well, most fund-raising discussions tend to break the subject down into two entities that from an agency standpoint must be treated separately. First, there is the mass solicitation, in which contributions of varying size are sought from a large number of donors—anywhere from several thousand to several million—each of whom is asked for and expected to give a relatively small contribution. Fund-raising sources also deal with a second, parallel fund-raising effort, in which a smaller number of (usually wealthy) individuals and institutions are singled out for special attention with the expectation that they will contribute large sums.

From an agency perspective, mass fund-raising is, like direct taxation, a rarity. While many agencies depend in part on revenues raised in this manner, it is extremely rare to find an agency engaged in its own mass solicitation. (Consequently, this subject is dealt with in Chapter 5, in the context of federated agency campaigns.) It is considerably less rare to find situations in which agencies approach large donors directly, seeking what are, in effect, private "grants." The expectations surrounding such an event are such that conditions similar to those found in the grants and budget contexts are created. Consequently, the principal assumption made in the following discussion is that the solicitation of large donors resembles closely the other two fund-raising contexts.

The similarities derive from three essential requirements in all types of fund-raising: first, the necessity to accurately recognize and make effective use of existing patterns of influence; second, the importance of careful planning and strategy; and third, the significance of a straightforward, honest approach in dealing with money sources. Each of these topics has already been detailed for the other two contexts. Let us examine them briefly in terms of three 'standard' works of fund-raising literature.

Irving R. Warner in *The Art of Fund-Raising* describes the two-tier, stratified approach to fund-raising. In discussing the large donor aspect of campaigns, Warner stresses the influential nature of such donors and their leadership potential. The ideal chairman of a fund campaign, he notes, is rich, powerful, generous to causes, well liked, well organized, a good speaker, a true believer in the cause, and fearless under community pressures.[25]

In addition to his role in leading the mass solicitation, Warner notes, such a chairman should be able to identify an "inner circle" of donors. As a rule of thumb, he suggests, the inner circle and the ten largest "outside" gifts should add up to about one-third of the collections expected for the entire campaign. Such an estimate clearly points to the importance of the "inner circle" approach to mass campaigns.

Warner also indicates that the best method for approaching large donors is to use "askers," who are selected by the chairman for their appropriateness. Although Warner does not deal extensively with the subject, it is reasonable to assume that askers are essential to the task of preparing a grant proposal. The askers should have a clear understanding of what they are requesting funds for, and be able to answer all questions on the subject. In many instances they may make what amounts to a formal proposal. However, it is unlikely that the detailed paperwork that goes into a grant proposal or a budget request is anything but a diversion in this context.[26] As this brief comparison should indicate the similarity among the approaches made to potential givers in campaigns, grants and budgets is so close, yet so strikingly dissimilar, in certain respects, that it warrants further investigation.

A dissimilarity worth noting is the stress laid on sacrificial giving in fund-raising literature. Grantsmen and budget officials are seldom expected to make a personal financial contribution prior to their asking others for funds. Yet a constant theme in discussions of large donors is the suggestion that they themselves must give to be effective as fund-raisers.

A second source on the subject, Seymour's *Designs for Fund-Raising*, deals less explicitly with the two-tier approach advocated by Warner.[27] Seymour's profile of the fund-raising campaign, however, agrees in its essentials with much of Warner's discussion, although it goes far beyond the other in seeking to probe the psychology of giving. (This topic will be dealt with in Chapter 5.) From the vantage point of large donors' relationship to grants and budget-making, Seymour's comments on the use of "case statements" are especially useful:

> The essence of the case for fund-raising, as determined during the original process of definition and design, will have been enough for establishing agreement among those in control with regard to the program to be financed and the list of needs comprising the campaign goal. *But something more will then be required for the enlistment of leadership, the enrollment of workers and the solicitation of the first pace-setting gifts.*
>
> The basic document for this purpose has come to be known as the "case statement." And this is the one definitive piece of the whole campaign. It tells all that needs to be told, answers all the important questions, reviews the arguments for support, explains the proposed plan for raising the money, and shows how gifts may be made and who the people are who vouch for the project and will give it their leadership and direction.[28]

As profiled by Seymour, the case statement of a fund-raising campaign sounds very much like the proposal discussed by MacIntyre. Furthermore, the points in the final sentence of the quotation read like a restatement of the standard elements of grant proposals. While many budgets forego letters of support or explicit reviews of the need for (that is, the "case" for) funding, testimonials and prepared arguments are also typically part of the preparation of the budget negotiators Wildavsky identifies.

Yet another similarity pointed up in the fund-raising literature is the need for strategic "calculations" (in Wildavsky's terms). Soroker, in *Fund Raising for Philanthropy*, notes, for example, the need for careful estimation of the likelihood of success in setting a financial goal:

> There are those who feel that the needs as validated by the Budget Committee should be translated into dollars, and that those dollars should then represent a campaign goal, regardless of how large a goal this might encompass. . . . The needs-goal philosophy is often opposed by hard-headed practical businessmen, usually the leading contributors and the campaign leadership, who feel that a goal that cannot be achieved is a suspect goal and when individuals working on a campaign conclude that the goal is unrealizable they lose heart and do not put in proper effort.[29]

Control issues

In each of the chapters in this section, the discussion of the types of fund-raising mechanisms employed in human service agencies concludes with the two principal management issues involved: control issues and planning issues. The former have to do with the adequate treatment of the various accountability claims by human service administrators, and the latter with the development of linkages between the fiscal and program structures of agencies.

In the case of grants, the control issues are relatively straightforward and found in virtually every discussion of grantsmanship. Nevertheless, they bear repeating here: adequate care should be taken in the preparation of grants that are to be negotiated to see that budgets, supplementary statements, reports of previous performance, and accompanying descriptive materials are accurate, suitably prepared, and not likely to prove unnecessarily offensive to funding sources or embarrassing to the agency. Moreover, all representatives designated to speak for the agency should be required to master the same pool of information (including the contents of proposals which have gone out). Whether it occurs at a public hearing, in a closed negotiating session with a federal agency, or over the telephone, nothing is more embarrassing or potentially damaging to the agency's position than having to reconcile two or more discrepant sets of financial statements. Proper preparation and management control of negotiations should, in the majority of instances, make such incidents completely unnecessary.

Planning issues

Perhaps the single most complex demand in preparing and submitting grants is "planning on the run." From a planning and decision-making perspective, human service grant negotiations take place in a very volatile environment indeed! In the face of pressures from the grantor to scale down (or increase) the amount of a grant request, adapt a proposal to changing guidelines, modify the work plan, revise the personnel plan, or make other changes in a grant proposal, the administrator must constantly consider the impact of such revisions on the agency and its programs. The issues that arise are seldom clear-cut or easy to deal with. How much can a request be decreased before it ceases to be worth pursuing? What are the recruiting and "start-up" implications of the proposed revisions? Can the proposed work plan be adapted to fit new (and seemingly contradictory) funding source guidelines? These are just a smattering of the important planning questions typically faced by the administrator charged with negotiating a grant. Furthermore, they are seldom faced under ideal planning conditions, allowing study, consultation, and consideration in detail. Instead, such questions often arise, and must be resolved, on the spur of the moment, and, not infrequently, when the administrator is away from the office and the needed information. In the present system of grant negotiations, last-minute decisions challenge the planning skill of human service administrators and may virtually nullify the deliberation and planning that went into the original proposal. Unfortunately, there appears to be little that any administrator can do about these circumstances at present. Perhaps the only option is to try to anticipate such situations with contingency plans asking which positions can be cut and what the essentials of this proposal are, and so forth.

Conclusion: a profile of the management fund-raiser

Beginning with a discussion of grants and the development of the present grants economy in human services, this chapter focussed on certain essential features of fund-raising in the human service agency. Certain key contributions to the literature on grantsmanship, budget-making, and fund-raising efforts directed at large donors were shown to be similar. Similarities in the expectations of the agency representatives functioning in these three different situations were also identified. Together, it was argued, they point up the requirements of effective management of fund-raising. It is now appropriate to review briefly the principal features of this profile.

In general, an agency fund-raiser in any of the three areas is a person who is both technically skilled and politically sophisticated. Because the daty-to-day work of grant and budget negotiation and fund-raising planning involve some considerable reference to dollars, the fund-raising agent must be comfortable with the necessary mathematics (principally arithmetic and simple algebra). Basic knowledge of accounting principles is certainly desirable. A second major technical requirement appears to be a high level of communications skills—both in speaking and writing. Proposals, memoranda to budget committees, and case statements are written documents basic to fund-raising efforts. If the agent is not able to prepare such materials personally, "back up" assistance appears essential.

Some skill in public speaking and small group discussion also appears to be basic to the fund-raising agent's task. Such skills will be employed both in the preliminary phases of the fund-raising effort and in the various meetings, negotiations, and presentations of the effort itself. A very high level of importance should be placed, therefore, on the rhetorical skills of persuasion, for it is clear from all three types of fund-raising efforts that face-to-face exchanges and speaking occasions form the principal arena for the exercise of influence in fund-raising.

In addition to technical proficiency of this type, the good agency fund-raiser must also be quite sophisticated politically, whether at public gatherings, in small groups, or in telephone conversations. The effective exercise of influence revolves around knowing when the point has been made, when the case has been won, and when to "apply the screws"—all of which require a knowledge and experience that can only be described as "sophistication." Indeed, this is one of the principal reasons why it was suggested above that a workable formula for fund-raising is not to be tampered with.

Finally, the above paragraphs point out the necessity of what might be described as integrating, or synthesizing, skills. The effective fund-raising agent in all three contexts should be able to translate the need for money from a dull, purely fiscal issue into terms that will be more persuasive and meaningful to those being solicited. In this way, the fund-raising agent must truly embody the integration of the fiscal and the substantive that has been mentioned elsewhere as a primary financial management concern in the human services.

CHAPTER 4

FEES AND
CLIENT CHARGES

*"Pay your bills,
so I can pay mine!"*
—Anonymous

In marked contrast to the perspectives on grants discussed in the preceding chapter are some approaches to fund-raising that have emerged in the peculiarly American setting of the voluntary sector of human services: fees and client charges. Rather than seeking the financing of human service ventures from sources "external" to the circumstances of service delivery, fee-based services seek to distribute the costs of service among those who directly benefit.

Fees defined

Fees may be defined as money payments collected from clients and "third-party" funding sources such as public welfare agencies, social security, vocational rehabilitation, and private or group insurance companies. The term is a generic one, interchangeable in this context with "client charges" for services rendered.

Fees are widely used today as a source of revenue in human service organizations, despite the fact that they present certain fundamental problems for social welfare theory, as well as requiring a distinctive management approach. From the so-called "macro" perspective, in which social welfare is seen as the pursuit of the social good or the public interest, fees present serious theoretical obstacles. How can

80

one justify, for example, the distribution of the economic costs of pursuing the social good among those very individuals singled out as the targets of social intervention? This issue has taken on substantial meaning since the rediscovery of poverty and social stratification in the 1960s and more recent interest in social policy and equality.[1] While it is beyond the scope of this book to deal with such matters, it must be noted that the subject of fee collections has important implications that transcend the purely fiscal management concerns discussed here. In many cases, for example, the presence or absence of fees is a good indicator of the "dual-class structure" of service delivery.[2] Generally, services available to inner city, rural, and other indigent populations are in some way publicly subsidized and available without charge to clients, while the more specialized, suburbanized "high status" services available to middle- and upper-income, educated clients are fee-based. In recent years much attention has been given to the problem of overcoming such dual service systems through the use of third-party payments.[3] In general, however, the problem remains, and practically minded financial planners and administrators should not fail to note the class implications that frequently arise in discussions of fees as a revenue source.

General principles

The use of fees as a revenue source in contemporary human service organizations is based on widespread recognition and acceptance of a principle that resolves, in specifics, the general problem raised above: fees-for-service are most useful and appropriate in those instances when the allocation of the costs of service delivery can be partly or wholly distributed among the recipients without violating any "side constraints."[4] Although the range of such constraints is, in fact, quite broad, a few guidelines can be drawn. For example, the collection of fees may be considered appropriate so long as a client's participation in the service is voluntary. Charging prison inmates for their custody, for example, seems absurd. Second, charging fees may be appropriate so long as fees do not place an excessive financial burden on clients. Herein arises the justification for the existing class system of services, as well as efforts to deal with it like ability-to-pay fees (discussed below). The circumstances of fee collection should not constitute a direct or serious threat to the physical, psychological, or social well-being of clients. The use of strong-arm tactics in the collection of past-due accounts, for example, would be considered inappropriate.

Other side constraints of this type can be spelled out in specific instances, but the essential point remains: unless such considerations arise, service providers and clients are free to "contract" with one another for services and payment.

Advantages of fees

The widespread utilization of fees as revenue sources is based on several advantages that characterize this form of revenue source. Four are particularly worthy of note. First, the voluntary, contractual nature of fee-for-service arrangements is considerably simpler in many instances than the complexities of allocation by some central budget authority. Second, except for instances when some specific side constraints are violated, fees are perceived as a fair form of cost allocation. That is to say, when clients can afford to pay, clients, agencies, and on-lookers alike will usually regard such fees as appropriate. Third, fees as revenue-generating mechanisms in human services have the additional advantage of maximizing choices. Choices are possible only if more than one type of fee-collecting service vendor is available. When such is the case, however, the fee-paying client is free to choose (within such well-known limits as available information). Finally, such options offer feedback to agencies on their performance, or, perhaps, their public image, or some other "irrational" factor of this type.

Disadvantages of fees

There are at least two well-known disadvantages to fee collections. First of all, since human service settings seldom approach market conditions in an economically meaningful sense, the above advantages may well appear to exist to those within the agency, but not to those on the outside. Because of this, there is likely to be a certain unpredictability inevitable in fee collections, even under the best of conditions. Second, it generally seems to be the case that fee collections are thoroughly unrealistic in virtually all crisis situations. Anyone who has ever visited the emergency room of a private hospital has an operational knowledge of this point! While you may be anxious to the point of panic about a serious injury, treatment may be withheld until the details of insurance and payment or credit arrangements are handled. In other instances, such as natural disasters, efforts to place the cost of service on individuals may be ethically repugnant, poor public relations, or both.

Furthermore, fees may be an inappropriate revenue mechanism for the simple reason that a realistic basis for distributing costs among clients cannot be developed. For example, financing professional education solely on the basis of student fees would not only place an enormous burden on students, it would completely ignore the ultimate benefits of professionally trained people to society. The economic value of services may not be clear, reducing the fee-charging question to one of "what the market will bear." Such a condition, in fact, already exists in many communities where essentially similar counseling services may go for anywhere from $5-$100 an hour.[5]

Pervasiveness of fees

Despite the complex issues involved, fee-based services are extremely common. The private practice of human services seems universally dependent on such fees. For most agencies, however, fees are an important, but seldom a predominant, source of revenues. In fact, in most public settings fee collections may be prohibited entirely. Nevertheless, it is likely that most human service administrators will, at some point in their careers, be exposed to this form of financing mechanism.

Types of fees

Regardless of the advantages and disadvantages, fee-for-service arrangements are a fact of life in contemporary social service operations. However, as Goodman notes, the percentages of total agency revenues derived from fees has probably declined since 1965.[6] This is largely due to the enormous inputs of federal funds since that time, rather than to any diminution in the use of fees as a fund-raising mechanism. In the following discussion, we will deal with five basic types of fees in addition to some others: (1) participation fees; (2) flat rate fees; (3) "sliding scale" fees; (4) "fair-share-of-cost" distribution fees; and (5) fees paid by a third party.

Participation fees

One type of fee often collected by human service agencies might best be termed a "participation fee." This fee involves the collection of a nominal amount (e.g., one dollar per client) as a "good faith" pledge on the part of the client to participate actively in the service experience. In community mental health, family service agencies, and other settings, practitioners have gone so far as to develop treatment rationales for the use of such fee collection mechanisms.[7] These justifications usually focus on the involvement and commitment symbolized by the payment of the fee. For our purposes, the primary significance of such fees is that they are likely to represent an insubstantial revenue source for the human service agency. Beyond that, they have very little significance to the financial management of an agency. Managers of agencies might delegate responsibility for such fees principally to a program supervisor. Delegation of them to bookkeepers or clerical staff could prove counter-productive unless the staff is carefully instructed in the programmatic purposes of the fees.

Flat rate fees

One of the most common means of fee collection in human service programs is a flat rate, or fixed fee, for services provided. Such fees may be fixed by the entire service episode (e.g., $50 for a weekend encounter or group experience), by the number of service encounters ($20 per office visit), by the amount of elapsed time ($35 per hour), and so forth. Whatever the basis of calculation, the distinguishing feature of fixed fees is their universality: they are intended to apply to everyone on an equal basis. Consequently, fixed fee or flat rate charges may or may not be related to fiscal concerns like the costs of the service and consequent revenue demands of the agency, or to program concerns like the client's ability to pay.

The virtues of flat rate or fixed fees are a result of the ease with which a fee structure for them may be administered. From a planning standpoint, it is relatively easy to project total available revenues as a straight linear function of the number of anticipated clients (number of clients times standard fee equals anticipated revenues). Likewise, from the standpoint of collecting accounts receivable, the procedures necessary to bill clients and follow up on delinquent accounts are relatively simple to establish and administer.

Furthermore, in many situations, flat rate fees are not necessarily inconsistent with the programmatic and policy objectives of human service agencies. For example, in those cases in which an agency serves a relatively homogeneous population with comparable incomes and family sizes, the inequities arising from fixed fees are likely to be minimal. The inverse is also true: in those situations in which clients of diverse income levels or family size are served, a fixed fee structure tends to place the largest economic burden on those with the lowest incomes and largest families.

Sliding scale fees

The development of sliding scale fee structures represents a recognition of the possible inequities of fixed fees noted immediately above. Fees as a revenue source must compete with considerations of the client's ability to pay in a sliding scale arrangement. As a result, unless a good deal is known (or can be accurately estimated) about the prospective client population, revenue projections based on sliding scale fee structures are relatively risky.

The principal administrative issue involved in establishing a sliding scale fee structure is determining the basis on which to adjust fees. The criteria employed by agencies include income, family size, severity of problems, and frequency of use of the service. In principle, virtually any characteristics that differentiate among clients using a service could be employed to establish a sliding scale fee structure. In actuality, the structures are usually closely linked to indicators of the client's ability to pay for services, such as those noted above.

In establishing a sliding scale fee structure, the financial manager of the human service agency may call upon several standard references. The profile of a community, based on such variables as age, income, and education level, may be obtained from the U.S. Census Information for states, metropolitan areas, municipalities, census tracts, and so forth. In addition, several federal agencies regularly prepare data that can be used to develop baselines for this type of fee structure. For example, the Department of Labor regularly publishes an "Urban Worker's Family Budget" for selected urban areas in the United States. The Bureau of Labor Statistics publishes a comparable "Retired Couples Budget" for older people. Each of these guides is computed at three levels ("high," "medium," and "low" budget levels), and offers guidance on normal family income and expenditure patterns. Similar data may also be obtained from surveys, such as those conducted by the Survey Research Center at the University of Michigan.[8]

The judgmental factors involved not only in the establishment of a sliding scale fee structure, but also in its administration, introduce certain possibilities for both abusing and favoring clients that need to be carefully monitored by agency administrators. This is also true to some extent of other types of fees. The therapeutic uses of participation fees noted above can, under certain conditions, degenerate into the inappropriate use of fees as rewards and punishments for clients.[9] Because of the discretion involved, sliding scale fees are particularly susceptible to informal or unofficial uses of this type. Therefore, agencies that use a sliding scale fee structure should also take steps to insure that the administration of the structure is fair and equitable to the client.

Fair share of cost fees

A fourth form of fee collection historically identified with the voluntary sector can be termed the fair-share-of-cost method. In this approach it is necessary to determine the total cost of the service or activity and then assess each participant an appropriate charge (total cost divided by number of participants equals fair-share fee). For reasons that should be obvious, this method of fee collection is most appropriate for short-term projects or projects in which clients form a closely knit group whose unity is reinforced by such "sharing." The fair-share method is usually less desirable than either of the two methods for generating revenues previously cited, unless both stable costs and a stable client population can be assumed. Otherwise, the risks of falling short of revenues or exceeding client expectations are too great.

The fair-share-of-cost method may be of greatest interest to those involved in community organization and group work activities, in which the collection of fees on an occasional basis for specific projects may be the only fund-raising activity necessary. Senior citizens groups taking bus tours, youth groups planning parties, and social action groups planning demonstrations or protest marches may best be handled using the fair-share-of-cost method.

According to Goodman there are two problems with using the fair-share-of-cost method. First of all, as in the costs of mounting a major demonstration, the expense may simply exceed the ability to pay of those involved (public housing tenants, for example). There is no simple solution to this problem, other than finding a large donor or somebody willing to pay more than his fair share. The second problem is the difficulty of anticipating costs. Particularly in cases where the project to be funded involves the purchase of services from an established service enterprise, such determinations can be extremely complex and difficult. Does a group planning a weekend retreat need to purchase the time of group leaders or will they donate their time? Will they donate all their time, or a portion of it? Who will pay travel costs for private autos, the owners or the group? What about space rentals? These are some of the questions that frequently arise in the context of efforts to determine the fair-share-of-cost allocation.

Fees paid by a third party

In addition to the basic forms of fee collections noted above, a variety of new and more complex fee-based funding arrangements are evolving in the human services today. For example, funding for programs under Title XX of the Social Security Act are frequently carried out on a modified fee basis. That is, the size of the grant (or third-party payment) made to an agency by the Title XX allocation operation may be based on a "unit-cost" computation times the number of client "units" served. Likewise, in some states, human service practitioners may receive third-party support from Medicare or Medicaid on a fee-for-service basis under payment schedules established by state or federal agencies.

In a limited number of instances, third-party payments on a fee-for-service basis are made for the delivery of various types of personal services. (The eligibility of psychologists, psychiatrists, social workers, and other helping professionals varies widely by state, insurance carrier, type of service provided, and other considerations. All insurance is based on the concept of pooled risk, whereby payments are made by those at risk for a service at a level determined actuarily, based on their presumed degree of risk. Payments from this insurance pool are then made to the service dispenser after the covered services have been provided.

Payee perspectives

This chapter approaches fees from an agency perspective, differentiating among types of fees by means of administrative criteria or circumstances. It should be noted that it is also possible to classify types of fees by the circumstances of those who pay the fees. This so-called "payee perspective" results in a slightly different list of fees, and is the basis for a number of commonly used terms. For example, we might identify "users' fees" as fees in which those who pay are those who actually use the service. (These fees are virtually identical to the participation fees discussed above.) These may be differentiated from third-party payments made in behalf of a client by a public agency, insurance company, or benefactor other than the client or the agency. In cases in which a fee-based agency or program acts as its own third-party payee, the concept of an internal subsidy or "write-off" of the fee may be introduced. Many variations on this practice can be found among human service agencies. When fees and grant income are mixed, for example, such internal subsidization may often be handled with virtually no bookkeeping effort. In other instances, such as when Title XX–supported clients and fee-paying clients are mixed in a program, rather complicated reporting schemes may be necessary to differentiate the patterns of client support (or even to subdivide portions of an individual client's support).

It may be possible to divide third-party payments into two broad classes: those that are made on the basis of a contract between the third-party donor and the service delivery agency for block purchases of services for a group of clients, and those made on the basis of a contract between individual clients and third-party donors (vendor payments). Title XX purchase-of-service contracts are an example of the former, while Medicaid is an example of the latter. Such purchase-of-service contracts are distinguishable from other types of block grants, principally because the question of the unit cost of service, essentially a fee calculation, is so central.

The terminology describing fees from a payee perspective is principally of interest to human service agencies only as it affects their relationships to funding sources. It matters less whether a particular payment is a block purchase or vendor payment, for example, than whether payments provide adequate reimbursement for real agency cost outlays in connection with delivery of the service.

Administrative implications

The administrative implications of fee collections for human services organizations tend to fall into two broad categories: control issues and planning issues. We shall discuss each of these in the remainder of this chapter. Major control issues under consideration will be the establishment of adequate administrative routines for recording and collecting fees and client charges, and the establishment of adequate follow-up routines, particularly billing and collection procedures. Four major planning issues will be dealt with: the problems of predicting income from fees, capitalization and third-party payments, the "social justice" implications of fee collections, and the problem of free goods.

Control issues

One of the most difficult administrative control problems arising out of fee-based services is the problem of insuring adequate procedures for recording and collecting fees. Regardless of the type of fee involved, the major steps in the process are the same: generating a "charge slip" or some other billing record, recording the charge as an account receivable, billing the client (or the appropriate third-party payee), recording payments received, "aging" unpaid accounts receivable, and collecting or writing off past-due accounts.

There are several points where a breakdown can occur. Although the problem of recording payments received is not as difficult to control as that of recording contributions received, there is still some cause for caution. Adequate procedures and safeguards (such as rotating personnel periodically, or requiring mandatory annual leaves for personnel) may be desirable, for example, to guard against embezzlement and theft by employees.

A major potential control problem with this kind of system can be avoided in most agencies if proper care is taken in the handling of initial charge records. If, for example, a central intake worker or receptionist logs in all clients entering the agency, and all service workers routinely report all clients seen, an adequate basis for cross-checking client charges will ordinarily exist.

It should be noted that an important feedback mechanism is inherent in the fee-charging system, particularly if clients pay their own fees: inaccurate, inappropriate, or other erroneous charges will usually be brought to the attention of appropriate officials by clients—sometimes with great vigor! Several encounters with angry mothers, whose children's visits with a child guidance worker have been misbilled, will usually provide the necessary incentive to establish accurate and timely billing procedures.

A more difficult control problem involves the question of what to do with unpaid accounts. While good "business sense" may dictate making efforts at collection (up to turning the account over to a collection agency), good "social work sense" often argues against such solutions. At least one mental health agency with which I am familiar has largely solved this problem by linking payment of fees to the clinical context: reluctance to pay fees is interpreted as a non-cooperative attitude on the part of the client, and the issue is taken up by the clinical staff. Such an approach, however, may strike some as taking unfair advantage of client vulnerabilities. Certainly, it can be seen that significant tensions can arise between the "helping" thrust of an agency and its need for fee revenue.

Most contemporary human service agencies are probably reluctant to turn uncollectable accounts receivable over to collection agencies—and with good reason.[10] Yet the problem is virtually unavoidable. All agencies that operate on a fee basis can expect to have at least some uncollectables. The primary question is how such uncollected fees are to be handled. One common approach is to write off uncollectable accounts receivable—that is, to enter them as an adjustment to assets. In such cases, the entry showing the net amount of such write-offs would probably show up on the trial balance, thereby bringing the matter to the attention of the board of directors and the public, which may be good management strategy (e.g., "In 1972 our agency provided $2,874 in services to clients for which we were not reimbursed"). In combination agencies, in which fee supported and grant supported clients may be mixed, there is the additional problem of maintaining a distinction between clients unsupported by any payments whatsover and those supported by grant revenues.

A major management problem in human service agencies is the question of how much is too much in the case of uncollected fees. Is the agency operating effectively if 5 percent of its fees are unpaid? 15 percent? 50 percent? Ultimately, the answers to such questions are dependent on a great many factors, including the type of client, size of individual charges, and importance of fees in total agency income. In cases in which small fees are collected simply as a means of regulating demand for services, 50 percent non-collection could be tolerated (see the discussion of the problem of free goods below). In agencies entirely dependent on fees assessed by problem episode, such as adoptions, even a very low percentage of non-collection cannot be sustained without systematic consequences for agency operations.

Planning issues

Predicting revenues from fees

The general problem of budget-making and allocations decisions in a fee-based system is discussed, along with other budget systems, in Chapter 8. In the present context we can identify the general problem to which such budget systems must adapt in fee-based agencies and programs: the problem of predicting income from fees. Three general approaches to this problem are identified below: one method involves estimation of fee income as a "linear function" of the number of clients and the amount of the fee, the second method involves procedures for establishing a range of probable revenues, and the third method involves the use of indifference curves from economics.

The linear function approach. Prediction of revenues using this approach requires two separate pieces of information: the number of clients to be served during a given period, and the charge per client. Obviously, the more accurate each of these "variables" can be made, the more accurate the predictions will be. In a day-care operation licensed to serve fifty children, for example, in which the charge is $200 per month, the computation of income from fees is straight-forward (ignoring for the moment the problems of collections noted above):

$$\$200 \times 12 \text{ months} \times 50 \text{ children} = \$120,000$$

Even in those cases where there is some slight variation from these estimates this approach may be usable. If, for example, one has access to the vacancy rates (for which charges are not assessed), it may be possible to determine that each child attends on the average 11.4 months rather than 12, or that each parent pays $180 per month rather than $200. Other adjustments can also be made to the product. For example, if the agency regularly writes off 2 percent of its collections, this figure can simply be subtracted from $120,000.

The range approach. If any of the above items (cost, time, clients) cannot be accurately estimated, some other approach to predicting revenue from fees may be necessary. For example, when the number of clients or appointments is a problem, or when charges per service episode vary significantly, use of the linear function approach may simply be impossible. In this case, the agency or program may use an approach to predicting fee revenues, perhaps by making at least two and possibly more predictions that fall over a range from high to low and are consistent with certain variable assumptions.

If the base of charges is variable, for example, it may be possible to determine that the agency delivers between 15,000 and 20,000 hours of service in a given year, with a hypothetical average of 17,500. If there is a constant charge of $10 per service hour, it is possible to estimate that agency revenues will vary between $150,000 and $200,000, with a hypothetical average of $175,000. While such information may be less exact than desired, it is certainly preferable to not knowing whether to expect $5,000 or $500,000 in the year!

In other cases, there may be the additional problem of estimating revenues when cost and time both vary (determining the number of service hours, in this case, treats both clients and time together). Thus, in the above problem, part of the estimated 17,500 hours of service may be at $8 per hour, part at $10, and part at $25. A prediction can still be made (or rather, three predictions can be made, and summed) by apportioning the 17,500 hours among the three rates. If one-fourth of the hours were billed at $8, one-half at $10, and the rest at $25, a pattern like that of Figure 10 would hold.

It should be noted here that when a "sliding scale" fee schedule is used, the prediction of revenues from fees is actually a variation of the range approach identified here—but one that requires several additional approaches. If, for example, scheduled fees "slide" in a number of steps, the problem of predicting income is identical with the range problem: the prediction is dependent on identifying the steps and the number of clients or hours of service expected at each rate, as in Figure 10. By contrast, if the "slide" is over an interval—that is, rather than being a series of steps, rates are a percentage of personal income and thus may amount to a number of whole dollars (see Figure 11)—the problem is more suitable to a linear or curvilinear regression approach.

Indifference curves. Finally, when quasi-market conditions exist, it may be possible to revert to a technique used by economists in predicting revenues. The technique is usually termed "indifference curves," and is appropriate for use in the human service context only in those cases in which it can be assumed that a relation exists between the size of the fee and the willingness of clients to make use of the service (that is, their "marginal propensity to consume"). The mere suggestion of such a relationship in human services may be enough to curdle the coffee cream of several veteran social workers, but there are quite clearly several occasions when quasi-market circumstances exist in human services. In sheltered workshops, handicraft groups, and other programs where items are manufactured for sale, for example, this is certainly the case. Likewise, this relationship may hold in instances where "social utility" services are made available to the general public for a fee—summer camps and swimming pools, for example. A family

FIGURE 10

A Range Approach for Estimating Revenues

$ 8 per hour	×	4375 hours	=	$ 35,000
10 per hour	×	8750 hours	=	87,500
25 per hour	×	4375 hours	=	109,375
Estimated fee revenues				$231,875

FIGURE 11

An Indifference Curve: Day Care Fees per Week

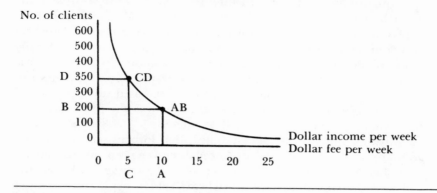

Note: A fee of $10 per week can be expected to yield 200 clients and a fee income of $2,000 a week (Prediction AB), while a fee of $5 a week can be expected to yield 350 clients and a fee income of $1,750 a week (Prediction CD).

willing to spend $35 for a pool membership is less likely to spend $150 for the same membership. Another category of services that may fit this model is day-care programs, in which the ability to pay for day care may correspond in a large degree to the relationship between day-care charges and the salary levels of working women.

The applicability of this model to human service revenue predictions is straightforward. Is the revenue to be predicted dependent on substantial variations in fees and, as a result, on corresponding increases or decreases in the number of participating clients? If the answer is yes, the indifference curve model may be useful. In a great many cases in the human services, however, the answer to this question will be "no," simply because agencies typically come nowhere near meeting the total need—and consequently the demand—for services. Situations in which there is a large "unmet need" are inappropriate for the kind of indifference analysis described here.

In essence, the indifference model involves identification of two axes, as in Figure 11. The vertical axis shows anticipated clients, while the horizontal axis shows the fee charged. In Figure 11 the fee varies from $1 a day to $25 a day for day care. The curved line ("indifference curve") displays the variable combination of clients and charges, with the resultant revenue combinations being derived by multiplication.

It should be obvious that this approach is based on the availability of sophisticated data, or at least the manager's ability to make sophisticated quantitative estimates. In this case, one could fit a curve to the graph by estimating that a $1-a-day charge would satisfy more than 50 percent of the total need for day care in a community (based on a random-sample survey), while a $25-a-day charge would reach only 2 percent of the working women in the community (those whose incomes exceed the daily charge by 50 percent). These estimates can be used to establish the range, with the curve based upon the law of diminishing returns. The assumption is that, as the price increases, correspondingly fewer women will be interested.

Because of the fact, previously noted, that human service agencies rarely approach satisfying the total need in a given problem area, as well as the bias against charges based on what the market will bear, the kind of indifference analysis outlined here is seldom explicitly employed in establishing fees. The ordinary practice, instead, is to predetermine an optimum level of services and base charges on the administrative and program costs necessary to maintain that level of service availability. From an administrative point of view there is relatively little in the latter approach that makes it either more humane or more farsighted than the approach of indifference analysis. It does, however, have a better image among human service professionals.

Whatever approach is used, the problem of predicting income from fees continues to be a major administrative headache in most human service organizations concerned with fees. In addition to the variables discussed there are countless other factors that affect fee income. For example, there is the influence of the well-known counter-cyclical function of human services: when unemployment is up and personal income down, the demand for community mental health services is likely to go up, along with the rate of non-collections.

The problem of capitalization

"Capitalization," as that term is utilized in business finance, involves the process of accumulating a substantial pool of capital with which to begin business operations or expand existing operations. Capital in this sense is obviously necessary—particularly to meet fixed and variable expenses in the period between the initiation of the enterprise and the beginning of the flow of income from sales.

Something of the same problem is often experienced in human services—albeit often under substantially different circumstances, and on an altogether different scale of operations. Because of the obvious inappropriateness of the term capital in the non-profit voluntary and public sectors, the term "seed money" is often used. The underlying dynamics are the same, however. In the case of the grant-supported, or fund-drive-financed agency, such seed money may temporarily compensate for unforeseen difficulties in the distribution of funds. An agency may have to temporarily borrow funds to meet its payroll, using the approved grant as collateral, or get a "grubstake" from a parent organization or federation to underwrite the initial costs of grant development or the expenses of fund-raising.

In the case of the fee-based agency or program, however, the problem is more like that faced by commercial enterprises: the procedures for *post-hoc* payment of fees inevitably incorporate a significant lag in the collection procedures of the agency, and this must be taken into account. Furthermore, since fee revenues are based on clients' actual use of services, and this factor may be something that builds up gradually over a period of time, it is very likely that fees will grow slowly during the initial phase of agency operations. By contrast, it is extremely unlikely that adequate levels of service can be made available if workers are added as money is available (with workers increasing gradually from five hours this month to six hours the next, and so on). Consequently, most fee-based agencies will require some assistance with initial capitalization in order to "get the program off the ground." This point is made here, in part, to underline the very real possibility that a number of human service programs that initially require grant support could, after a start-up period, revert to a self-sustaining basis, if fees are phased in properly.

The social justice perspective

The question of whether, in fact, shifts in funding support from a grant-supported to a fee-supported basis *should* be made introduces for us the third, and final, planning issue to be considered: the social justice implications arising from fee-based services.

There is no avoiding the fact that the delivery of services on a fee-for-service basis directly conflicts with the presumed objective of many human services to make service available to clients solely on the basis of need. If one adopts a fee perspective completely, for example, one recognizes the "legitimate needs" only of those who can pay, leaving the entire low-income population out of the picture. If, on the other hand, one adopts the perspective that services must go to everyone

regardless of ability to pay, equally serious questions about the capability of agencies to provide such services are raised.

As a result, most people and most agencies are inclined to adopt a
compromise position: a fee structure is established, with explicit recognition of a sliding scale provision, or "informal" arrangements are
made for fee waivers, "client grants," "stipends," and other arrangements. The difficulty is that relatively wide discretion must be granted
to staff members in the handling of such arrangements, and as a result,
substantial potential for unfairness and abuse can be introduced into
the system. It also should be apparent that from a larger perspective,
the fee-for-service arrangements in human service agencies are fundamental factors in the existence of "two-class" service delivery systems
of the type discussed by Hollingshead and Redlich.[11]

While third-party funding is sometimes suggested as a partial solution to this problem, recent evidence suggests that such arrangements
may not entirely eliminate differences in the quality of services, but
may instead shift the issue from one involving different agencies to
an internal agency matter. ("They know who pays their own bills
around here," clients may be heard to remark, "and it makes a difference
in how they treat you!") Regardless of how one interprets such comments, they do point up the on-going difficulties of fee-based services
in the human services. It is both poor administrative practice and
contrary to program objectives to simply sweep aside such concerns
and concentrate only on the revenue potential of fee collections. Revenues and the just treatment of clients are both part of the permanent
reality in human services, and seldom can one be considered without
the other.

The problem of free goods

There is yet another social justice aspect to the subject of fees.
Although it is seldom explicitly dealt with in human services, we
may identify one of the problems of fees as their use in manipulating
services toward those who (in their own opinion) need a service and
away from those who (in their own view) don't.

This matter is frequently treated by economists as the problem of
free goods: where there are no costs to the consumption of goods and
services, users will tend to "overconsume." Perfect illustrations of
this are the free newspapers and handouts that one may take, then toss
aside a few steps later. Totally free services, it could be argued, may be
used by people who don't really need the service and who would
not be willing to pay even a nominal fee for it.

To avoid the problem of overutilization of free services some agencies require clients to pay a minimal fee ($ .50 a visit). A different perspective on the same phenomenon, of course, is the view that payment of a minimal fee signals the client's minimal commitment and willingness to seek help, as discussed at the beginning of the chapter. We have a rare instance here in which "economic wisdom" and "psychodynamic wisdom" offer differing explanations but a common conclusion: minimal fees have a very practical use as an instrument for encouraging the legitimate use of services and discouraging casual or inappropriate use.

Conclusion

This chapter has been addressed to the question of fees as a basis for financing human service agencies and programs. On the assumption that an on-going fee-based program can be established, the chapter on budget-making (Chapter 6) pursues the question further in the context of fee-based budget systems. In addition, questions of more sophisticated planning and control techniques useful in the fee-based situations are discussed in Chapters 9 and 10.

The essential observation here is that several types of fees are employed in human service settings. Regardless of the forms, however, certain generalizations can be made about fees. For one thing, the fee-for-service system that has grown up in various branches of human services in the United States shows no signs of decline. Fees give every indication of continuing to be a mainstay in service delivery operations.

From an operational viewpoint the principal question with fee-based services involves the establishment of adequate procedures for the recording and collection of fees, whether from clients or from agencies. From a broader perspective the context of fee-based services raises additional questions: particularly important here is the difficult problem of predicting fee revenues, for which several approaches have been set forth in this chapter. Also problematic are the social justice implications of the effect of fee collections on the availability and utilization of services. These are long-standing issues, and one suspects they will be with us as long as services are available on a fee basis.

CHAPTER 5

FUND-RAISING CAMPAIGNS FROM AN AGENCY PERSPECTIVE

It may strike the reader versed in the traditional perspectives of social services as curious indeed to find a chapter on fund-raising campaigns in a book on social *agency* management. Roughly since the end of World War I there has been a widely accepted view of the division of labor in the social services between public and voluntary auspices.[1] Furthermore, while public services are seen as entirely tax supported from this standpoint, the voluntary sector are seen as relying primarily on various fund-raising techniques.[2] Within the voluntary sector, therefore, one finds specialists in fund-raising who deal "outwardly" with the community, as well as administrators and service workers who deal "inwardly" with the agency and its clientele. This has been supported and institutionalized over the years by the growth of community-level federated funding organizations that embody such a division of labor. For example, it is common for fund-raising to be supervised by a "campaign committee" composed of prominent citizens and community leaders while the allocation of funds is handled by a "budget committee" with a different composition.[3]

In this orthodox view public and voluntary administrators alike deal directly with allocations committees, but neither deals with fund-raising per se. To those accepting this world view it may appear to border on heresy to suggest, as this chapter does, that there are a number of things that agency administrators need to know about the fund-raising arts. Like Victorian brides, social agency administrators apparently are better off not knowing certain things!

The neglect of fund-raising knowledge and skills represents a serious lacuna in the curriculum of human service professional programs, and is a particularly glaring omission in many human service administration programs.[4] If anything, this oversight is becoming increasingly serious, due to the impact of some of the trends noted in Chapter 1 on the pattern of funding support for human service organizations.

Since the mid-1960s, at least, a more heterodox pattern of agency funding, characterized principally by the breakdown of major distinctions between "public" and "voluntary" agencies, has become apparent.[5] Today, as a result, the purely tax-supported public agency and the purely contribution-supported voluntary agency are more often viewed as opposite ends of a continuum of funding possibilities than as qualitatively distinctive entities. Probably the most common form of human service agency to emerge in recent years is the hybrid "multi-funded" agency in which public funds, voluntary contributions, and third party and client fees in varying combinations are merged into a more or less coherent program package.

The reasons for the emergence of this new type of agency—typically organized as a not-for-profit corporation—are related to the factors discussed in Chapter 1. Pressures for new types of services, together with the relatively high accessibility of federal funding, for example, have forced many organizations in the traditionally voluntary sector to compete with entirely new agencies in such diverse programs as Model Cities, the War on Poverty, the Older Americans Act, Developmental Disabilities, and Title XX.

In the context of this new form of service delivery organization, many of the traditional distinctions regarding the division of labor in fund-raising have broken down or been seriously undermined. For example legislative requirements for matching funds or in-kind contributions are part of many of the federal programs mentioned above. In many cases as well, evidence must be provided that such matching is over and above current "community effort" in the problem area in question. The efforts to raise these funds most typically fall outside the traditional federated funding system, which has developed a logic and timing of its own. Consequently, the burden of fund-raising usually falls directly on the management and staff of the agency pursuing the grant.

Furthermore, the incorporated status of multi-funded agencies often places them outside the traditional strictures against "fund-raising" by public agencies, leaving them largely free to pursue their fund-raising activities in the traditional voluntary sector manner. Thus, such publicly created entities as community action agencies, local aging agencies, and community mental health centers typically possess the legal sanction to participate in such federated fund-raising campaigns as United Way, or to create their own independent campaigns.

The perspective on fund-raising taken here is, therefore, an entirely pragmatic one. Agency financial managers need to understand the basics of fund-raising both because it is an important factor in the milieu of most agencies, and because, in all likelihood, they will be called upon to engage in this practice at some point. Even those administrators who never engage in any direct fund-raising effort, however, may be called on at some point to engage a professional fund-raiser for a "capital campaign" or the establishment of an endowment for the agency. Whether one is seeking to raise $10 million for a construction project, or $2,500 in matching funds to obtain a federal grant, the basic principles of fund-raising identified in the literature are applicable.

Terminology

As in previous chapters, we begin the discussion here with the clarification of some basic terms. "Fund-raising," as that term is used throughout the book, refers to the administrative process of locating and securing money or in-kind contributions with established monetary value. In this broad sense, fund-raising in human service agencies involves allocations budgeting, grantsmanship, third-party payments, and fee collections, as well as the organizing of solicitation campaigns and special events. Throughout much of the literature cited in this chapter (and in the discussion immediately preceding), the term fund-raising is used in the more restricted sense of organized solicitations and special events. From a management perspective, however, this usage is not justified. First, as noted in Chapter 2, "funds" are defined as collections of assets and their attendant accountabilities. Consistent with that usage fund-raising refers to any effort contributing to (and raising) the total assets of a fund. The activities that go into this function, as noted above, are several.

Use of the generic meaning, however, leaves the problem of what to call the set of fund-raising activities of greatest interest in this chapter.

They fall into two discernible categories. Annual fund drives and other organized fund-raising events shall be referred to as "campaigns." Other activities such as bake sales, talent shows, celebrity appearances, and testimonial dinners shall be referred to collectively as "special events."[6]

Numerous other terms also should be noted, if only to caution the reader unaccustomed to their use that no precise or consistent definitions are to be expected. Among the terms that fall within this caveat are "charity," "philanthropy," and "volunteer." Each has at least two meanings—a traditional usage and a modern idiom—and the reader who confronts these terms is cautioned to try to sort out their meanings by context.

Campaigns as peculiarly American

Present descriptions of fund-raising campaigns represent a fairly clearly articulated "technology," or body of how-to-do-it knowledge, and it is a peculiarly American invention. Although the first recorded fund-raising campaign was conducted in Liverpool, England, in 1873, it was in the United States that this form of fund-raising came into its own. Probably no other population in human history has granted such widespread legitimacy to this particular form of economic exchange.[7]

In a very real sense fund-raising campaigns also represent a major contribution of the human services to American culture. Orginally conducted for charitable purposes, the fund-raising campaign is employed today for educational, political, and religious purposes as well. And while church members may have given offerings for centuries, the tactics and organizational strategies employed in such campaigns today were largely worked out in the "federated funding" efforts of councils of social agencies in the early years of the twentieth century.[8]

This form of fund-raising is considerably older and more established than some of the other forms used by agencies discussed in this book (e.g., grantsmanship). In essence, the "principles" of fund-raising campaigns were established in outline after the First World War, and have been an essentially stable body of knowledge since the Second World War.[9] Wars, in fact, played an important role in the development and dissemination of this knowledge. Although the first organized community fund-raising campaign in the United States occurred in Denver in 1887, the widespread proliferation of campaign organizations came with the "War Chests" of World War I. In the peacetime demobilization, a large number of these campaigns were converted to peaceful pursuits directed at community well-being. Between the wars such local campaigns, then known as "Community Chests," became a standard feature of life in the large cities. Following World War II, a similar resurgence of interest in smaller cities occurred, with the result that today there are several thousand local fund-raising organizations in cities of all sizes throughout the United States.[10]

During the late 1960s, community campaigns came under widespread criticism for their "elitist domination." Such charges placed a negative value on what appears throughout the fund-raising literature as one of the principal virtues. An effective campaign, it is suggested, must begin with "top-flight leadership," a phrase that normally means the recruitment of rich, powerful men. One recent publication, for example, identifies the ideal campaign chairman as rich, powerful, generous to causes, well liked, a good speaker, a true believer in the cause for which funds are sought, and fearless under community pressures.[11] The observation that the chairman should begin the campaign with a large donation of his own before asking others is also common.[12]

The social agency administrator embarking on a fund-raising campaign, then, is faced with a clear-cut choice. According to the fund-raisers, it is essential for the success of a campaign that community leaders be involved. On the other hand, critics argue that such involvement unfairly biases the event against minorities, women, and unpopular causes. In all likelihood, the choice will depend on the particular situation.

The art and science of fund-raising

Close scrutiny of the historical development of the fund-raising enterprise in the United States suggests the articulation of two interrelated models of practice: an organizational model, which addresses questions of interaction, authority, responsibility, and systematizing of the efforts of volunteer workers in a successful fund-raising campaign; and a motivational model, which focuses on the relationship between asker and giver and attempts to identify the most appropriate and effective ways of asking. The first of these models is only of passing interest in the agency context, since it is principally concerned with creating a campaign organization where none presently exists. Those interested in this topic should consult some of the standard sources.[13]

On the other hand, there is very great interest in the agency context in the issue of motivation: the motives, reasons, and compulsions attributed to people who give to campaigns and to those who do not.

Perhaps no statement appears more frequently in the fund-raising literature to summarize this motivational concern than the following: "People don't give to causes. They give to people."

As with most homilies, it is not immediately apparent whether this is a profound statement or simply trite and self-evident. (Try handing a fifty-dollar check to a cause some time!) The usual meaning given to this statement in the literature, however, is that the secret to successful fund-raising campaigns lies in direct, face-to-face encounters, preferably between people who already know one another. Fund-raising campaigns, the literature suggests, are not built on the "positive sentiments" of good will, altruism, public spiritedness, and humanitarianism. Only by the subtle coercions of those whom they admire and respect, and whose ill opinion they fear, can people be counted on to contribute at satisfactory levels.

This basic postulate normally takes two distinct forms in a campaign, presumably in recognition of the elitist/public view of society already noted. On the one hand, the identification of a singularly effective community leader who is able to chair the entire campaign, make a substantial contribution, and solicit his friends for similar donations should account for approximately one-third of all collections. Concurrently, a cadre of volunteers (presumably not rich, but also contributing) is identified, recruited, and trained before being sent forth to garner the remaining two-thirds.[14]

And a dissent

Not everyone agrees, however, with the consensus regarding the face-to-face dynamic of fund-raising psychology. Levy, for example, states:

> It no longer seems sufficient to assert that "people don't give to causes; they give to people" or that "the fund-raising process and medium are more important than the funds actually raised." There is just too much ambiguity and ambivalence about statements like these and they often contradict one another. If people really do give to people, or if fundraisers and volunteers continue to act as if they do, then what happens to the developmental and enduring consequences of the intensive process that so many fundraisers and volunteers really believe that fundraising ought to be?[15]

Fund-raising principles are, according to Levy, much like administrative principles—often contradictory, with no clear-cut "rules" to justify choosing one over the other.[16] The issue raised by Levy ultimately revolves around the model of human behavior one assumes: an economic one, of persons giving in light of the expectation of some unspecified good; a psychological one, of persons giving to satisfy some basic need; a sociological one, of persons responding to the expectations of face-to-face encounters; or a moral one, of persons giving from a sense of obligation or duty.

Unfortunately, in most instances this issue is thoroughly clouded by the strategic and instrumental interests that dominate the typical campaign. "I don't give a damn why people contribute," one volunteer reported, "so long as they do!" From this perspective the motivational model one adopts is less important for its overall validity than for its immediate value in motivating volunteers and reinforcing their sense of the importance of their work. In the administrative setting, the instances in which an administrator is using a fund-raising drive to encourage the "developmental and intensive process that so many fund raisers believe it ought to be" are most likely to be related to organizing, strengthening, or expanding a constituency for the agency (see Chapter 5). In most instances, however, the purpose of the fund-raising campaign is straightforward—to raise funds. The principal motivational question is "What works?" and from the testimony of the fund-raising literature, face-to-face encounters do.

Knowledge and skill of volunteers

Another point on which there is agreement in the literature is that volunteers should be trained for their task before being sent forth. A major question that arises is what kinds of knowledge and skills must the volunteers possess? The range is quite broad. Volunteers agreeing to distribute canisters to local merchants, for example, may need to know little beyond the basic purpose of the campaign, their delivery route, and the basic elements of courtesy. For other procedures, far more elaborate preparation of volunteers may be essential. One of the critical questions here involves the "division of knowledge" among agency administrators and staff, fund-raising consultants, and volunteers. Ordinarily, one would expect all persons connected with the campaign to possess certain knowledge and skills: (1) an understanding of why people do and do not contribute to causes; (2) the practical influences on givers (taxes, business conditions, laws, etc.) and ways in which these intrude on giving; (3) the cause for which funds are being raised; (4) its relation to the larger human service system.[17]

In addition, however, the person in charge of the campaign must possess additional knowledge and skills. The general profile of the fund-raiser offered in Chapter 4 begins to identify some of these. Over and beyond that sketch, however, Levy offers the following specific suggestions: (1) individual, group, and mass approaches to education; (2) administrative process, organization and necessary equipment of the campaign; (3) statistical, financial, and other administrative reporting formats; (4) planning techniques, such as needs assessment and needs-meeting techniques.[18]

Levy also notes numerous skill requirements for fund-raisers: (1) skill in persuasion, interpretation, and education; (2) the highly valued "ability to unearth relevant facts or to facilitate their discovery as a basis for setting campaign goals"; (3) leadership, sensitivity, skill in group dynamics and problem solving; (4) the ability to "rate" givers (that is, to estimate accurately how much they might contribute).[19] Communication skills, personnel management skills, and the ability to operate office equipment are also mentioned as important.

Ethically speaking, a fund-raiser should be committed to the cause, possessed of a sense of higher purpose or greater good, able to restrain "rating" and other procedures to avoid excessive invasions of the privacy of potential donors, have a helping attitude, unusual seriousness and breadth, and objectivity without dispassionateness, and be directed toward encouraging giving as altruism.[20]

After noting all of this. Levy rhapsodizes:

> Can anyone alive do all these things, know all these things and be all these things? Probably not. But when one teaches or tries to learn a worthy occupation it is well for him to start with the aspiration to master all that is worthy to be mastered, and then to use his education and the rest of his career to try to master it—never making it perhaps, but never feeling convinced that it was not worth the attempt; never feeling that whatever degree of mastery he did attain did not help him to be that much more effective and gratified as a fund raiser, and that much more a boon to the community.[21]

In summarizing his views thus, Levy also imparts the fervid, emotion quality of the fund-raising literature (and not a few of the practitioners!). Furthermore, a goodly number of the knowledge and skill areas mentioned (particularly in the ethical area) are perhaps less taught than caught; that is, enthusiasm, a sense of higher purpose, and the like are more readily acquired by contact with others who already possess them than they are taught in any usual sense of that term. Nevertheless, the prospects for including many of these items in the curriculum of human service training programs appear good.

Organizing a campaign

Very little has been said thus far about the task of organizing or structuring a fund-raising campaign. If the agency is part of a federated campaign group, or employs a professional development expert, these matters will be handled in due course. Assume for the moment, however, that even in such cases it is advisable for agency officials responsible for financing to have some basic understanding of the directions to be taken.

The essential task of creating a campaign organization can be viewed as the creation of a temporary, voluntary organization—that is, the recruitment of a sufficient number of volunteer workers to solicit funds on a face-to-face basis; division of the task among members of this group in a way that responsibilities, offices, assignments, and other matters are clear; and the provision of the necessary logistical supports, which must be at the right place the first time around. This task is made doubly difficult by the fact that the organization is built around the assumptions of inexperienced, unpaid people who do not have long experience working together and cannot be controlled by the kinds of inducements and constraints that apply to full-time, paid employees.

Of critical importance in the creation of such a fund-raising organization is the appropriate assignment of responsibilities. In many instances such organizations assume a formal committee structure, with officers (chairperson, secretary, treasurer, etc.) instead of some other form of organization or assignment of titles. Regardless of organizational labels, however, the respective duties of the various officials should be clear to all concerned. If some solicitors expect to turn in funds to the treasurer, and others to the secretary, and these officials themselves are not clear as to who gets the money or what to do with it, the result may be confusion or disaster for the campaign.

From a management perspective, the task of creating a fund-raising organization is not fundamentally different from any other organizing task: the critical initial step is for clear, unambiguous delegations of responsibility throughout the fund-raising organization.

Several of the works on fund-raising cited above recommend a command-like organizational structure—with the leaders delegating specific assignments (publicity, mailings, contacting large donors) and assigning specific territories to "precinct captains" for door-to-door contact. An often-cited and highly important fiscal control objective is the earliest possible separation of funds and receipts recording those funds. Thus, each solicitor who gives the actual money collected to a block captain—who in turn gives it to a precinct captain, and so on through the organizational ranks to the treasurer—should be required to submit a simultaneous report directly to the treasurer that indicates how much was taken in. Otherwise, the organization is entirely dependent on simple trust in the volunteers at each level—and experience in this area suggests that occasionally such trust will be violated, and violated badly.

Before such an organization can be converted from a plan into a reality, however, a cadre of volunteer workers must be recruited, identified, and trained. Recruitment is one of the essential tasks of this type of fund-raising, and is also subject to the face-to-face rule stated previously: just as people don't *give* to causes, a good many people do not *work* for causes, but rather for people. Consequently, some sources in this field suggest that the single most essential task in organizing a campaign is the selection of a chairperson for whom recruits are willing to work.

Volunteers for a fund-raising project should always be assumed to be in a blissful state of ignorance with respect to the particulars of your campaign, and you provide them with detailed information about what is expected of them in training sessions. How much time will they have for collections? How should they present the case for funds? What do they do with the money? Will there be others competing with them in their territory? What if they fall off someone's porch and break an ankle? The well-organized campaign should be prepared in advance to provide satisfactory answers to these, and innumerable other questions. Those volunteers already informed on such matters will usually be tolerant of repetition and the rest will be grateful.

Third, it is essential in organizing a campaign to plan very carefully the distribution of equipment and supplies. If there are to be appeals in various churches on a particular weekend, will the religious leaders get the necessary information in order to present it satisfactorily? If there is to be a special event requiring public address equipment, have arrangements been made to get the equipment to the event and back? Do volunteer solicitors have ample copies of handouts and promotional literature? Again, from a fiscal control standpoint, if volunteers are expected to submit reports on their collections directly to the main office by mail, do they have the report forms, envelopes, and so on that will ease this task?

Finally, it is probably a good idea in organizing a campaign such as this to provide some advance planning for dealing with crises. One rule of thumb here would be to apply the "management by exceptions" principal discussed elsewhere, and designate in advance the chairperson or some other official to be responsible for dealing with crises. Everyone working on the campaign is then told to report serious problems directly to this person. ("If you think it's serious, call Jane at 555-4141" is the kind of message one might have printed on handouts to volunteers.) It is important for some explicit name recognition to be involved. To many people, the phone number may seem mysterious and slightly forbidding, but a name adds an ingratiating personal touch—even in those instances in which the scale of the campaign is such that "Jane" is the codename for a corps of operators manning a bank of phones!

The ultimate task of organizing a campaign or organizing any other voluntary group of people for some specific tasks is essentially a matter of creating or inspiring a satisfactory level of orderliness, predictability, and routine performance by seeking and keeping the volunteers' co-operation.

A caution

Many persons engaged in fund-raising as a full-time occupation identify their efforts as professional, and as with many other human service occupations, fund-raising has, indeed, assumed some of the trappings of professionalism.[22] It remains true, however, that unlike brain surgery or the representation of clients before federal courts, the voluntary setting of fund-raising activities makes any exclusive prerogatives of professional fund-raisers impossible to enforce. Although subject to the loose limits of state and federal law, virtually anyone is free to engage in directing or consulting fund-raising campaigns. This raises certain inevitable questions about the proper relationship between agencies and "outside" fund-raisers, which can only be considered briefly here.

For many in the human services, propriety, as noted at the outset of this chapter, is best maintained through the traditional division of labor. Leave the fund-raising to "them" and "we" will provide the services. Unfortunately, this attitude is unrealistic in the context of the multi-funded agency.

Another approach involves the direct employment of a fund-raiser on the staff of an agency. Using our broader definition of that term, such a person might spend part of his time organizing campaigns and special events, part of it in grantsmanship, and part of it collecting accounts receivable. This approach, however, is likely to be workable only in those instances in which the fund-raiser can "pay his own way," that is, raise enough money to cover the costs of fund-raising as a relatively low proportion of the total funds collected. Two additional problems arise, however, in the decision to hire a fund-raiser. The first involves the question of recruitment. Where should one look for such a person? And when applicants with less than all of the qualifications apply, which traits should be most valued? A partial solution to this problem is offered by the credentialing procedures of the American Association of Fund-Raising Counsel, whose members ascribe to a fairly explicit code of ethics. Beyond that, of course, many of the usual assessment considerations that go into staff recruitment and selection are also important. Perhaps the most difficult aspect of this choice for many agencies will be the tradeoff between "experience" in fund-raising and "ability" to learn the tricks of the trade.

A second set of management concerns applicable to all fund-raising efforts involves the assessment of performance. Several possibilities exist. First, the criterion of fund-raising being at least self-supporting seems essential. It is unlikely, however, that any agency will be able to sustain for very long a fund-raising operation that pays only for itself—for reasons of external accountability. How does one explain to contributors, for example, that all of their contributions (or even most of them) are spent on raising their contributions? Consequently, the proportion of fund-raising costs to total funds raised may be a useful, if relative indicator of effectiveness in this area.

Likewise, the proportion of funds raised by the fund-raiser to total agency revenues may be a good indicator of the importance of this activity to organizational life. Certainly another indicator of fund-raising performance may be the proportion of projected goal or target funds actually collected. This factor may reflect, for example, how successfully the fund-raiser can plan and forecast.

In the vast majority of instances, however, agencies are unlikely to have a staff position assigned to fund-raising even on a part-time basis. Consequently, it is far more likely that a consultant will be retained for those occasions—such as a capital giving campaign—when expert advice on the dynamics of organizing and carrying out a major campaign is required. Under such circumstances, most of the above considerations relating to the employment of fund-raising personnel are also applicable to consultants. In addition, one should note that professional fund-raisers consider one of the ethical canons of their work to be working for a fixed fee. One should never retain a consultant for a "percentage of the gross" or some other variable-fee formula, according to most sources.[23]

Special events

Up to this point, the discussion has been restricted almost completely to the topic of organized solicitations or fund drives. Another related topic receiving increasing attention in the fund-raising literature in recent years involves the use of "special events" for fund-raising purposes. According to one source, a special event is defined as "a dramatized effort to promote an idea, a cause or a program. Its purpose is to improve the relationships with an organization's public, develop understanding, and strengthen support through increased effort and contributions.[24]

The possibilities of such events are virtually endless. One source provides a list "From A to Z." Others mention some of the following: public meetings to report on events or introduce new activities or services; "follow-up meetings to report on completions of projects or services;" building or room dedications; open houses; annual meeting dinners; testimonial dinners; inauguration or retirement dinners or receptions for chief executive officer; outstanding service testimonials; kickoff dinners, meetings for fund-drives, or membership drives; balls; theater, movie, or concert benefits; fashion shows; bridge, wine, or cocktail parties; car washes, paper drives, clothing or furniture drives; tree or plant sales; pancake breakfasts; and candy or magazine sales.

In general such events are likely to be of two types, with respect to fund-raising activities. One is the direct fund-raiser, in which admission to the special event is in some way contingent on making a contribution. (So-called $1,000-a-plate dinners for political candidates fit into this category.) In the other case, no actual fund-raising activities may be linked directly to the special event. Dinners to honor employees, volunteers, or supporters are often of this type. Usually the connection to fund raising in such events is obvious to all concerned but not linked directly with the event itself, which is ostensibly either in appreciation for past contributions or in anticipation of future ones.

Whether or not to engage in a special event for fund-raising purposes ought to be a top-level management decision (or, a board decision in cases in which there is one). Formalizing the decision in this manner should provide at least minimal insurance against "getting carried away" with what seemed like such a terribly good idea at the time, but which winds up costing more than it brings in. Planning for special events requires fairly deliberate examination of the fiscal possibilities. What will this event cost? How much can we realistically expect to "net" after expenses are paid? Do the potential benefits in public relations, good will with constituents, and so forth make up for the outlays in those cases in which fund-raising is not the principal purpose?

Further guidance on the planning of special events is offered in the following "checklist" offered by Liebert and Sheldon:

The event must be important enough to attract the attention of groups the organization wishes to reach. It must be the right kind of event, suited to the tasts of the audience in order to draw the attendance in competition with other events. It must be significant—identified clearly with some aspect of the organization's overall program, policies and purposes—to warrant the time, effort and cost involved. It must be interesting—presented in an entertaining or dramatic form that will hold the attention of the audience. It must be convincing—creating a desire in people to respond in some way, to make a decision, to join, to participate, to support through volunteer service, or to make a financial contribution. It must be interpreted—promoted effectively in advance through printed pieces and other methods to build attendance. It must be publicized through communications media—covered or reported by newspapers, radio, television to arouse interest and encourage response. Thank you letters should go to volunteers, local business firms, and groups who have contributed in any way to make the event a success. There should be a final report, telling of the mistakes and successes, for use in planning the next special event. Follow up with cultivation materials to reach members, volunteers, contributors and people on other mailing lists beyond the range of local publications. The followup may be for information or cultivation purposes or may be a direct appeal for funds or volunteer service. Producing an event without adequate insurance coverage is asking for trouble. . . . Checklists are a must. They provide a step-by-step guide and serve as a working tool.[25]

From a management perspective, some such special events may be large enough to justify their treatment as separate budgetary projects, as discussed in Chapter 7. If so, careful use of a project budget should offer additional management control over such events, and prevent things from getting out of hand. In particular, careful attention should be given to the projections of cost and anticipated revenues, unless as noted the concern is not primarily fund-raising.

Even when project budgets are used, however, actually enforcing or living by them may well be another matter. A further suggestion here would be to employ the kind of "lines of credit" discussed in the chapter on programming, so that those responsible for the special event have a clear understanding of what they can—and cannot—spend.

In the final analysis, the criteria for deciding to hold a special event should be primarily fiscal if the purpose of the event is principally to raise money. If not, some attention must be given to attempting to "cost" the objectives for the event. How much is good will with our staff, supporters, or clients worth? Such questions may be unanswerable, but the context of special events necessitates at least an approximation.

Management of collections

Whether one is concerned with the operation of fund-raising campaigns or with special events, the circumstances of this type of fund-raising activity require some special fiscal control procedures and precautions not required in other fund-raising contexts. The 1964 *Audit Guide* prepared by the National Social Welfare Assembly, for example, states the nature of the problem in this way:

> The voluntary nature of revenue received by health and welfare organizations causes internal accounting procedures and administrative controls to take on added significance. In manufacturing or selling organizations, the purchase-sales-gross profit relationship provides overall useful checks which are not present in voluntary health and welfare organizations. In a business situation, cash and checks received through the mail are normally in payment of an account or accompany an order for goods. Consequently, the initial record is usually subject to subsequent verification through statements mailed to customers and merchandise shipped. However, a procedure requiring the mailing of receipts for all voluntary contributions, besides being expensive, does not provide full control since there is no assurance that a contributor would follow up if there was no subsequent communication from the organization.[26]

In the context of human service organizations, therefore, both management controls and certain specialized auditing procedures must be utilized to compensate for the natural incompleteness of accountability.

The method preferred by the American Institute for Certified Public Accountants for handling contributions received in the mail involves assigning two employees joint responsibility for controlling incoming mail and recording amounts received—either in a prenumbered receipt book or a day book that is totalled and initialed by each employee. These records should, according to the AICPA, be routinely compared with bank deposits by someone not having access to the deposits. Alternatives to this approach also suggested by AICPA include assigning mail contributions directly to processors at the agency's bank, or having a test mailing of contributions done by a protective agency or other collaborators. Furthermore, in conducting an audit, the independent auditor may wish to contact a sample of contributors listed in the receipt or day book to verify their contributions.

In the case of door-to-door campaigns, each level of the hierarchy of block captains, neighborhood captains, district captains, and so forth should be responsible for obtaining a signed report of the total collections from those below them. Alternatively, depository bank accounts in which withdrawals may be made only by authorized campaign officials (such as the treasurer) may be used. In such cases, workers may deposit their collections directly, giving the deposit slip to their supervisor.

In the case of special events, pre-printed tickets represent a major fiscal control devise if they are prenumbered and allocated to workers in amounts that are carefully recorded. Further, the AICPA recommends that detailed records of all costs incurred in special events be maintained, since the agency is responsible for advising contributors of the tax-deductible proportion (the non-fund raising costs) of the contribution.

Other management procedures suggested by the 1964 guide that may be useful include: (1) comparison of results from prior campaigns or special events or with "expected contributions" projections; (2) staff knowledge of the type and intensity of fund-raising activity occurring in the area or territory covered; and (3) feedback reports from key personnel, such as team leaders, in each area.[27] While these procedures may fall short of the strict standards and expectations of AICPA auditors, each of them appears to make a potential contribution to solving the knotty problem of the adequate fiscal control of contributions.

The problem of fund-raising costs

A significant management problem for which no ready solution is presently at hand involves the question of the establishment of adequate and convincing limitations on fund-raising costs. Perhaps no single problem has so consistently plagued fund-raising over the years as the suspicion that too great a proportion of funds is going into "overhead" (in contemporary terms, "administrative costs" and "fund-raising costs") (See Chapter 2). Newspapers and magazines routinely "reveal" new or continuing excesses in this area, and a large number of innocent agencies are regularly tarred and feathered for this.

No one can say with any certainty how much per fund-raising dollar should legitimately be allocated to these supportive purposes. However, one does not need very exact guidelines to become suspicious of those few agencies that expend 80 per cent or more of their funds for fund-raising purposes.[28] Until quite recently, there was some doubt over whether such costs could even be computed accurately. Recent elaborations of the AICPA guidelines, however, appear to have mitigated that problem, at least theoretically.

What remains is essentially a problem of comparability. Based on the standard definitions now widely disseminated, there is a need for some agency or organization to begin routinely collecting and collating national trend data on the total, administrative, fund-raising, and program expenditures in human service agencies. By disseminating such data in an accurate, reliable manner, the agency will simultaneously be providing guidelines against which agencies and their constituencies can contrast their own performances. In this way it should become increasingly possible to provide a level of self-regulation among agencies and federations raising funds, and to identify and isolate the agency whose performance is out of line.

Conclusion

Fund-raising campaigns and special events are a part of the province of human service financial management. The realities of the multi-funded human service agency are such that human service administrators can no longer afford to remain aloof from the realities of these important forms of voluntary fund-raising. Throughout this chapter an effort has been made to survey some of the most important trends apparent in the fund-raising literature and to identify their implications for fund-raising carried out in the agency context. While adequate justice could not be done to the depth and nuances of this topic in a single chapter, it should be clear to the reader at this point that the subject of campaigns and special events must be integral to human service finance. Therefore, considerable effort is needed in the present era to more thoroughly integrate this form of expertise into all types of training programs in the human services, and to compare it with and contrast it to other forms of fund-raising.

Part III

Allocations

The first two parts of this book are devoted, respectively, to an overall view of the historical and theoretical context of human service management, and to fund-raising as the first of five central topics that together define human service finance. In the three-chapter unit that follows, the second major topic is explored. The section is entitled "Allocations," although "Allocations and Distributions Through Budget Decisions" might be a better, if more awkward, title.

In truth, it is almost impossible to completely separate fund-raising and allocations activities in human service agencies. The one is concerned essentially with

115

finding and gaining access to large blocks of revenue that can be used to support diverse agency activities, and the other is concerned with the assignment of those revenues to various agency activities and purposes: now funds may be used to pay certain personnel costs, and later other funds may be used to pay building rent and the like. In public budgetary settings United Fund and other community federated funding enterprises, public grant-in-aid programs, and possibly other funding contexts as well, agency fund-raising and allocations activities are intimately interwoven. In some instances an agency may develop a budget for a program of activities and "go shopping" for funds, while in other instances the funds may be directed toward the agency subject to a developed budget.

This on-going relationship between fund-raising and allocations may explain why it is that some authorities in social work have traditionally referred to both topics using the single term "budgeting." That particular approach was rejected in this work, however, as insufficiently sensitive to the unique as well as the common elements of the two topics.

Budget-making, in either the broad or the narrower sense intended in this book has, for many years, occupied a relatively ironic position in the literature of human service administration. Everyone, it seems, concedes a central place to budget-making not only in financial matters, but in the entire spectrum of agency decision-making. Furthermore, some recognition of the importance of this topic goes back to the days of the National Association of Corrections and Charities at the turn of the century. Yet, for all the much-vaunted importance of budget-making, there is not a single fully developed theoretical work published on the subject, and there are only a handful of journal articles and booklets that offer much beyond simple homage to the subject. In preparing this volume, in fact, I encountered a number of articles that attempted to treat the subject with no reference whatsoever to matters financial—to deal with it as entirely a matter of responsiveness, interpersonal relations, and motivations. Similarly, despite widespread fascination with the technology of budget-making over the past two decades, one is hard pressed to cite more than a handful of demonstrations of this new technology actually "up and operational."

One is tempted to conclude from all this that, like the classical dieties, budget-making is to be approached with fear and trembling. Tempted, but not convinced. Therefore, several related attempts will be made in this unit to deal with this dreadful topic. The chapter that follows is an attempt to bring some order to existing budget theory and to identify some major implications of the current consensus on agency operations. It is less "theoretical" as that term ought to be used, than it is "conceptual." That is, the chapter is organized around the recognition of certain key concepts that can be found or inferred from existing writings on the subject of budget-making, and applied to the human services context. Especially important in this regard is the distinction between two types of "budget systems"—public appropriations, grant distributions, voluntary federated distributions, and fee-based budget systems—and "budget decision systems"— traditional incrementalism, and proposed reforms, primarily PPBS and zero-based budgeting. In the case of budget decision systems no attempt is made to present the proposed reforms in anything approaching their resplendent complexity. Instead, the focus is on the consequences of the adoption of such systems in agencies.

In the second chapter in this unit the rubric "information theory" is used to make a case for examining the formats of budget-making— the documents, forms, and stylistic devices used to organize and convey budgetary information in the budget process and beyond. The elements of budget formats are identified, and certain standard features of human service budget formats are singled out and discussed. The discussion of fund accounting in Chapter 2 is used as the basis in this chapter for further exploration of the relationship between budget formats and decisions: in particular, fund decisions, sub-fund decisions, and supra-fund decisions are linked with different formats for budget documents. In Chapter 7, a number of different forms (some currently in use, others logically justified but borrowed from other contexts) are also identified and discussed.

Finally, the concluding chapter in this section asks the provocative question, "What happens then?" Specifically, upon completion of a successful round of negotiations, is there any further use for budget documents and related agreements, or should these simply be shunted aside until the next fiscal period? Unfortunately, in far too many agencies the answer to that question seems to be, "this is when we turn all the financial stuff over to the bookkeeper and get on to other things." The answer to the question suggested here is found in the often cited concept of "programming." After the budget, it is suggested, human service administrators must attend to a number of discrete and specific tasks if they expect their "budget plans" to be realized.

The discussions in this chapter are divided into two parts. In the first part, the focus is on the programming activities most relevant to a newly created program of activities, while in the second part the focus is on the implementation of a funding continuation. The end of this chapter attempts to raise, in an orderly manner, some of the programming questions one is likely to encounter in the critical implementation phase of activity.

CHAPTER 6

BUDGET-MAKING IN
THE HUMAN SERVICES

In a world without scarcity there would be no need to choose among desirable ends and preferable courses of action.[1] In this chapter we shall examine, in some detail, various concepts that approach the issue of how one should go about organizing ideas for agency decisions allocating scarce resources. The discussion begins with the introduction of a number of very basic terms whose implications are easily overlooked in human service settings. Following this, we shall examine the concept of a "budget system," looking at both systems internal to, and broader than individual agencies and programs.

After examining the evolution of budget systems in human services we shall look at a number of specific proposals for improvements in budget systems set forth in recent years. In concluding this chapter a number of issues basic to the organization of a budget system in human services will be identified.

Basic terms and concepts

The first major task essential to a fuller understanding of budget-making in the human services is to set forth those terms and concepts that form the scaffolding on which further discussion of the subject rests. For greater understanding, these terms will be presented within

119

the context of the discussion of accounting presented in Chapter 2. This approach is built on the awareness that fiscal, internal, and community accountability, as outlined in that chapter, form a strong bond between the post-implementation activities of accounting and the pre-implementation efforts of budgeting.

Five terms are essential to an adequate understanding of budget-making in the human services: budget, balance, budget analysis, budget-making, and budget system. Let us briefly examine each of these in order to lay out a common ground of understanding for the later discussion.

In a certain, limited sense, a *budget* is a "document" made up of words and numbers in paired sequences, which reflect anticipated levels of expenditure (and, either explicitly or by inference, income) for a given period of time. Such documents may be organized in a number of different ways. (See Chapter 7.) For example, the most common form of budget found in human services today is probably the *functional budget,* in which items included on the budget are categorized and summarized by functional expenditure areas, such as personnel costs, office space costs, supplies, travel, and the like.

In large, multi-organizational budget systems, such as state government appropriations, or even within large agencies, the demands of a parsimonious presentation of data may result in the presentation of entire programs, agencies, or other budget entities as a single line entry, giving rise to the term *line-item budget,* which is also applied to this type of budget. This term highlights the informational difficulties that can arise in the context of functional budgets. Frequently, the *budget entity* for which the budget was prepared is a purely fiscal creation and is not meaningful in program or goal terms.[2] As a result, the making of budget decisions using this type of format is often highly constrained, from a programmatic point of view. For this reason, many authorities on the subject have, in recent years, endorsed some version of *program budgets,* in which, by design, the entities around which the budget is constructed are programmatically meaningful. Another means of making this conceptual leap is through the use of *project budgets,* in which the emphasis is on a known and determined set of activities to be completed during a given period of time. Because of the growth of grant support for social services, budgets that are negotiated are often of both a program and a project nature.

The accounting concept of entity and the derivative concepts of financial statements measuring performance and position are also useful in understanding the "principles" that govern most budget documents. First, it is important to understand that regardless of the entity involved, budgets are ordinarily constructed as *balanced budgets*. That is, they incorporate the break-even principle discussed in Chapter 1. They incorporate either directly or by implication, assumptions that projected revenues and projected expenditures will be equal in the period in question.[3] In a number of instances the question of matching revenue and expenditure estimates is difficult, but a number of technical shortcuts to balance may be included. The accompanying table (Figure 12), for example, shows a budget with an entry for an anticipated surplus as the difference between income and expenditure. Even the federal budget, which perennially operates at a deficit (that is, expenditures exceed revenues), is theoretically constructed on an assumption that the budget will balance at full employment.[4] For very good reasons, however, social agencies cannot continue to operate for any length of time at a deficit without literally consuming themselves (that is, consuming all their assets), so in most instances, budget

FIGURE 12

Statement of Support, Revenue, and Expenses and Changes in Fund Balances (same form as Balanced Budget)

Year Ending December 31, 19—

	Total All Funds
Revenues	
Fees	$ 51,642
Grants	175,000
Public support	4,780
Miscellaneous revenue	1,200
Total revenues	$232,622
Expenditures	
Program expenditures	$200,502
Management and general	23,939
Fund-raising	3,841
Total expenditures	$228,202
Excess of revenues over expenditures	$ 4,340
Fund balance, January 1, 19—	20,072
Fund balance, December 31, 19—	$ 24,412

adjustments of the type noted above involve excess revenues rather than excess expenditures.

A related point is that budgets, as normally employed in human services, are future-oriented statements of operations.[5] While there is not adequate theoretical reason why budgets could not be prepared as projected statements of financial position at the end of the next budget period, the general consensus in the field and outside holds that such information would be less useful for agency management and decision-making than budgets as statements of operations. A modified form of a statement of future position, however, is often part of the process of capital "budgeting" (See Chapter 9) for such projects as the construction of a new building—an observation that suggests that there may well be some future insights to be gained from budgeting in both the operations and the positions modes.[6]

We must be careful not to overstress the analogy between accounting and budgeting. In doing so, it is relatively easy to reduce budget-making to a refined technical exercise performed according to a set of operational rules. Indeed, it could be argued that a number of proposals for budget reform put forth in recent years attempt to do precisely that: to define budget-making as an optimization problem, in which those in a position to decide are seeking the optimum mix of benefits; or as a maximization problem, in which they are seeking the most benefit per dollar. While both of these decision models have some applicability to the human services, it is doubtful whether either is a paradigm around which to build an adequate theoretical approach to the subject.[7] What goes on in budget-making in human services is simply too complex to be reduced to such terms.

Many in the human services of the opposite point of view may be inclined to reject a sophisticated technical perspective on budgeting, and with it the analogies between budgeting and accounting. The position taken here is that both perspectives are needed, but that some care is needed in delineating concepts, so that needless confusion and pointless disagreements are avoided.

As suggested previously, the focus of this work is on both analytic and behavioral techniques useful in financial management. From this point of view, it is useful to reject the conventional term "budgeting" and to speak, instead, of *budget-analysis* when one is interested in the construction of budget documents and the attendant mental, arithmetic, and notational activities; and to speak of *budget-making* when one is interested in the interpersonal negotiations and decisions that convert budget documents and decisions into authoritative controls over aspects of agency operations and staff behavior. Ordinarily, in human service agencies, preparation of agency budgets involves both budget-analysis and budget-making. While such tasks will be performed jointly and serially by the same persons in the smallest agencies, in the largest agencies such tasks may be divided so that entire departments are assigned to each. In either case, it is important to remember the symbiotic relationship that exists between the analytic and behavioral dimensions. Budget decisions are ordinarily made in light of some problem analysis, for example, whether it is the kind of economic analysis favored by proponents of PPBS, cost-effectiveness analysis, or the explicitly political analysis of a vote-counting congressman. Likewise, even the most sophisticated budget analysis cannot be freed from the expectation that it be understood by those whose decisions it is intended to influence. Although they are often treated as separate dimensions, or even as separate approaches to the subject of budget decisions, the analytic and the behavioral dimensions are necessary to an understanding of the allocation of resources in human services.

The final term with which the reader need be concerned is that of *budget systems*. This term refers to a large number of elements that work together in a systematic way to facilitate the task of budget-making. Two types of budget systems will be dealt with below: arenas and decision models of budget-making.

Together, these five terms—budget, balance, budget-analysis, budget-making, and budget systems—form the matrix of our terminology in this area.

Types of budget systems

Budget systems of greatest interest to agencies in the human services can be classified in two different ways. First, there are what might be termed the arenas: organized situations or contexts in which human service organizations compete among themselves, or with other organizations and interests for portions of a distribution of funds. There are four such arenas of critical importance to most contemporary human services organizations: public appropriations, such as the Congress, state legislatures, or city councils; public distributions, such as the several hundred federal and state agencies involved in the distribution of funds through grants review and contracting procedures; federated distributions, such as United Funds, in which groups of member agencies divide revenues generated in a consolidated fund-raising campaign; and fee systems, in which budgetary decisions must rely on projections of income from fees. Second, budget systems of interest to human services can be classified on the basis of how the budget-making task (especially decision-making) is conceived and organized. Five conceptions of budget-making are mose relevant: the incremental model, performance budgeting, program budgeting, program planning and budgeting (PPB), and zero-based budgeting. Because a good deal has been written on each of these topics much of which fails to make clear distinctions between what such systems actually accomplish, and what their designers intend for them to accomplish, each discussion will be of an evaluative character.

The term budget system is intended to refer to a relatively broad range of situations, from the allocations activities of a local United Fund organization to the appropriations activities of a state legislative committee or the internal decision-making of a particular agency. The essential reference, in each instance, is to the systematic and interrelated character of certain common events and processes. Among the principal elements in many budget systems, for example, is a summary or consolidated budget document, which represents an authoritative statement by the principal decision-making authority of the results of their efforts.[8] At the federal level, the federal budget serves this purpose, as do comparable state budgets. Local governmental practices, as well as those of the voluntary sector, vary widely—sometimes they produce a consolidated budget and sometimes not. In either case, however, an equally important source of information in understanding the actions of any given budget system are the intermediate documents produced along the way—committee minutes, hearing transcripts, newspaper accounts, staff reports, letters, and memoranda, as well as the interpersonal agreements and understandings. Because of the brief, aggregate nature of the final budget statement, it is almost inevitable that the full import of budgetary actions cannot be found in the final budget but must be gathered from the intermediate sources, as well. In a very real sense, budget-making at the working level is often a veritable subculture of meanings, attitudes, agreements, and decisions. Gaining insight into this "working level" of budget-making and its implications for administrative action is the single greatest challenge to the human service administrator.

Whether one is operating in the most highly professional context imaginable or in the worst rotten borough the essential insight remains constant: budget-making, ultimately, is not the solving of a scientific problem or mathematical puzzle. It is, instead, an intensely human encounter in which different groups seek to gain scarce resources for their own purposes. Authoritative decisions must be made. We cannot escape the fundamental observation that conflict is an inevitable element in all budget-making.

Typically, there are a number of regular events that define the full cycle of a budget system.[9] Most budget systems affecting human services are annual, with many state governments operating on a biennial cycle (cycles as long as five years not being unheard of). To maximize accountability, the budget cycles of an agency should coincide with its accounting cycles. During the typical budget cycle, it is likely that several standard benchmarks can be detected. These may include a request from the funding authority for a preliminary proposal, or budget request, which may be accompanied in some instances by a set of "guidelines" or criteria to be used in creating budgets. A third element in most budget systems is a deadline for submitting a specific (and often documented) budget request to the staff of the budget authority. The proposal may be reviewed and modified by the staff (with or without entity participation) and presented to the formal decision-making authority for consideration. Typically, such consideration is accompanied by an opportunity for a "hearing" or formal presentation by the requestee, and is followed by a decision from the authority, the various stages of implementation of that decision (notifying the recipient, drafting a legal contract or agreement as needed, and actually distributing the funds), and the follow up of the patterns of utilization of the funds by the recipient. These steps appear to be fairly universal, regardless of differences in individual budget-making contexts.

One of the principal characteristics of a budget system in the human services is that several of these activities may be occurring simultaneously, and programs or agencies receiving funds from more than one funding source may be involved with several budget systems at the same time. In many instances the activities of a budget system's cycle are spread out so that budget-making is a more or less continuous management concern. In other cases the entire process may be telescoped into a brief and intensive period of activity. In multi-funded agencies, minor differences in the phasing of different budget cycles, or overlapping or simultaneous events in different systems can present major management headaches unless these contingencies can be adequately integrated into agency routines. (The following chapter offers several helpful hints for staging such integration.)

It is worth reiterating here that some budget systems may be strictly internal, while others serve to link the agency or program to a larger bureaucracy, a federation of agencies, or some other broad configuration. Furthermore, some budget systems will be on-going appropriations systems in which the principle of continuity may be implemented both through a funding *base*, to which each participating entity is ordinarily entitled, and an *increment* of increased funding over last year, for which agencies must compete.[10] Other budget systems will be zero-sum systems, in which no secure funding base is assumed. This distinction does not apply, as one might suspect, to the difference between line-item and grant funding. The history of many of the grant-in-aid programs created in recent years is strongly suggestive of a pattern in which funded programs tend to be the first in line for refunding, and although all applicants supposedly receive equal consideration, some are, in Orwell's phrase, "more equal than others." The upshot is that something like funding *base* assumptions appear to have grown up in a number of grant programs, a fact that should give pause to the most zealous proponents of zero-sum budgeting.[11] The reasons for the growth of such stability even in inherently unstable funding patterns are quite reasonable: a disinclination to disrupt the lives of clients and employees of defunded programs, an effort toward efficient resource use through avoiding constant start-up costs, and so forth.

Public appropriations

The American form of government, we are often reminded, is the oldest constitutional democracy in the world. While many of the institutions of American government were in existence from the beginning and others developed quickly in the new republic, significant progress in the management of finances in the public sector has been a comparatively recent development.[12] At the federal level a coordinated executive budget was not presented to the Congress until the 1920s and some states and localities continued to request funds from the legislative branches "as needed" until quite recently.[13]

Today, however, annual or biannual appropriations made to administrative agencies following legislative scrutiny of budgetary proposals, and with some provision for executive review and release of funds, are the norm for the handling of public funds at all levels of government in the United States.

Because of the pattern of funding of social services which has developed since the 1960s, however, the effects of public appropriations budgeting are primarily indirect for most human services agencies.

At the federal level the Department of Health, Education and Welfare, actively participates in public appropriations through the Congress.[14] However, most HEW funds for human services are "passed through" to state and local governments, rather than going into direct service expenditures.[15] Likewise, the participation of human services in municipal-level budget-making remains relatively limited, even with the advent of revenue-sharing.[16] Only at the state governmental level is participation in public appropriations of direct concern to the human services. In public welfare, mental health, corrections, child welfare, and other fields, state budgetary action is a critical factor in the continuance and expansion of human service programs. Unfortunately, the significance of state-level funding has only been dimly perceived by human service professionals, and, as a result, knowledge in this area is woefully inadequate.[17]

In most states, a detailed understanding of the budgetary process is limited to a few key "insiders" employed by large public bureaucracies, and perhaps members of legislative liaison committees, professional associations, public interest groups, "trade associations," and private interest groups. The majority of human service professionals today operate with an understanding of state budgeting at the level of high school civics text books, possibly supplemented by a flow chart showing the major steps in the formal budget process of their state. This is clearly an area in which a great deal of detailed work needs to be done before more sophisticated understanding of the exigencies of state appropriations will be conceivable in the human services.

An initial distinction can be made between appropriations, authorizations, and actual expenditures. Since these distinctions are often blurred in small contexts, they are critical in the complex, modern state budgetary arena. Appropriations are amounts of funds designated by official action for various general purposes. The typical appropriations budget in a state government continues to be a line-item budget, despite some interesting forays into the program-budgeting arena. Appropriations may equal authorizations, which are the expenditure ceilings identified in legislation. The practice of including authorizations in enabling legislation varies widely, being common at the federal level and in some states, and unheard of in others. For a large number of reasons, including the withholding of funds by an executive-level agency (a bureau of the budget or department of finance, for example) and internal factors such as staffing levels, actual expenditures by public agencies seldom coincide with and are often well below both appropriation and authorization figures.

Other critically significant factors for understanding the participation of human service agencies in public appropriations processes are the three levels of operations that obtain. Students of organization should be familiar with the common distinction between "formal" and "informal" organizations.[18] In addition to these, public appropriations processes typically include an additional level of "official" or ceremonial organization, and participants in these processes are expected to operate effectively at all three levels. At the informal level, agency efforts may include intelligence gathering about the leanings of key legislative figures, social contacts with relevant officials, "idle" conversations with committee staff members, lining up interest group support, and the like. At the formal organizational level, budget-making efforts by an agency may be directed at preparing and delivering budget proposals that are in line with guidelines or prior experience, revising these submissions, and participating in formal in-house budget hearings with departmental superiors, representatives of the governors' office, or others involved in the process. At the ceremonial level, agencies often prepare and present public testimony supporting their requests before a public meeting of the appropriate legislative committees. This is frequently ritualized and highly ceremonial. It may also be a unique public opportunity to dramatize agency accomplishments, plead for legislative (and public) support for programs, or pursue other strategic objectives.[19]

Useful strategies on such public occasions are discussed in detail by Aaron Wildavsky in *Politics of the Budgetary Process,* and veteran participants and observers of such events will have lists of their own to add. The critical point, however, is not what strategies are employed, but rather the fact that the true purposes of such hearings are seldom apparent on the surface. While everyone present may publicly endorse the fact-finding and informational character of the meeting, the real budget work is seldom done in public meetings today.

Another factor of considerable significance in public appropriations budget-making is the existence of a politically viable constituency that an agency can rely on in the context of formal and informal budget negotiations, and occasionally for public or ceremonial support, as well. Whether one sees such "power plays" as the normal way of doing business or as the height of chicanery and unprofessional conduct, it must be conceded that effective agency performance in the public budget arena would be virtually impossible without some level of constituency support.

Our present understanding of the dynamics of human service performance in the public appropriations arenas is markedly limited. A great deal of additional research will be necessary before we are able to state with much certainty what factors beyond these sketchy details contribute to success in appropriations. One of the areas in need of study is the degree to which public allocations decisions are, or can be planned. Looking at the range we find the model of legislative "pork barreling" at one extreme and centrally planned allocations at the other.

Public distribution [20]

Most contemporary accounts of budget-making in the public sector concentrate on the appropriations processes noted above.[21] During the past decade, however, there has emerged within the federal government (and in state governments, as well) a type of budget system whose importance to human service agencies rivals, and in some respects surpasses that of appropriations. The growth of grant-in-aid funding of human service programs has meant the institutionalization of a separate level of budget-making activity largely carried on as transactions between administrative agencies.

Although some of the "public" aspects of the appropriations system, such as public notification requirements, have been carried over to the new system, and other requirements, such as the publication of guidelines governing the distribution of funds have been developed, the fact remains that the circumstances of this distribution system as it operates within federal government agencies in the Department of Health, Education, and Welfare, the Department of Housing and Urban Development, and other federal and state agencies grant relatively large discretionary opportunities to relatively unaccountable public officials. Furthermore, as Lowi has pointed out, the characteristics of the distribution system make centralized control and planning virtually impossible.[22] With relatively few exceptions, legislative oversight of these distribution systems has also been limited or non-existent.

The budget system should be thoroughly integrated with the programmatic goals of agencies, and many of the ills of this system of budgeting are a function of the sheer complexity and numbers of programs involved. Estimates of separate federal programs ordinarily run from the hundreds to the thousands, with the result that the process of seeking initial funding by an agency is often reduced to a game of roulette.

At least at the formal level a principal difference between the appropriations and distributions budgetary arenas derives from the question of continuity. As Wildavsky and others have noted, public agencies are created by law, and some level of appropriations is more or less assumed, virtually as a right, by these agencies.[23] Such a funding base can be expanded, typically, by increments of increased funding in a pattern Wildavsky terms "incrementalism." In this way, an agency may come to control an increasing base of funds with which to operate, irrespective of its accomplishments. By contrast, agencies operating in the public distributions context have no such assurance of continued support, at least formally. Most grants and contracts are for short periods of time (often one year or less) and no commitments are made or implied for continued support.

This formal difference may be more apparent than real, however, for experience over the past decade has shown time and again that agencies already receiving funding are most likely to receive future support from a funding agency in the public distribution system.

The formal differences between the appropriations and distributional budget systems on matter of membership can also be overcome. Ordinarily, public appropriations considerations are restricted to budget entities created by the legislative branch, while individuals or organizations that meet the criteria for funding spelled out in the guidelines may negotiate for funds in distributional systems. Initially, this means that a relatively large number of potential applications will not receive funding, a factor that may be a kind of crude "quality control." In any case, a number of public agencies publicize the percentages of grant applications funded to support their claims of high selectivity, discriminating judgement, and high standards. What is seldom reported, however, is the percentage of funded projects and programs that are more or less continuous. A kind of "closed membership" of agencies and programs that are, in effect, first in line for funding is a common feature of most public distribution systems. While any public or non-profit organization was free to participate for community action funds during the War on Poverty, the bulk of such funds inevitably went to designated Community Action agencies. Likewise, at present we are witnessing the stabilization of funding patterns in state and local Title XX planning systems, and the emergence of recurrent support for on-going funding in many communities.

The reader should not assume that such comments are intended as criticism of the operation of public distribution systems. Realistically, they probably cannot operate any other way: funding agencies accountable for their performance to Congress or legislative groups are not likely to pursue "high risk" funding strategies. And, there is something reassuring about funding an agency previously funded and performing acceptably. Likewise, from the agency standpoint, the circumstances of funding are largely a matter of indifference, provided some degree of certainty and continuity is assured. It's frustrating to jettison programs because grant support is lost, and difficult to seek out new sources of grant money each year.

There are good reasons on both sides for the arrangements that have emerged. The principal questions remaining concern efficiency. If the extensive documentation and support that goes into grant preparation is largely superfluous, would it not be more efficient simply to openly acknowledge funding continuity in grant-in-aid programs? Such acknowledgement flies in the face of the current interest in fiscal accountability, and runs counter to proposals for zero-sum budgeting (discussed below) as well as "sunset laws" providing for the systematic termination of programs. If these approaches are premised, as they seem to be, on the assumption that a certain level of uncertainty about continuity is conducive to better performance and high quality services, the experience of the past decade in the public distribution system is highly relevant. That experience does not seem to support the view that the prospect of disrupted funding results in discernably better quality services, and in some cases, where anxiety is high, it is more likely to produce exactly the opposite effects. For example, uncertainty over continued funding under Title-IV-A kept one agency I am familiar with in a state of disorganization for the better part of a year. While the parts of proposals that focus on performance measurement are highly laudable, the difficulties of such measurement should not be taken lightly, and the strategy of deliberately provoking anxiety is likely to prove both inhumane and counterproductive in the long run.

As with public allocations, the degree to which public distribution decisions are planned is a crucial concern. Do public agencies, as they claim, distribute funds more in response to measurable needs or effective grantsmanship?

The long-term future of distribution budgeting is not at all clear. In addition to zero-sum budgeting and sunset laws, revenue-sharing and numerous other fiscal reforms have been cited in recent years as replacements or modifications of this system. Nevertheless, the system of grant-funding that has developed shows a great many signs of vitality, and relatively few human service agencies are able to avoid at least minimal contact with it.

Voluntary federated distributions

Next to the two budget systems discussed above, perhaps the most significant type of budget system affecting human service agencies today is the federated distribution system, in which a number of member agencies divide among themselves the revenues generated by a federated or consolidated fund-raising campaign. Most widely known among such campaigns are the local affiliates of United Way of America. Less well known, perhaps, but equally relevant in this category, are such diverse enterprises as the black United Funds, Red Feather, and the like. These fund-raising enterprises can be distinguished from single-agency fund drives, such as the American Heart Association or the American Cancer Society, and from national agencies with local affiliates (many of whom participate in United Way) by the manner in which decisions on resource allocation are reached.

As with state and local governments, the sheer number of federated distributions systems makes generalizing about their budgetary operations difficult. In some communities, for example, the United Fund operates like a public utility, with public budget hearings, newspaper accounts of transactions, and so forth. In other communities, allocation of funds to agencies are handled by community leaders serving on the budget committees in a manner once described by one of them as "discretely and appropriately." In at least one community budgetary decisions are handled in total secrecy, with members of the budget committee alone knowing the full picture, and agencies being informed only of their own appropriation.

However, several tentative generalizations appear appropriate. First, distributions decisions are typically handled in federated distributions as a "community trust" by a board or committee of laymen rather than through direct negotiation among agency representatives. This fact alone should insure the presence of some minimal levels of community accountability in the federated distribution systems.

Second, there is a long tradition among federated funding entities to engage in social planning, priority studies, and needs determination studies to create a data base for allocations decisions.[24] As a result, funding decisions are likely to take into account factors other than the pattern of demands expressed by the member agencies. Third, although it is still not widely recognized, federated operations, in particular the United Way of America, have emerged as significant forces in improving the financial management capacities of agencies in the voluntary sector, because of their recourse to coercing, pleading, and reasoning with member agencies.[25]

The future of federated social welfare ventures and their unique budgetary systems is genuinely uncertain.[26] Because voluntary contributions available to human service agencies are relatively paltry compared with federal funds, many agencies once supported entirely through this mechanism are now partly, or largely supported by public distributions. As a result, some serious questions about the tail wagging the dog come up.

Another related, essentially voluntary form of budget system affected by the growth of federal funds is the foundation.[27] While foundation giving has grown steadily in recent years, this growth is relatively miniscule in comparison with the growth of federal funds. (See Chapter 3.) One feature of the budget system developed by the foundations, however, which was adopted wholesale by federal research agencies, and which deserves further scrutiny in both public appropriations and federated distributions, is the use of the advice of expert review committees in decision-making. To some degree the Congress is moving in a similar direction with the Congressional Budget Office, and a number of states have had legislative research operations for many years.[28] In general, however, the systematic utilization of various forms of "peer review" and expertise in the budgetary process at all levels of human service budgeting has not been what it could be.

Fee systems

In all the above budget systems, agencies request revenues from outside sources, using for "collateral," as it were, past performances and promises about future effort. They are also in direct competition with other agencies. A substantially different budget system is created when an agency generates large amounts of revenues from fees and client charges. In this context a budget involves juxtaposing equal or balanced revenue and expenditure estimates and providing supporting documentation that is consistent, convincing, and acceptable to the funding sources. This phenomenon, like fund accounting, is found only in the public and voluntary sectors of American society. In some instances, human service agencies may be involved in a substantially different form of budgeting, one that corresponds more closely to that found in the business sector. Rather than forming a contract between two parties—the third-party fundor and the funded agency—this budget involves predicting income in the most reasonable manner possible, and developing expenditure patterns in light of the income prediction.

This type of budgeting is essential when agencies have programs supported by fee collections or other charges assessed against individual clients (including third-party payments from Medicaid or insurance companies).[29] The balance of revenues and expenditures is a subordinate consideration to the accuracy of the income prediction. Such budgets have the virtue of not requiring extensive negotiations outside the agency, but they also have the defect of uncertainty—any number of contingencies during the budget period may upset the delicate balance of income and expenditures. This situation can be highly problematic for the human service agency, since it ordinarily has no cash reserves, capital, or other financial devices (such as a stock issuance or bond sale) to fall back on. Even borrowing to cover an income shortfall will probably have to be short-term and unsecured (unless the agency owned a building or other tangible assets). In this context, the critical dimension in fee system budgeting is how agencies can make the most accurate income predictions possible. (This question is explored, in some detail, in the discussion of fees in the preceding chapter.)

Where fee collections are a part of total revenues, the remainder coming from ear-marked or designated program funds, a human service agency may have an unrecognized element of flexibility. Unless fees are in some way tied to specific program operations (by grant agreement, board of directors action, or some other similar arrangement), it may be possible to use them as a kind of contingency fund—one year supporting the staff in defunded programs until different grant funding arrangements can be made, and another year providing matching moneys for a grant, or "risk capital" to start a new program, research, or training activity. Even if amounts are quite small, the careful administrator can get considerable use out of such discretionary funds. An ever present problem in such instances, however, is the unintentional loss of their contingency powers by tying them to other dedicated funds. Matching money linked to a grant this year will not be free for some other use next year if the grant is to be continued. With such funds the difficult management problem is to keep enough capital free to maintain some flexibility while making effective use of funds instead of simply banking them.

Summary

In sum, then, human service agencies are likely to be involved in one, or all, of four distinct budget systems. Public appropriations systems assume on-going operations. Negotiations therein tend to be concentrated, prior to zero-sum budgeting, around the increments of increase or decrease. While operating in many ways like the appropriations systems, membership in a public distribution system is not assured, and the potential for a zero-sum mode of operations always exists. Federated appropriations systems, by contrast, possess restricted memberships and operate like public appropriations systems, with negotiations focussed largely on the increment. The fortunes of agencies in such arrangements have a considerable degree of uncertainty, however, tied as they are to the success of the annual fund-raising campaign. (In recent years, many state and local agencies have faced similar uncertainties in tax collections.) Budgeting in agencies and programs supported by fees takes on a substantially different character, for the entire budget operation must by focussed on income projections rather than negotiations with a funding source.

Further investigation of these four types of budget systems would reveal additional differences. However, this discussion should serve to alert the human service manager to the principal differences among such systems, and to the need for adjustments of strategy and approach to the search for scarce resources.

Models of budget decision-making

In this section we shall forego further discussion of the question of the organization of budgeting, and concentrate instead on the elements of budgetary decisions. We will examine six "models" of budgeting that have emerged over the years, both as proposed reforms of budgetary practice and as arguments against reform.

The critical question, which will seldom be far from the center of focus in this discussion, is how appropriate budget choices are to be made. Over thirty years ago, the political scientist V. O. Key expressed the question as one of how decisions regarding the allocation of scarce resources were to be made among competing claimants.[30] This approaches the question from the point of view of funding sources. From an agency standpoint the comparable question may be how one is to succeed in attaining one's objectives in a context in which only a few can succeed. Running through five of the six approaches is a "meritocratic" assumption that criteria of worthwhileness (usually economic criteria) can be employed to answer such questions. The sixth proposal—for incremental budgeting—represents a fundamental rejection of criteria of any sort, and an appeal for a reliance on the social forces of what Lindblom has called "mutual partisan adjustment." Let us begin, therefore, with this last position, usually called incremental budgeting.

Incremental budgeting

The approach to budgetary decision-making called incremental budgeting is ordinarily associated closely with two social scientists—Aaron Wildavsky, a political scientist who discovered the phenomenon in research on the U.S. Bureau of the Budget and its relations to Congress, and Charles Lindblom, an economist who with David Braybrooke, a philosopher, and Robert Dahl, another political scientist, developed a substantial theoretical base for incrementalism as a general theory of decision-making.[31]

While critics have attacked incrementalism for its conservatism and attachment to the status quo, it would be more accurate to view it as the most sociologically and psychologically sophisticated of decision theories. While most decision theories, such as the budget decision models below, begin with "rational economic man" paradigms in which a complete knowledge of the world and the world's infinite mallability are assumed, incrementalism acknowledges quite forthrightly that knowledge of the world is always partial and incomplete, and that the world cannot be changed instantaneously. This acknowledgement is the source of most criticism—both informed and idle.[32] Lindblom further adds fuel to the fire by explicitly linking the style of decision with the degree of change—a linkage that may not be theoretically justified or necessary.[33]

A substantial difference should be noted between the descriptive work of Wildavsky, addressing the federal budgetary processes premised on the "aids to calculation" of the base and increment, and the more elegant theoretical prescriptive work of Lindblom and Braybrooke. While Wildavsky has emerged as a critic of proposed modifications of the status quo in budgetary decision-making, the incrementalism of Lindblom and Braybrooke can be used to support modifications in current practice. For this reason, it might be better to refer to Wildavsky's approach as "political rationality" and the Lindblom-Braybrooke approach as "marginal analysis," thus abandoning the overwrought term incrementalism.

In the Wildavsky view, budgets in the public sector are less significant as management instruments for public operations than as occasions for the working out of interpersonal political understandings.[34] The political is stressed here to accentuate its superiority over the economic, and also to legitimize the log-rolling and partisanship that characterize so much of budget-making in the legislative arena, but have been thoroughly shunned in budget theory. Since Wildavsky's view does not focus on the concerns of administrative agencies (other than to identify them, quite correctly, as political entities), we can safely abandon it here, and concentrate on the more cogent Braybrooke-Lindblom approach.

From the vantage point of marginal analysis, a broad range of decisions, including budgetary ones, are made marginally, sequentially, and in successive incremental steps. Seldom, if ever, in the budget process of an agency can one expect to see the profoundest questions of purpose faced forthrightly, with a willingness to stick by the answer, no matter what. Such an approach to decisions is suitable for philosophers and zealots, but is demonstrably out of character with the fluid context of agency and program administration. Instead, we all generally tend to "satisfice"—considering only those factors and alternatives of which we are aware, by habit or choice, and those factors we cannot avoid.[35]

Such behavior is often linked with the various weaknesses of a "bureaucratic person." Far from being a deficit, however, Braybrooke and Lindblom argue, it is the peculiar strength of the incremental method that it provides the maximum opportunity for the adjustment of the claims of the future to the legitimate claims of the past. Nor is this view conservative, being both realistic and consistent with extensive research data on social change from sociology, social psychology, and American history.[36]

The critical question for consideration here, however, is how one can approach budgetary decisions marginally in the context of agency decisions about budgets. One answer is, "pragmatically," by taking budget questions and issues on their own terms. That is, one assumes that there are no fixed set of questions (economic or political) that represent the most important considerations, to which all budget matters must be reduced. In some situations, questions of goals and objectives will seem all important, while in others, efficiency and productivity will seem critical. In the marginal analysis view, whatever seems important to the participants *is* important, and should be dealt with. There are no "rules of conduct" in budgeting that can be appealed to in order to dismiss the concerns of participants as unimportant. If lay board members are concerned with the high cost of lighting, and disinterested in the cost-effectiveness of services, the proper budgetary strategy for management, according to the marginal analysis approach, is two-fold: to satisfy their demands for data on lightbulbs *and* seek to interest them in cost-effectiveness questions as well (perhaps by linking this issue to the cost-of-lighting question). In this modest example, as well as in the more profound issues of budget-making, marginal analysis tends to dissolve the distinctions, which often emerge in budget theory, between the experts who truly understand and the laity who do not.

Second, the marginal approach emphasizes the significance of past performance for future projections. Even if the past is rejected, it still represents an important point departure in the marginal perspective.

Third, to apply marginal analysis in budget-making one must recognize the legitimacy of the "toehold," or "foot in the door." Whether one is a funding source or a seeker after funds, minimal psychological insight should make one aware of a number of the important interpersonal bases for this phenomenon. For one thing, most contemporary human service systems operate on norms of trust, friendship, and collegial respect that are not allowed for in "rational economic man" approaches to the subject. Rejection of the claims of a presently funded agency or program is not regarded simply as a matter of the dispassionate consideration of the public good, but rather as a direct assault upon the legitimacy of the funded activity and hence upon the integrity of those operating the program. Consequently, it is not conservatism that sustains the marginal nature of budgetary decision-making in human services, but rather such "trivialities" as the threats of embarrassment, of giving unnecessary offense, or causing suffering to colleagues. In certain circumstances, for example, cutbacks of funds are tolerable simply because it is clear to all that, in this case, cuts do not reflect negatively on those funded. In other instances the personal objectives, insensitivity, or power of key actors in the budget process may be sufficient to override such implications. As on on-going phenomenon, however, the significance of interpersonal factors can not be overlooked. Cast in political terms, the most common conflicts of interest experienced in budget-making are not clashes of class or economic loyalties, but diagreements over how best to "satisfice" the largest number of persons and interests.

Fourth, marginal analysis is a workable approach in human services because of the enormous area of uncertainty involved. If it were known exactly which services, in what quantities, delivered under what circumstances to which clients would definitely resolve certain problems, perhaps we might be able to approach budgetary decisions in another way. In the absence of such assurances we are all inclined to proceed cautiously, less from a sense of conservatism than from a sense of genuine concern lest we compound the problems of clients. Under such circumstances of uncertainty a marginal approach is the most natural, and consequently most appropriate reaction for most people.[37]

Finally, it should be noted that marginal budgeting is, by its very nature, "unsystematic" budgeting. Outside the immediate context it is not possible to state definitively what the essential questions are. Neither is it possible to define definitively what the criteria for assessing results are. Marginal analysis explicitly fixes budgeting as a vehicle for the attainment of other purposes. Budget-making is not an end in itself, and cannot be judged as such. The final assessment of budgeting, therefore, must be in terms of results. Two kinds of results are likely to be of great concern in human services: the simple completion of the process and the political ramifications implied by Wildavsky. The bottom line is who gets what from the process.

Financial management and marginal budgeting

The biggest criticism that can be levied against the marginal approach is not its conservatism, but its lack of explicit guidelines for how to proceed with budget tasks. Particularly for those seeking a "cookbook" approach to rules and principles there is something inherently unsatisfactory about the marginal approach to budget-making. Where other approaches offer specific, if misleading or impossible guidance, marginal analysis offers only pragmatism: do what you have decided to do in the best way you can. Some work, therefore, is needed to elaborate budget methodology.

The elements of such an approach can be identified from other social scientific perspectives. From interactionist social psychology, for example, we can identify the importance of situational assessment: those factors that the participants of the situation believe are important will be important.[38] There must also be explicit recognition of the roles of authority, power, and influence in differentiating the abilities of participants to define what is important. Rational economic approaches to budget-making have a much greater likelihood of success in situations controlled by economists than in situations in which budget participants are largely lacking in economic insight.[39] Similarly, marginal analysis must recognize the reality of conflict—not only over the allocation of resources, but also over the criteria to be used in choosing.

The endorsement of marginal analysis in human service budgetary decisions has an additional advantage: the partial, sequential, and remedial approaches to decisions also provide the basis for the pragmatic treatment of other proposals for budget systems (that is, in terms of what they will do for an agency). Consequently, from the marginal point of view, it is less important than an agency engage in a budget analysis system that is logically complete and internally consistent than that participants in the process get satisfactory answers to the questions that arise. In this way, we can approach budget systems not for their elegance or profundity, but in light of our experience with budget-making. Since such a procedure makes no pretense of objectivity, but relies instead on inter-subjective assessments among participants, we must state at the outset that the following analyses are somewhat idiosyncratic and tailored to match as closely as possible the author's assessment of agency financial management interests.

Performance budgeting

The very idea of public allocation budget systems, which constitute a kind of early "flow chart" procedure in which key events and activities in a process are specified in advance and for the benefit of participants, is, as noted previously, something of a recent occurrence. As part of the climate of expectation about the rationalization of budget-making and the improvement of the decision process, at the federal level in the immediate post-war period there emerged particular interest in what came to be identified as "performance budgeting."[40] Although the nuances separating this approach from other approaches to budget-making are subtle, the central issue from the standpoint of human services administration is simple: the performance of agencies should be evaluated by funding sources as part of the on-going budget review process. The essence of performance budgeting is summarized by Due:

> The budget is organized on the basis of various programs and activities to be carried on; and in turn, each program is broken down on the basis of the performance of the agencies involved in its accomplishment, in such a manner as to facilitate measurement of performance and ascertainment of cost.[41]

It is important for students of human service budget-making to recognize that the performance budget model was developed explicitly in the public sector, and incorporates some ideas that have since become essential elements in the accountability movement—particularly the emphasis on the measurement of performance and the determination of cost.

Shoup suggests that the term "output budget" is preferable as a label for this approach:

> Because of the many different senses in which the term "performance budget" is commonly taken, it is preferable to use the term "output budget" to designate those plans and records of accomplishment that are cast in terms of quantities of defined units of output.[42]

Regardless of the term employed, the systematic linkage of considerations of past performance with allocations is certainly an innovation in public budget practice. In all likelihood today this linkage would be regarded as merely a truism by most of those interested in the applications of economic analysis, evaluation research, and other accountability techniques to the budget process.

An important distinction between the present and previous preoccupation with output budgeting needs to be drawn with respect to the types of measures used. The initial formulations of performance budgeting came primarily from economically oriented public administrators, who consequently placed great stress on the measurement of output in productivity terms (that is, who desired to measure outputs as a ratio of resource inputs—both measured in dollar terms). Over the past several decades, however, substantial improvements have been made in non-economic social science measurement techniques. As a result, more recent output measurement efforts in the human services have often been directed at the measurement of social and psychological variables. It remains to be seen whether such measures can be systematically linked to budget indicators in the ways suggested by the performance budget-making model. As Due suggests, a continuing problem in performance budgeting is how to measure the units of the end product.[43]

The initial efforts to measure the performance of public agencies in productivity terms proved to be, with a few notable exceptions, an extremely difficult methodological task, one that has still not been completely resolved. This has tended to limit the applicability of the approach to several clearly defined fields of public activity (generally not including the human services). As Shoup says, "The activities of government that can be planned and controlled by output budgeting are those that yield a bundle of products that are more or less homogenous in quality."[44] Since the dynamics of quality assessment in human services can seldom even be clearly defined, much less incorporated into administrative routines, it is easy to see why performance budgeting has generally not been widely used in human service contexts. The primary significance of this approach, however, has not been its successful resolution of budget decision problems. Rather, it serves both historically and conceptually as a transitional phase in the history of budget practice. Prior to performance budgeting the principal focus in budget reform was on the formulation of formal budget systems of the type discussed above. Since that time, budget reformers in all settings have devoted almost exclusive attention to the questions of budget decision. Each of the budget-making models reviewed below is based on assumptions consistent with the budget problem as outlined in the performance budgeting model.

Program budgeting

It is, on the whole, only a very small step from the concept of performance budgeting to the concept of program budgeting. As the Due quotation above indicates, the identification of "programs" is an important prelude in identifying agency outputs in the performance model.[45] Common sense dictates that a performance approach and a program budget approach—in which budget decisions are made by grouping expenditures for similar sets of activities—are virtually synonymous.

Appearances can be deceiving, however, as is the case in this instance, for the term "program budget" is frequently used in at least two important senses that are not entirely consistent with the performance budget approach. In the first sense, program budgets are differentiated from traditional functional line-item budgets. Thus, rather than displaying budget breakdowns based on standard categories like personnel and supplies, the typical program budget attempts to link breakdowns with the "goal matrix" of the organization—essentially "pricing" the various organizational objectives. Second and equally important, the logic of most program budgeting ventures and the emphasis on goals leads to a breakdown of the integrity of organizational units in the budget document. Thus, proposed expenditures for similar activities from an objective standpoint are linked under a common heading (e.g., income maintenance intake), regardless of the organizational units in which they are to be performed. While program budget information will provide, in theory at least, much more accurate perspectives for decision-makers on the overall performance patterns within the budget system, its value to the line administrator is clearly limited. Likewise, at each programmatic level one is likely to find a similar situation—the information, in effect, is clear principally to those at the next highest level at which expenditure is to occur.

In contrast to performance budgeting, which was limited almost exclusively to the public allocations arena, program budgeting has been a popular reform idea with those in public distributions and federated allocations systems. It is not too difficult to extend the perspective to the fee-system context, as well. Both PPB and zero-based budgeting discussed below, represent variations on some of the essential notions of program budgeting models. There has been a great deal of superheated rhetoric on both of these subjects from both sides in recent years, with the result that one is inevitably expected to take a stand either for or against program budgets.

A black-or-white approach, however, fails to do justice to the very real management potentials of program budgets, on the one hand, and the very real difficulties of implementation of an adequate program budget scheme within existing budget arenas, on the other. We need to differentiate, in particular, the inflated claims for program budgeting markedly improving the performance of budget decision-makers from the more modest and realistic claims for program budgeting serving to clarify and identify budget choices. By failing to differentiate these two perspectives the Wildavskian critics of program budgeting are simply failing to allow any legitimacy to agency perspectives. If political decision-makers wish to continue making their choices on the "pork-barrel" potentials of public expenditures, for example, they should be as able to do so under programming budget formats as under existing line-item formats. The incremental gains in budget control and planning that the latter allow administrators will be substantial indeed. In brief, much of the debate over program budgets has simply failed to adequately sort out the different legitimate uses of budget information. No budget system, per se, is going to exercise a controlling influence on the way decisions are made. However, the critical step, from an agency standpoint, is to link budget decisions and implementation. In this context, program budget approaches offer enormous possibilities for extending the capabilities of management control and planning. Furthermore, the integration of program budgets and program accounting schemes offers some unique opportunities for direct feedback from the accounting system to agency decision-making, both in budget-making and operations.

Since only a handful of agencies in human services have any extensive experience with working program budget systems, and since much of that experience is quite recent and tentative, it can truly be said that the jury is still out on the question of the utility of program budgeting in human services.

Programming-planning-budgeting systems

One of the most fascinating, and in some respects, curious, episodes in the history of budget reform in the United States was the rise and fall of Programming-Planning-Budgeting Systems (PPB) during the latter half of the 1960s. In many respects, PPB represented a radical alternative to present budget practice, because it combined uncompromising notions of program budgeting (as outlined above) with extensive use of cost-effectiveness techniques and a synoptically rational model of budget arenas as scientific problem-solving bodies. PPB began in the Rand Corporation as a way of making sense of the Department of Defense budget in programmatic terms, and was subsequently mandated for the entire federal government by President Johnson in 1965. It was quietly "deactivated" by the Nixon Administration at the end of the decade.

The PPB approach is perhaps the penultimate rational model of budget-making—beginning with the definition of the objectives of all operating programs, and proceeding through the analysis of alternative strategies, the adoption of preferred strategies, and the creation of management information systems for monitoring the performance of implemented strategies. It boasts certain novel features, such as the introduction of zero-base budget decisions—an approach in which each major budget choice is subject to renewed consideration each year—program structures that are linked to objectives and extended across agency or departmental lines, and complete integration of budget and accounting systems. Ultimately, however, the comprehensive rationality of PPB proved to be too unrealistic in its assumptions, too difficult to implement, and too clearly conducive to increasing the political power of "neutral" economists (whose cost-effectiveness determinations become the only *real* decisions in PPB) to warrant much interest. PPB proved to be especially difficult to deal with in the ambiguous, inconsistent, and often conflicting climate of goals in the human service arena.[46] Whose goals, for example, does one identify and measure in a complex and controversial program such as public welfare? PPB ultimately would have necessitated a virtual remodeling of the entire governmental system in order to accommodate its logical requirements—a slightly excessive demand for a budget system!

Nevertheless, one should not conclude that the PPB venture was entirely in vain. In the human services, for example, it is largely because of PPB that we are aware of the tremendous armory of economic analysis tools that can be used to deal with financial problems. Also, the growing awareness of a linkage between planning and budgeting must be credited, in part, to PPB.[47] Furthermore, it was largely in reaction to PPB that Wildavsky's elaboration of the politics of the budgetary process was made, and the recent impressive accomplishments of the UWASIS system are founded on PPB—like assumptions.[48] These are substantial accomplishments for a reform that failed.

Zero-based budgeting

One is tempted initially to dismiss zero-based budgeting as simply another unrealistic effort by economists to de-politicize the budgetary process. Closer examination, however, reveals a critical distinction to be made between the unrealistic zero-sum assumption of PPB that every expenditure should be completely justified every year, and the zero-based budgeting assumption that every expenditure should be subject to periodic reexamination and justification (although not necessarily every year.)[49]

Zero-based budgeting, as implemented in the state of Georgia, also incorporates a more realistic approach to program structures than the PPB model: originally formulated at Texas Instruments in 1968, and subsequently implemented in the city of Garland, Texas and the state of Georgia, a zero-based approach has been proposed by President Carter for the U.S. Budget, and it is certain to receive extensive discussion in future years.

The essense of the zero-based approach is a combination of the linkage of planning and budget decisions found in PPB (this time, in what are called "decision-packages") with an essentially incremental decison model that serially and marginally makes decisions on decision packages. At each level in an organizational heirarchy, a manager works with sets of "decision packages" (essentially "work programs") of proposed objectives and sets of alternatives for attaining objectives, each "costed" with a proposed budget. In the true marginal manner no effort is made to list all possible alternatives, but only to concentrate on what appear at each level to be the most likely options.

While the steps involved in implementing a zero-based approach vary by setting, Pyhrr notes four common steps:

1. Identification of "decision units."
2. Analysis of each decision unit within a package.
3. Evaluation and ranking of all decision packages to prepare an appropriations request (a top management activity).

4. Preparation of a detailed operating budget reflecting those decisions packages approved in the budget appropriations.[50]

It appears very likely that in many operational settings, zero-based budgeting may turn out to be a minimal merger of planning and decision-making in the budget arena: the incorporation of concern for the identification of objectives with concern for performance in existing budget systems and incremental decision protocols.

In general, the recent history of budget reforms is not a particularly optimistic one. It remains to be seen whether zero-base budgeting will turn out to be just another good idea or a radical improvement in our capacity to orchestrate budget decisions.

Profile of a budget official

In a previous section several points were made about the implications of fund-raising requirements for the fund-raiser. In a similar vein, one can make a number of interrelated observations about the person whose responsibilities include the development, negotiation, and implementation of an agency budget.

Perhaps the single greatest talent required of such persons might be termed "numerical imagination": the ability to mentally link the substantive, program activities of the agency with the abstract, numerical world of the budget. This talent consists, in brief, of the ability to visualize or conceptualize in "real" (that is to say, program) terms the implications of changes in the various numerical qualities of a budget.

This talent is demonstrated in different ways at different times in the budgetary process. In its most elementary form, a numerical imagination differentiates novices from those with experience and knowledge in budgeting. Most novices, faced with a starting point like a $50,000 expenditure ceiling and a progam concept, experience great difficulties in envisioning the expenditures necessary to bring that program into reality, and with good reason. After all, who really knows how many sheets of typing paper or even how many staff persons at what salaries are necessary for a projected program? The answer is, "those with the kind of numerical imagination suggested above!"

One can routinely expect projections from even the most minimal data from an experienced budget official possessed of this particular talent. He will divine, for example, that with $50,000, one can't expect to hire ten or more staff. And he can answer questions. Will the project pay its own rent and utilities? Are there any overhead charges? If so, what's the overhead rate? And on and on.

In a somewhat more advanced form a numerical imagination is also manifested in the ability to anticipate certain scale effects: if the number of staff on a project are increased, additional office space and secretarial assistance may be necessary—do these items need to be built into the budget?

In its most sophisticated form, one finds among budget officials a truly remarkable form of numerical imagination. This is the ability to routinely incorporate speculations on the program implications of the manipulation of budget items into active, on-going negotiations over budgets. For example, it is proposed in a meeting that the total expenditures in a proposed budget be increased by 2 percent. Will these funds be added to those already included in the miscellaneous item, on the assumption that some later use can be made of them? Or, will someone notice that the increase is just enough to make a slight adjustment in the travel projections and support a needed half-time aide position?

Conclusion

The phenomenon of budget-making emerges in human services largely because certain resources are scarce and must be allocated carefully. Budget-making, we have seen, arises out of a pragmatic necessity for choice within human service agencies and in larger budget systems. We identified four budget systems external to human service agencies and incorporating them in various ways. These were termed public appropriations, public distributions, federated distributions, and fee systems. Each of these was labeled a budget arena in which agency participation is strategically directed at seeking out and capturing scarce resources.

Five other budget systems were also identified and discussed. Each of these systems was characterized by a particular approach to the problem of budgetary choice. The five systems are: marginal budgeting, performance budgeting, program budgeting, programming-planning-budgeting systems; and zero-based budgeting. The chapter analyzed each system for its internal and external effects on human service organizations, and made recommendations for the incorporation of valuable features of each system into the management routines of the human service organization. In the following chapter some of these suggestions are followed up systematically, as we examine the budget-making phenomenon as a problem of information gathering, and concentrate on the preparation and presentation of a number of different types of budget documents and formats.

CHAPTER 7

BUDGET
DOCUMENTATION

"It's in the budget
—somewhere"
—Anonymous

In the preceding chapter, the problem of budget-making in human services was approached as a problem of organization and decision-making. In this chapter, we will examine the same area of budget-making from the vantage point of information. Budget-making, it will be shown, has certain important dimensions best perceived as problems in information generation, organization, and diffusion.[1]

Practical discussions of budget-making with new administrators and students of human service administration often move very quickly to informational issues. The problems of budget organization and decisions previously discussed are, apparently, much more elusive and difficult for many people to grasp than the more concrete search for the "right" budget format. Unfortunately, scholars whose primary interests are on the former topics have far too often neglected the latter topic as trivial and uninteresting—the results of such neglect can be seen in the chaotic handling of financial information in most human service fields today.

Unlike financial statements of operations and position, which come under the watchful eye of the accounting profession, no person or group has assumed responsibility for the formats of budget documents in the human services.[2] As a result, at present the art of preparing and disseminating budget information leaves much to be desired.

In this chapter we will focus on two issues necessary for the movement of the field toward more standardized reporting of budget information. First we will consider the general subject of the internal logic of budget documents, borrowing from both business and human service budgets. Budget documents, or more simply, budgets is usually used to refer to statements of projected or anticipated financial operation. Second, we will approach the general issue of a Budget Information System (BIS) from the vantage point of the human services. The basic question considered here is whether it is possible to identify a comprehensive system suitable to the information needs of budget decisions in human service organizations. (This relates closely to the discussion of ratio analysis in Chapter 11.)

We shall take as a departure point for this discussion the simple observation that the fundamental purpose of the preparation of budget documents is the communication of information. That is, the person constructing a budget document, whom we shall call for simplicity, "the analyst," seeks to convey, using a standard format, certain bits of information critical to those persons in the organization charged with making policy and management decisions.

Three guiding principles, borrowed from the accounting profession, appear especially relevant to this objective. They are accuracy, balance, and brevity. It goes without saying that *accuracy* is important in all financial information, even allowing for a certain "fudge factor" in budget negotiations: persons who overstate their budgets for strategic reasons should not be mislead by their own overstatements. *Balance*, while important, cannot always be achieved in budget statements. In some cases, we are only interested in dealing with the expenditure side of the equation, or with revenues, and consequently, simple mathematical balance is not possible. Even so, however, it is possible, as we shall see below, to build a kind of inferential logic into budget documents that serves as a good substitute for true mathematical balance. In other instances the true advantage of conceiving of a set of budget documents as a management information system becomes apparent, in that we can substitute the use of external reference points in other report formats in the system for the lack of balance in a budget format.

Finally, the significance of brevity in communicating financial information cannot be overstated. Indeed, one of the principal criticisms of several existing efforts to develop budget information systems in the human services is the fact that such a tremendous range and number of reporting formats are included that the forms themselves impede the information flow.[3] It is also easy to find budget formats that err in the other extreme. Many state government line-item budgets reduce the entire annual or biennial operation of complex departments like public welfare or mental health to half-a-dozen lines with colorfully descriptive labels like "total expenditures"! One does not have to be a zealot for comprehensive budget reform in order to see the need for more meaningful presentation of information.

The elements of a budget format

Is it possible to state with any certainty the minimum elements that should be incorporated into a budget statement to make it meaningful for decision purposes? Yes; an examination of forms used in a broad range of human service contexts suggests that there are a number of common elements, like a heading, which make identification possible. A heading should contain names of agency and/or program entities, the location or other identification, and the period under consideration. Second, there is likely to be a set of category labels (and, perhaps, subcategory labels) identifying or naming the major groupings of revenues and/or expenditures. Third, the minimal unit, or "building block" of most budget formats is a column listing of discrete revenue or expenditure items (each of which is, of course, an aggregate of discrete financial transactions anticipated). Each listing is likely to include brief, identifying words or phrases in one vertical column and dollar entries in another, as in Figure 13. In some instances, budget formats also include a computational formula indicating how the dollar figure was arrived at (e.g., $1,000 = 200 hours at $5 hour). Such formulae are often enclosed in parenthesis or brackets.

In the remainder of this chapter approximately two dozen separate budget formats of interest to human services are presented. Most of them are currently in widespread use. Most have already received acceptance in human services. Several are used in business settings or public organizations, and appear to be adaptable to the human service context. A few are experimental. They all are potentially usable with questions either of internal or fiscal accountability, and some are appropriate to community accountability issues, as well. The following discussion does not address at all the question of the audiences of such documents, since this is a pragmatic issue that must be resolved within individual agencies. Some administrators will find it helpful to use all of these types of formats to disseminate financial information to board members and

FIGURE 13
Budget Format Elements in Sub-Fund Budgets

(Title Of Statement)
(Name of Agency)
(Time Period Covered)

Sub-section labels (if appropriate)	
Resources on hand, beginning of period	Amount
Income during period (by source)	Amount
Total resources available in period	Amount
Labels (if appropriate)	
Anticipated expenditures (by line item, chart of accounts headings, or program category)	Amount
Anticipated revenues, end of period*	Amount

*Difference between revenues and anticipated expenditures. In most public budgeting this item is eliminated—revenues and expenditures are expected to match, or "balance."

even the mass media, while others will prefer to keep some or all budget information confidential. Such issues of utilization patterns are beyond the scope of this discussion.

Basic budget formats

Three types of budget documents correspond to the breadth of agency budget decisions. First are the *fund decisions*, that is, decisions concerned with major changes expected in given accounting entities in a given budget period. Some possibility exists, at present, for identifying standard types of budget formats for this. Program budgets and project budgets, for example, are computed on a fund-entity basis, and fund budgets are presented in "balanced" format—with both expenditures and revenues listed.

Second, are the *sub-fund decisions*. In this case, decision-makers are concerned with a specific aspect of fund operations, and budget documents must be prepared to focus on that aspect only. Such a budget will usually focus on either a set of expenditure items or a set of revenues, but seldom on both. Consequently, in contrast to fund budgets, sub-fund budgets rarely can be presented in a state of balance.

Most efforts at identification of budget formats in human services occur with one or both of these levels of information demand. However, the emergent problems of the multi-funded agency in human services raise an additional level of information demand that is seldom taken into account in the literature. This is the problem of the *supra-fund decision*. There are, in most human service agencies, a number of financial decisions (ranging from such relatively mundane matters as the design of the telephone system to extremely complex questions of the appropriate formula for determining contributions from each program-fund to the central administrative staff costs of the agency) that cannot be approached at either of the above levels. Consequently, there is occasional need in human service agencies for integrated budget information on the entire agency or a major program involving more than one fund. Essentially, what is needed is a consolidated budget format incorporating all of the needed information in summary form into a single document.

All of the budget formats discussed in this chapter are classified under one of these three headings—we begin with consideration of fund budgets, proceed to consideration of sub-fund budgets, and conclude with a discussion of a proposal for a supra-fund budget format for the human services.

Budgets for fund decisions

The logical starting point for any discussion of budget formats in the human services is to deal with those budgets that purport to tell "the whole story" about agency revenue and expenditure patterns. Such budgets ordinarily are organized to present statements of projected operations for a fixed future period, although there is, as already suggested, no inherent reason why fund budgets reflecting assumptions about future conditions could not also be developed. Such budgets would usually be less than helpful, however, since human service budgets use a zero-balance assumption: all revenues coming in during a period will be consumed during that period, leaving a zero-balance at the beginning and end. While such assumptions are seldom actually met (there is almost always some surplus revenue or deficit at the end of a fiscal period), this assumption makes a handy departure point for the necessary computations. Unfortunately, it also often sets up the year end mad scramble of agencies seeking to "spend it or lose it."

For human service purposes, there are three general types of fund budget formats we need concern ourselves with: line-item formats (see Figures 14 and 15), program formats (Figure 16) and project formats (Figure 17). The three formats differ principally in the headings

FIGURE 14

Line-Item Entries

Tennessee State Budget, 1975
Sub-Program F. Medicaid–Intermediate Care Nursing Home Program

Purpose: The ICF program is to provide and insure proper medical and nursing home care to eligible recipients including those in State hospitals and schools for the mentally retarded.

Personnel
No personnel

Funding

Appropriation	$ 3,918,495.73	$ 6,925,500	$10,418,100
Federal	13,315,850.37	22,305,000	30,183,800
Local	675,338.33	769,500	1,157,600
Total	$17,909,684.43	$30,000,000	$41,759,500

FIGURE 15

Project Budget

Foster Family Placement
Bethlehem Children's Homes
(date)

	Last Year	Projected
Salaries and fringe benefits		
Professional	$ 71,841	$ 87,000
Clerical	8,299	10,000
Fringe benefits (17%)	15,032	16,490
Office rental	4,108	5,000
Staff travel	2,742	4,000
Telephone	977	1,000
Office equipment	1,203	1,500
Office supplies	1,806	2,000
Total project costs	$106,008	$126,990

FIGURE 16

Revenue/Expenditure Budget

Family Services, Inc.
(date)

	Revenue	Expenditures
Counseling program		
United Fund	$ 25,000	
Title XX	71,000	
Private insurance	28,600	
Fixed expenditures		$ 98,000
Surplus (for allocation)		26,600
Total	$124,600	$124,600
Outreach program		
United Fund	$ 8,000	
Action	8,000	
Admission fees	250	
Fixed expenditures		$ 16,000
Surplus (for allocation)		250
Total	$ 16,250	$ 16,250

FIGURE 17

Project Budget: Personnel

Juvenile Drug Outreach Program
Appalachian Mental Hospital
19— Fiscal Year

Employees	No. of Employees	Salary	Time	Amount
Senior social worker	1	$17,500	100%	$17,500
Gang worker	1	12,500	75%	9,375
Psychiatrist	1	75 per hour	100 hours	7,500
Testing psychologist	1	40 per hour	100 hours	4,000
Case aides	4	7,100	100%	28,400
Clerical workers	3	6,000	100%	18,000
Total personnel cost				$84,775
(Less 28% first year for start-up delays)				23,737
Total				$60,938

employed and the method used to aggregate revenues and expenditures. Line-item budgets, for example, present highly aggregated information in a very small number of categories (as in Figure 14) or listings of revenues by source, with expenditures listed in standardized functional categories (as in Figure 15). Program formats, by contrast, seek to employ some minimal concept of goals or objectives to organize budget items.

Frequently, in such efforts, the resultant program structure includes a matching of revenues and expenditures, as in Figure 16, although this need not be the case. Program budget formats are explicitly assumed to refer to on-going activities, while project budgets refer to activities with identifiable beginning and ending points. In these terms a YMCA budget presented would be a program budget while a summer camp budget (or basketball program budget) would be a project budget. Although they use the same fundamental formats, project and program budgets differ in certain significant ways, the most important of which is the assumption made about the duration of activities. For example, in dealing with project budgets, decision-makers may wish to explicitly take into account "start-up" and "wrap-up" cost variations. Therefore, in doing a project budget one may seek to explicitly build in some recognition of this (as in Figure 17). Likewise, a major problem in project budgeting in cases in which federal funds are involved is unrealistic expectations about when expenditures for the project may legitimately begin.[4] It may be desirable in most instances, therefore, to give some consideration to the establishment of a broad enough project period to realistically incorporate all relevant expenditures. For example, if a summer camp program is to operate from July 1 to September 1, but the director is to begin working—and expects to be paid—on June 10, the operational period for this program must be set accordingly.

Although actual practice varies widely, it is assumed here that it is desirable in the preparation of program and project budgets to include both revenue and expenditure entries, which presumably will balance, if for no other reason than to make the arithmetic task easier and less susceptible to errors. A key question, then, is how much detail to show in listing revenue sources: whether to list no separate revenues entry (as in Figure 14 and 15), by categories (as in Figure 18), or by specific sources (as in Figure 16).

An additional variation that can readily be incorporated in any of these formats is "retrospective" data. By adding one column, or several, one can provide comparative information from last year, five years ago,

FIGURE 18

Line Item/Program Matrix Budget

Save The Seniors of Our City (STSOC)

	Program 1	Program 2	Program 3	Program 4
Expenditures				
Personnel	$120,000	$65,000	$28,000	$15,500
Office	15,000			
Travel	6,000	3,000	2,000	1,500
Communications	1,200	1,000	8,000	600
Equipment	1,000	1,000	1,000	1,000
Supplies	1,200	650	280	155
Total expenditures	$144,400	$70,650	$32,080	$18,755
Revenues				
Fees	$ 4,000	$ 2,000		
Grant no. 1	140,000	15,000	$10,000	$10,000
Grant no. 2		53,650	5,000	5,000
Grant no. 3			16,980	3,755
United Fund	400		100	
Total revenues	$144,400	$70,650	$32,080	$18,755

or any appropriate period. Some care must be exercised in so doing, however, particularly in the case of project budgets, lest false comparisons be established. If prior summer camps operated for eight weeks, and this year's camp will only operate for six weeks, serious questions would have to be raised about including retrospective data in a project budget. Furthermore, high rates of inflation in recent years may make the adjustment of such prior expenditures to "current dollars" necessary, at least in those cases where very large sums of money are involved.[5]

Other interesting variations on these budget formats are also possible. For example, many human service organizations find themselves enmeshed in bewilderingly complex patterns of federal, state, and local funding, with variable allowances for "matching" contributions by the agency. In such cases, presentation of revenue entries in line-item, program, or project budgets in a manner consistent with Figure 18 may be desirable. Anyone who has ever attempted to explain to a lay board of directors the sort of byzantine funding patterns shown in Figure 18 will appreciate the importance of visual and graphic presentation to support such explanations.

Finally, in some cases the types of fund budgets discussed above will be large and complex enough to encompass several major organizational units. In such cases, it may also be desirable to devise what are, essentially, departmental budgets, as in Figure 19. In such cases, to be consistent with organizational patterns one lists revenues in consolidated fashion (revenues of the fund) rather than by department, and breaks down only the expenditure items to reflect organizational units. Such sub-division of a single fund-entity, it should be noted, is similar to, but distinguishable from, the situation in which the organizational sub-units correspond, wholly or in part, with separate fund-entities. (This last case is discussed in the final section of this chapter.)

Special purpose budgets

All of the fund budget documents presented up to this point have been general in the sense that they were reporting on generic sets of planned activities of overall accounting entities. In addition. virtually any component of these budgets (whether programmatic as in the project budget already discussed, or functional, as below) can be identified,

FIGURE 19

Departmental Expenditures

County Aid Association	
(date)	
General administration costs	$ 80,000
Food stamps department	
Distribution	3,637,000
Administrative costs	82,000
Public aid department	
Distributions	1,471,000
Administrative costs	67,000
Social service department	320,000
Medical aid department	
Distributions	3,272,400
Administrative costs	333,000
Total	$9,262,400

broken down, and examined in a special purpose budget. The use of special purpose budgets in human service organizations is minimal, and many of the budgets presented in this section are taken from business. However, many are already in use in agency settings, and there appears to be no reason why special purpose budgets could not be more widely used in the human services (subject to the general observations made at the beginning of this chapter). As a general rule of thumb, the special purpose budgets discussed below can be used whenever it is convenient or appropriate to present information on programs in dollars and cents.

Sources of revenue table

One of the simplest adaptations of a budget is to convert actual dollars into percentages. In the example shown (Figure 20) budget revenues *and* expenditures are converted to percentages, with the added feature of percentages listed in ranges, rather than as exact figures. Such a "sources of revenues table" can be a highly informative addition to planning studies or proposals that are under review by a board or committee because they offer fairly clear indications of where and in what relative strength agency resources originate. Revenue sources, in this instance, might also be listed by agency or entity, by program structures, and by programs rather than options (or in addition to options). (The listing of revenue source agency broken down by program structures is the beginning table in the "consolidated budget reference sheet" discussed below and shown in Figure 35).

FIGURE 20

Sources of Revenue Table

	Social Services Dept. (date)		
Revenue Source	*Option A*	*Option B*	*Option C*
Dues	75.6–78%	61–92.1%	99.1–100%
Fees	1–6	1.3–8	
Third-party payments	6–14	0–10	
Sales	0–4.1	0–8	
Other income	5–8.3	6.7–13	0–9

Source: "Sources of Revenue Table," Department of Health, Education, and Welfare, Health Services and Mental Health Administration, *Financial Planning Manual for Health Maintenance Organizations* (Washington, D.C.: G.P.O., 1973), p. 4.

Administrative (or overhead) cost budget

One of the more interesting special purpose budgets, which is finding increasing utilization in personal service and is absolutely essential to program budgeting and cost analysis schemes, is the administrative (or overhead) cost budget. In this case, we are concerned only with "cost" items—as measured by real or projected expenditures. Matching these with revenue estimates would ordinarily be futile. The principal task in estimating administrative cost is one of isolating those actual or projected expenses that cannot properly be attributed to an agency program or the creation and dissemination of services. A complete listing of the cost elements subsumed under administrative cost is included in the AICPA definition of such costs cited in Chapter 2.

The format in Figure 22 is illustrative of what might be included in an Administrative Costs Budget. The term overhead budget might be more meaningful in the case of voluntary sector human service organizations, to describe all non-service expenses—combining administrative cost and fund-raising expenses together (see Figure 22). Acceptable accounting practice, according to AICPA, requires separating these expenditure categories; however, presentation of any or all of them together on an overhead budget should not pose any problems so long as they are properly identified.

Accounts receivable budget

Of considerable use in an agency or program dependent upon client or user fee for a substantial portion of its revenues is the "accounts receivable budget" (Figure 21).

FIGURE 21
Accounts Receivable Budget

Arapaho Guidance Center
January–June, 19—

Accounts receivable (January 1, 19—)	$ 40,000
Estimated charges during period	$600,000
Total accounts receivable for year to date	$640,000
Desired accounts receivable balance end of period	$ 35,000
Necessary collections	$605,000

FIGURE 22

Quarterly Administrative Cost Budget*

Rock County Department of Public Welfare
January–March, 19—

	Fixed	Variable	Total
Executive salaries	$200,000	$40,000	$240,000
Clerical salaries	110,000	25,000	135,000
Telephone	10,000	10,000	20,000
Depreciation—equipment	30,000		30,000
Insurance	10,000		10,000
Office supplies	20,000	10,000	30,000
Legal and audit fees	5,000		5,000
Total administrative expense	$390,000	$85,000	$475,000

*Overhead costs not assigned to major program or functional areas.

In this case, "accounts receivable" best refers only to those accounts receivable directly from clients. In principle, however, all receivables can be shown on such a statement. Many agency accounting systems differentiate receivables from clients and institutional funding sources in the form of appropriations, grants, and so forth. Other "modified accrual" systems do not regard outstanding grant revenues as receivable at all. Determination of an estimate for necessary collections during a

FIGURE 23

Accounts Payable Budget

Center City YMCA
Second Quarter, 19—

Accounts payable, March 31	$3,900
Budgeted purchases in quarter	3,200
Total accounts payable in second quarter	$7,140
Desired balance, July 1	1,000
Necessary payments in quarter	$6,140

given fiscal period may, by itself, justify the use of this format in the human services. In the example shown (Figure 21) a number of decisions are implied: the beginning-of-period and end-of-period balances are different by $5,000, implying an explicit decision by management to reduce outstanding accounts receivable by that amount during the period. Without this decision, necessary collections for the period might equal charges during the period. In some instances, the use of write offs may occasion an additional line as follows:

Uncollectable accounts, written off $100

Accounts payable budget

The logic of the "accounts payable budget" is directly comparable to that of the accounts receivable budget, except that what is being communicated is information regarding the amount owed by the organization to its creditors (in accounting terms, liabilities rather than assets). The primary reason for using an accounts payable budget (shown in Figure 23) in human service organizations, is to project the effects upon cash flow of accounts payable during a given period (month, year, quarter). (See Chapter 10.) However, the desired or expected balance at the end of period may be only partially a matter of organizational planning and control. Credit terms covering the accounts payable often dictate when they must be paid. Consequently, examination of bills and statements may be necessary to determine a

FIGURE 24
Capital Improvements Budget

Jane Austen Girls' Club
19—

Replacement of typewriters	$ 1,745
Copiers—lease charges	4,580
Repairs on office equipment	490
Renovations—counselors offices	6,840
Purchases of gym equipment	18,700
Pool repairs	6,000
Total capital equipment costs	$38,355

feasable and reasonable figure for the end-of-period balance. And, if, after this examination, it is found that the organization will be unable to meet all of its obligations during the period, several options are open. One is to seek some means of speeding up payments (from grantors, or other funding sources). Another would be to scale down budgeted purchases during the period. In most instances, it will be possible to put off purchasing one or more items in order to reduce the total amount of accounts payable during the period. In all cases, however, the first item to be checked should be the necessary payment figure, which can be compared with expected cash and liquid assets during the period.

Capital improvements budget

The name of this budget (shown in Figure 24) is taken directly from business usage. Because, strictly speaking, human service organizations do not have any capital to improve, we might more appropriately label this an "equity improvements budget," or perhaps merely an "improvements budget." In any case, the principle behind the budget is the same: it represents a project budget for major improvements in the physical plant, equipment, or permanent facilities owned or controlled by a human service organization. Since such facilities are usually expected to last long into the future, an integral aspect of capital budgeting is the inclusion of interest and other charges in the consideration.

Most readers are perhaps familiar with a version of this budget because it is used by the churches or other organizations, which often present such budgets to their membership in seeking approval for construction projects. In large organizations such budgets might also take into account major equipment purchases (copying machines, typewriters, computing facilities). In such cases the "lease or purchase" decision (discussed in Chapter 10) is a major administrative issue, and a formal listing of several options may be a useful way to present the capital improvements budget.

Unit cost budget

One type of budget that cost-accounting techniques have made an every-day reality in business is the unit-cost budget. This budget consists of a series of "factor costs" derived from actual performance, rather than the kinds of "raw" estimates that cost human service managers are familiar with.

In the human service context, unit-cost budgeting should be ap-

FIGURE 25

Unit Costs Budget

Whole Blood and Serum Vending, Inc.
January–December, 19—

	Units	Unit Cost	Total
Last year's volume	12,500	$100	$125,000
Unit increase projected	1,500	100	15,000
Cost increase projected	14,000	25	4,500
This year's costs			$144,500

proached with "kid gloves." Advances in non-profit accounting, standardized definitions of service components, and a general growth in management sophistication have brought the field to the point where cost-accounting techniques and the integration of accounting and budget data are technically feasible.[6] However, the actual design and implementation of a workable cost-accounting system that would allow the preparation of budgets using standard factors rather than raw estimates still requires a substantial, on-going commitment on the part of an agency.

Perhaps the greatest problem with unit costs in the present is the tendency to simply select an arbitrary unit (say, the number of clients served) and divide it by the total program expenditure to determine a unit cost figure.[7] This approach, while it may have a certain usefulness in facilitating decisions, may be just about as appropriate as rolling dice. In human service usage, terms like clients, programs, and service units seldom have very precise definitions, as noted previously. Different programs may have different procedures for including and categorizing various types of cost-items, such as administrative, personnel, or travel costs. Furthermore, some "client contacts" may be with single individuals or for long periods of time, while others are with large groups or for brief periods. Unless the unit-cost budgeting format recognizes, and incorporates standardized procedures for the treatment of these and related matters, the results can be genuinely chaotic. This however, is an argument for caution and prudence, not for abandoning the use of this approach entirely.

We are truly concerned here with an "apples and oranges" comparison. What is easily overlooked, however, is that apples and oranges can indeed be compared if one is aware of, and has carefully defined the qualities or traits being compared: the thickness of peels, color, calories, acetic acid content, and so forth. The handling of unit-cost budgeting must be approached similarly, through standardized definition and careful, precise measurement.

One of the most common approaches to definition and measurement of unit-costs involves the use of "production," or "output" units. Such units may be defined in terms of physical quantities (pints of blood collected, birth control devices dispensed, number of lunches served per day, books read per student), procedures performed (number of clients admitted, number of social histories completed, number of interviews conducted), or clock-time (number of minutes spent with each case). In all cases, however, the critical question is one of standardization. Ideally, not only the average (or mean) unit values should be known, but the other parameters, as well (standard deviation, range, etc.).

Provided such standard units of production can be identified and satisfactorily defined, it should be possible to systematically relate them to each of the discrete supportive expenditures. Thus, rather than aggregating expenditures by "functional" budget categories (personnel, travel), aggregation is by "cost centers" based on the production units noted above. Budgeting, in this context is essentially a matter of adjusting the various cost factors to changes expected during the budget period.

Even without full articulation of cost-accounting schemes, however, unit-cost approaches are currently being used in several contexts in human service budgeting. For example, following media criticism early in the War on Poverty, the Office of Economic Opportunity developed a unit-cost method for setting ceilings on requests for grant funds to operate Head Start programs. Based on a calculation of reasonable cost-per-child-per-day estimates, the agency was able to use this approach to shield itself from funding requests that sought excessively large sums of money in the name of high quality programs. A similar approach has also been used successfully in a number of manpower programs, where key cost factors (hourly salary, number of hours of training) are predictable.

In other contexts, however, such unit costs approaches are routinely abused or misapplied. The comparison of general unit costs (costs per client) in a setting where a wide variety of different programs are funded—such as Title XX, Model Cities, Community Action, or

Community Mental Health—is a questionable practice at best, and often inappropriate. Without the defining and standardizing practices noted above, such comparisons are worse than misleading, they are downright unfair to those being compared.

The principal virtue of this approach is in the standardization. The need to recompute at each step in the budget process can be seriously diminished, with a consequent savings in time and effort. Conceivably, this approach could also expand the use of planning in budget-making, by allowing widespread consideration of options without a lot of laborious computation. Furthermore, the incorporation of units of production enforces a link between fiscal and program goals, and the quantification of the latter. In the absence of careful definition and delineation however, the unit-cost budget is likely to amount to no more than meaningless numbers on a page.

Direct labor budget

In essence, the unit-cost budget focuses on the total cost of producing a unit of service. It is also possible to partialize some of the cost elements of such an approach, and prepare budget statements on these. One of the most likely candidates is the direct labor budget, which measures the amount of labor involved in producing a unit of service. Widely used in manufacturing organizations, this budget also appears to have some uses in human service organizations with established, on-going unit-cost systems. (See Figure 26.) In this case, two unit figures are necessary: the total number of production units (such as service hours or number of clients seen) and the direct labor content per unit (which, in this case, is simply the total amount of employee time involved in a unit of service).

FIGURE 26
Direct Labor Budget

May 1, 19— to April 30, 19—

Units to be produced	194,000
Standard direct labor content/unit	2 hrs.
Production hours required (units × hours)	388,000
Average wage rate	$2.50/hr.
Total direct labor cost (total hours × wage rate)	$795,400

A note of clarification here: "direct labor" in the human service context refers to personnel costs associated with program (rather than administrative or fund-raising) costs. With these figures, it is possible to project the total direct labor costs of an agency or program. In fact, with two additional pieces of data, one should have the basis for projecting an entire budget. They are the non-direct labor (that is, non-personnel) costs, and the administrative costs (or overhead costs) rate. With these figures, it is simply a matter of arithmetic to determine total budget figures:

$$T = L + (ML)$$

where T equals total program costs; L equals direct labor costs and M equals a percentage of administrative labor costs.

Production budget

It also should be possible to devise a budget for either an on-going program or a special project that takes into account both anticipated expenditures and variable revenues (generated through fees, sales, and the like). In fact, such a budget would be very similar in format to a standard production budget employed in manufacturing concerns. Figure 27 shows a typical version of such a budget.

In Figure 28, this basic format has been adapted and simplified to fit the circumstances of a common event in voluntary organizations, the fund-raiser—a special event such as a bake sale or craft fair. The same

FIGURE 27
*Production Budget**

Non-Profit Craft Sales, Inc.
Calendar Year, 19—

Desired ending inventory, finished goods	$ 12,000
Expected sales (or, units required)	200,000
Total units required (or dollar value)	$212,000
Present inventory, finished goods	18,000
Necessary production (units required—inventory)	$194,000

*In dollars or material units produced.

FIGURE 28

Fund-raising Budget

Bay City Friendly Visitors and Hospital Auxiliary
(date)

Gross revenue ($5 × 30 members)		$150.00
Expenses		
Building rental	$15.00	$ 15.00
Materials	8.50	8.50
Total expenses		$ 22.50
Net revenue from project		$127.50

two elements remain: estimates of anticipated costs and expected revenues. For example, let's assume that the Bay City Friendly Visitors and Hospital Auxiliary is planning a bake sale. Each of the thirty members is expected to bring $5 worth of baked goods at the following rates: $2 each for cakes; $1.50 each for pies; $1 per dozen for cookies; and $.75 a loaf for bread. The auxiliary pays $15 a day to rent the building where the sale was to be held, and expects to spend $8.50 for materials. In their enthusiasm, the planning committee predicts that the event will bring in $150. However, as Figure 28 shows, they failed to take expenses into account.

Supplies budget

For those agencies and projects involved in the use and consumption of large amounts of supplies (office supplies, food, or birth control and other clinic items), a format comparable to the capital equipment budget may be useful for projecting the pattern of expenditures and its effect on inventories during a given period (month, quarter, or year). As Figure 29 shows, the internal logic of the format is comparable to that of statements of financial position—containing beginning position, changes and adjustments during the period, and anticipated position at the end of period. In this case, there are three manipulable variables that can be altered to affect the outcome in the desired direction: supplies on order could be cancelled, routine orders budgeted for the month could be increased or decreased, and expected use of supplies could be increased or decreased. (Discussion of these various options will be included in Chapter 9, under Purchasing and Inventory Control.)

FIGURE 29

Supplies Budget

Family Planning Clinic
October, 19—

Clinical supplies on hand, October 1	$21,740
Supplies on order	870
Budgeted purchases for month	4,100
Total supplies	$26,710
Expected use of supplies this month	9,400
Total estimated supplies on hand, November 1	$17,310

Costs of debt budget

Deficit financing is not, ordinarily, an acceptable state of affairs in non-profit human service organizations, primarily because they seldom have fixed (or, for that matter, liquid) assets sufficient to secure major debts. There are a couple of major exceptions to this generalization, however, and in these cases, a "costs of debt budget" may be a useful format for planning and keeping management and the board of directors informed about the impact of debts on the operation and financial position of the agency.

The two circumstances in which debt may be a consideration in human service agency will go into debt simply to finance an ongoing construction of buildings or additions), and the purchase of major "capital equipment," that is, equipment that will be a part of the permanent "plant" of the agency—perhaps playground equipment, shop equipment, maintenance equipment, vehicles, and printing or duplicating equipment. In no instance is it reasonable to expect that a human service agency will go into debt simply to finance an opening operational program. It is conceivable, however, that short-term loans may be necessary, as in the case of some federal grants, to avoid serious cash-flow problems. In such cases, however, the likelihood of interest charges being charged against the federal funds should be determined in advance, since federal agency practice varies on this.

The cost of debt budget shown in Figure 30 lists two separate types of debt, in the language of finance, one "secured" by bank notes, and the other by mortgages. The period covered by this budget is one year— during which, the budget tells us, $14,000 in short-term notes is due and

FIGURE 30
Costs of Debt Budget

Holy Name Children's Home and Retirement Center
Fiscal Year Beginning March 1

Notes payable	$14,000
Interest expenses on mortgage (7% of $1.2 million)	84,000
Principle total, debt service	$98,000

---

payable, and $84,000 in interest payments is due on the various mortgages held by the organization. In this instance, the item listing the principle payable on the mortgages has been eliminated from the budget (and presumably, listed as expenditure items charged against the various project budgets). The net effect of this is that the agency is charging each of its programs "rent" for the facilities they use, and using this money to pay the mortgages.

Professional and paraprofessional services budget

The final budget format outlined here is an adaptation of a general "personnel costs" budget to the human service organization, where by convention most employees can be divided into professional and paraprofessionals. In the example shown (Figure 31), all costs pertaining to employees (salaries, fringe benefits, educational payments, travel and conference expenses) have been pulled together into a single budget that reveals the total costs of personnel for the organization. For a specific program, this format could be used to compute some of the percentages and figures discussed in the direct labor budget section above. Another variation on this budget that may be of some value to administrators includes the estimated value of volunteer time, perhaps to obtain a truer estimate of the "economic value," as opposed to the cost outlay of services delivered. In such cases, the value of all volunteer services should be estimated as accurately as possible. Volunteers performing paraprofessional tasks should be tabulated at prevailing wage and hourly rates, while professionals donating their time should be tabulated at either the predominant rate for comparable professional services in the organization, if there is one, or at their "usual and customary" rate.

FIGURE 31

Professional and Paraprofessional Services Budget

Brown County Retardation Center
November, 19—

Executive salaries	$ 27,400
Professional staff salaries	
Education component	47,680
Counseling component	16,750
Sheltered workshop	22,875
Cafeteria	81,450
Legal aid	24,790
Paraprofessional staff salaries	
Education component	12,000
Cafeteria	76,420
Counseling component	4,000
Total	$313,365
Fringe benefits (14% of total)	43,871
Staff travel and conferences	18,770
Consultants	4,780
Liability and malpractice insurance (paid by agency)	16,271
Total professional and paraprofessional services	$387,057

Old year / new year tables

A good deal of useful management information can sometimes be developed through the use of comparisons of past revenue or expenditure categories with present or projected ones. In this particular analysis, the program-by-program expenditures of an agency are compared for two year periods (one past, one present; one present, one future). The analysis can be conducted in two forms: using dollar figures or standardized coefficients. The first form (Figure 32) will yield information about the positive or negative changes in the agency as a whole as well as component programs. The second form as in Figure 33, will give an estimate of the relative importance of different types of changes.

This table is not terribly useful, except that it shows clearly and graphically, and perhaps misleadingly where major changes have occurred. By a simple change, however, we can also come up with a crude quantitative estimate of the relative fiscal importance of these

FIGURE 32
Old Year/New Year Table (dollars)

Child and Family Services

Program	Old Year	New Year	% Change
Alcohol	$ 50,000	$ 50,000	00
Drugs	1,000	10,000	+1000
Marriage	33,000	66,000	+ 100
Schools	100,000	110,000	+ 10
Aging		10,000	

changes for the agency. We do this by "standardizing" the numbers—that is, by dividing each of them by the same number. In this case, divide each number by 10,000 and you will get Figure 33.

This table has a number of advantages. For example, the use of percentages in the first table makes it appear that the "1000 percent" increase in the drugs item is really significant, when in reality, its overall contribution to the agency program is fairly slight, as is shown by the second table. Also, using percentages, there is of course, no way to indicate a change starting with "0" since such a percentage cannot be computed. However, using these standardized index numbers, one can compute the value of this change, and note, for example, that it compares almost directly with the fiscal changes in the schools and drugs programs (+.9). The use of a percentage change table is

FIGURE 33
Old Year/New Year Table (standardized)

Child and Family Services

Program	Old Year	New Year	% Change
Alcohol	5.0	5.0	
Drugs	.1	1.0	+ .9
Marriage	3.3	6.6	+3.3
Schools	10.0	11.0	+1.0
Aging		1.0	1.0

FIGURE 34

Affirmative Action Budget

Brown County Retardation Center
November, 19—

Employees	White Males		Minority Males		Women	
	$	%	$	%	$	%
Executives	$27,400	100				
Professional staff	67,369	34.8	$21,412	11	$104,764	54.1
Paraprofessionals	1,971	2.1	6,456	6.9	83,993	90.8
Consultants	2,800	58.7	1,980	41.3		

recommended in cases in which internal, or intraprogram comparisons are to be made, as in, "our program is ten times what it was last year." When the principal concern is the overall pattern of changes, the standardized figure is more suitable.

Affirmative action budget

One of the principal points underlying the presentation here of sub-fund budgets is that such statements are ways of focussing on information about particular aspects of the revenue or expenditure performance of an agency. As such, they are constrained only by the problems facing agency decision-makers and the data available.

For example, it is possible to compute a variant on the "professional and paraprofessional services budget" that breaks personnel expenditures into categories for women and minority males, as shown in Figure 34.

Budgets and the multi-funded agency

The preceding discussions have been premised on the information demands of sub-fund decisions. As noted previously, however, an increasingly common management problem in human service organizations arises in the situation in which multiple sources of fundings for distinct program entities must be integrated into a meaningful whole.

One problem that constantly occurs in the "information system" of budgets, financial statements, and the like grows out of the multi-funded character of human service organizations. Government agencies ordinarily have a single source of income—taxes. Businesses, too, depend primarily on income from sales. By their character, however, many human service organizations have all of the types of fund-raising discussed earlier (fees and charges, grants, and fund-raising campaigns), often with several different revenue sources for each. Little attention among accountants and management personnel has been devoted to this vexing question.

The problem may be further compounded by the fund-accounting basis of the agency's financial records, which often completely segregates information about expenditures in one area from information about other areas. Such a scheme is clearly supportive of a decentralized, almost feudal system of independent programs rather than an integrated managed agency. The recent development, by the American Institute of Certified Public Accountants, of the *Audit Guide for Non-profit Health and Welfare Agencies* is a real advance on this problem—since the resulting financial statements offer a realistic assessment of the performance of the entire agency (all of its funds and programs) during the fiscal period. This, however, is a report after the fact, and can only provide data on where the agency has been. What about those critical periods of budgetary planning "before the fact"?

The simplist budget format for integrating the revenues and expenditures of separate programs is to operationally define a "departmental" structure for the organization based upon the AICPA-type of fund structure, with each separate fund constituting a separate department. In its simplist form, an inclusive budget like this might list revenues by source and total expenditures by "department" (that is, fund). In this way, the vagaries associated with the term, program, can be largely ignored, and some picture of the overall financial structure of the agency described.

A further refinement on this idea (shown in Figure 35) would be to combine data on revenue sources with categorical breakdowns of projected expenditures in a matrix format.

Desk-top budget reference

In fact, the matrix format shown in Figure 18 can be further extended in a number of interesting directions to incorporate several of the budget formats previously presented into a single format suitable for handy reference as a composite of the entire budget of the agency. For example, the "Desk-Top Budget Reference" shown in Figure 35 begins with the matrix format identified above, and adds a breakdown of "federal and "non-federal" funds for each major program and entity, monthly cash flow estimates, and can be extended by the user to include additional reference data.

FIGURE 35

*Desk-Top Budget References**

1. Revenues

Item	Amount	Program 1	Program 2	Program 3	Program 4	Unallocated	Earmarked	Unearmarked
Fees	$ 6,000	$ 4,000	$ 2,000					$6,000
Grant no. 1	175,000	140,000	15,000	$10,000	$10,000		$175,000	
Grant no. 2	63,650		53,650	5,000	5,000		63,650	
Grant no. 3	20,735			16,980	3,755		20,735	
United Fund	500	400		100				500
Total	$265,885	$144,400	$70,650	$32,080	$18,755	0	$259,385	$6,500

2. Expenditures

Program	Personnel	Office	Travel	Communication	Equipment	Supplies
1	$120,000	$15,000	$ 6,000	$ 1,200	$1,000	$1,200
2	65,000		3,000	1,000	1,000	650
3	20,800		2,000	8,000	1,000	280
4	15,500		1,500	600	1,000	155
Total	$228,500	$15,000	$12,500	$10,800	$4,000	$2,285

3. Quarterly Projected Revenues (by program and source)

Item	First	Second	Third	Fourth
Program 1				
Fees	$ 1,000	$ 1,000	$ 1,000	$ 1,000
Grant no. 1	35,000	35,000	35,000	35,000
Grant no. 2				
Grant no. 3				
United Fund		400		
Total	$36,000	$36,400	$36,000	$36,000
Program 2				
Fees	$ 500	$ 500	$ 500	$ 500
Grant no. 1	3,750	3,750	3,750	3,750
Grant no. 2	13,412	13,412	13,412	13,412
Grant no. 3				
United Fund				
Total	$17,662	$17,662	$17,662	$17,662
Program 3				
Fees	$	$	$	$
Grant no. 1	2,500	2,500	2,500	2,500
Grant no. 2	1,250	1,250	1,250	1,250
Grant no. 3	4,245	4,245	4,245	4,245
United Fund	25	25	25	25
Total	$ 8,020	$ 8,020	$ 8,020	$ 8,020
Program 4				
Fees	$	$	$	$
Grant no. 1	2,500	2,500	2,500	2,500
Grant no. 2	1,250	1,250	1,250	1,250
Grant no. 3	938	938	938	941
United Fund				
Total	$ 4,688	$ 4,688	$ 4,688	$ 4,691

FIGURE 35
Desk-Top Budget References (continued)

4. Monthly Expenditure Projections (with end of month surpluses)

Program	Jan.	Feb.	March	April	May	June	July	Aug.	Sept.	Oct.	Nov.	Dec.
1	$12,034 (23,966)	$12,034 (11,932)	$12,034 (-932)	$12,034 (24,264)	$12,034 (12,230)	$12,034 (196)	$12,034 (24,162)	$12,034 (12,128)	$12,034 (94)	$12,034 (24,060)	$12,034 (12,026)	$12,026
2	5,887 (11,774)	5,887 (5,888)	5,887 (1)	5,887 (11,776)	5,887 (5,889)	5,887 (2)	5,887 (11,777)	5,887 (5,890)	5,887 (3)	5,887 (11,780)	5,887 (5,893)	5,893
3	2,670 (5,350)	2,670 (2,680)	2,670 (10)	2,670 (5,360)	2,670 (2,690)	2,670 (20)	2,670 (5,370)	2,670 (2,700)	2,670 (30)	2,670 (5,380)	2,670 (2,710)	2,710
4	1,580 (3,108)	1,580 (1,528)	1,580 (-52)	1,580 (3,056)	1,580 (1,476)	1,580 (-104)	1,580 (3,004)	1,580 (1,424)	1,580 (-156)	1,580 (2,955)	1,580 (1,375)	1,375

*Data are from Figure 18.

CHAPTER 8

PROGRAMMING AND
BUDGET IMPLEMENTATION

There are in the financial management of human service organizations an important set of concerns that follow from successful completion of necessary budgetary negotiations, and logically precede those tasks that arise out of the actual operation of services. It is this intermediate set of concerns that we shall address in this chapter, under the general heading of "programming."

In a much-quoted line from the "Waste Land," the poet T. S. Eliot touched on what may be the universal dilemma of all efforts to convert human intentions into action:

> Between the idea and the reality
> Lies the shadow.

For a very long time, we have operated human service agencies with a financial management programming model not much more specific than Eliot's metaphor. Indeed, this "three-stage model" of programming, in which "ideas" become "realities" through the "shadows" is probably at the root of all efforts at implementation. For our purposes, however, the essential concern is to identify what "shadows," must be passed through in order for the plans set in the budget to become program realities.

Some divergent views on programming

Among the contemporary policy sciences it is possible to identify a number of divergent views of what we are calling "programming" in this chapter. The term itself is most commonly employed in the helping professions, where it is generally used to refer to the range of activities between planning and the operation of service programs, and carries implications of preparation for actions that have largely been determined already. A similar usage has emerged in recent years among the public service professions of urban planning and public administration, except for them the term refers to the act of creating or modifying programs. "Implementation" appears to be the preferred label for this activity. The issue of terms is a continual problem for those interested in human service administration. For example, a recent piece by Kamerman, published in *Social Service Review*, develops a model in which implementation is one of the three major stages of program-mining.[1] One is reminded of Winston Churchill's witticism about the British and Americans being divided by the Atlantic Ocean and a common language. The terminology set forth in this chapter attempts to bridge such gaps and provide recognition of the relevant phenomena dealt with by both the helping professions' focus on programming and the public service professions' interest in implementation.

Programming defined

Programming, for our purposes, is an on-going process in which agency and program administrators seek to translate program goals and fiscal generalizations, such as those which appear in line-item budgets, into meaningful work routines that will result, eventually, in the production of services. Overall, the principal skills in programming are not logical or legal, but negotiational. The main tasks of programming involve fitting together the understanding of constituencies (discussed in Chapter 7) of "how things are" and "what will happen now" with that of employees and clients. In other words, programming is the creation of behavioral routines, rules, and understandings that will insure the realization of goals and objectives worked out in budget planning. Programming is, in this sense, *follow-through planning* in which the implications of prior financial planning must be worked out in detail.

Central aspects of this task involve: the establishment of a suitable distribution of work, authority, and responsibility; creation of formal patterns of communication (and encouragement of appropriate informal patterns); establishment or revision of operational policies and procedures; and other facets of organizing. Some features of programming such as the recruitment and selection of personnel may be essential only during the start-up phase of new ventures. Other programming tasks, such as reassignment of work loads, amendments in policies and procedures, and adjustment of salary levels may recur with each budget cycle. Both types of post-budget programming are discussed below. First, we shall examine the major financial implications of starting up a new program. Following that we shall look into the financial decisions that must be attended to on a regular recurring basis.

Programming and time sense

Most of the major differences in uses related to programming, particularly those between planning and managerial roles, can be attributed to what might be termed different "time senses." Time senses may be seen as consisting of at least three different components: a *time-frame*, within which the attention of the planner or manager is principally focussed; a *time-horizon*, which is the most distant point in time of this time frame and delimits the bounds of interests in such matters as the consequences of decisions or actions; and a *time-sequence* which involves the selection and arrangement of major events in a temporal order that seems "right," "natural," or "appropriate."

All three aspects of time sense can be expected to be different for those engaged in planning and those engaged in management, and the differences are reflected in the different perspectives on programming found in these two groups. For managers, financial management programming is merely a companion to personnel programming and other managerial programming concerns. The managerial time-frame is not only shorter than the planning frame, it is also more filled with benchmarks or delimiters or "subframes." While the planner is encouraged to think two, five, or even ten years ahead, the manager must be concerned about this week, next week, and next month. Second, while the planner is usually concerned only with a master time-frame within which all events are to be fit (often logically), the manager is frequently faced with reconciling time-sequences that are often unrelated. Finally, the time-horizon of the manager is often coincidental with the budget cycle of the agency (see Chapter 7)—a much-remarked phenomenon that often precludes concern with long range consequences of programming in the manager's agenda.

Starting a new program

The management focus in starting a new program is multiple. The manager must simultaneously (1) deal with immediate problems as they arise; (2) anticipate major problems before they arise; (3) maintain a personal sense of the focus, direction, and sense of the program amid a welter of seemingly insignificant details; (4) and impart his sense of mission and direction to others. Many of the financial management concerns in starting up a program strike most human service professionals as uninteresting details. Nevertheless, they are matters that must be attended to and often cannot be delegated. The questions that may arise are myriad. (A partial list is included in the Programming Checklist.) In some instances, the new program manager will have to personally attend to all these and other matters, owing to the size, newness, or ineptness of the staff. In other instances the "dual track" nature of many agencies will tend to congregate the financial aspects of programming in the business manager or comptroller's office, leaving the program manager completely free for other matters. In such cases, however, care should be taken to insure that the bookkeeper does not become the de facto program manager because of his control of expenditures. (Some of the purely fiscal issues involved here are discussed in Chapter 10.)

A number of topics of management concern emerge in this context: clarifying the legal status of the new program, the use of departmental or sub-program budgets and "lines of credit," policy guidelines and precedents, personnel recruitment and selection, and office set up procedures. In all instances the proper management focus is on adapting fiscal limits, constraints, and requirements for the program mission and objectives.

One of the things that sociology has contributed to the general understanding of economic phenomena is a clearer view of the necessity for legal order to underly economic order. Ordinarily an obtuse, vague theoretical point for administrators, this matter becomes of critical importance in the creation of new service programs. Although the legal order enabling the management of services is likely to take two forms, the underlying point is still the same. In the case of public agencies, it is unlikely that any new major programming will be undertaken in the absence of some specific "mandate"—explicit legislative sanction or administrative consent that justifies the new enterprise. In the voluntary sector such an explicit mandate is not necessary. It is likely that new agencies or programs will require explicit sanction by a governing board, however, and also the explicit recognition of legal status as "not-for-profit" corporations. The absence of such explicit non-profit sanctions can create tremendously complex ethical, legal, and financial problems in the human service setting. Such "legitimization" efforts are important aspects of the successful financial management of human services, and should be attended to with great care.

Over and above questions of legitimacy, however, are questions of financial liability. Public employees are ordinarily exempted from financial liability that results from the performance of their regular duties. The problem of liabilities in non-profit agencies and membership associations is somewhat more complex. If, for example, a group of persons form an "agency" to operate a program such as a day care center, and constitute themselves as a board of directors overseeing the management of the center without incorporation, then the group also constitutes a "partnership" in the legal sense. Two consequences follow from this. One is that the agency is liable for the payment of corporate income taxes on revenues generated, and second, each member of the group, by virtue of his board membership, is individually liable for a proportionate share of whatever liabilities are accrued by the agency.

Departmental budgets

A continuous programming problem for human service organizations is the operational link between fiscal and program objectives that should occur following successful funding of a program. In general, existing patterns of fiscal accountability do not extend inside an agency. Short of unit-cost and program budgeting of the type discussed in Chapter 7, there seems to be no practical way to fully extend such accountability to sub-organizational levels.

There are, however, a number of specific steps that may partially overcome these deficiencies. For example, one may "departmentalize" program budgets into various categories with some program relevance (e.g., "classroom," "kitchen," and "playground" in a day care program). By monitoring the proportion of funds spent to funds available over the year, administrators and supervisory staff (lead teachers and chief cooks in the above example) can keep a working idea of how their performance compares with fiscal expectations. Together with program and agency managers, then, they may be able to suggest ways to more effectively utilize available resources. Such an approach will work best in cases in which the "department" includes something more than one or two salaries or similar fixed expenditures (about which little discretionary decision-making is possible).

Lines of credit

In cases, in which a full disaggregation of the program budget may be inappropriate, an alternative for the program manager is to identify some key variable expenditures and assign expenditure guidelines or limits, termed "lines of credit," to various staff members. These are useful less as a control device than as a means of facilitating more intelligent planning of resource utilization.

In this way, the worker who knows from the beginning of the year that his travel line of credit will allow 1,000–1,500 miles per month can plan more intelligently in both the short and long term than the employee who receives a memo from the director in the ninth month of the project saying, "Because the staff has exceeded travel expectations, we are nearly out of funds, and therefore, I must ask you to severely limit your travel for the rest of the program year." Limit travel? One is inclined to react, "How much? What about my clients?" Such double binds for workers can, in many cases, be avoided by the kinds of line of credit allocations discussed above. The approach is also amenable to a more unambiguous modification of the above message: "Our travel funds are being depleted too rapidly. Therefore, effective immediately staff mileage limits are reduced to 750 miles per month until further notice. Compliance with this guideline will reduce the risk of complete curtailment of travel later on."

Similar kinds of lines of credit arrangements can be made for a broad range of variable expenditures—conference travel, office supplies, consultants, contracted speakers, and more. In fact, such arrangements are particularly appropriate with limited resources that the staff may regard as unlimited, such as photocopying expenses.

A critical feature of the successful management use of lines of credit, however, is a provision for monitoring staff performance and feedback. If the staff is limited to 1000 miles of travel per month, requests exceeding that limit should be denied, or at least a "tickler" memo or warning should be issued. Without such provisions, the staff may find it altogether too easy to ignore the limits entirely. Various approaches are possible, and punitive sanctions are not always advisable or possible, but some kind of feedback is essential.

Policy guidelines and precedents

In setting up a new program the most difficult set of tasks involves the conversion of the rhetoric of goals and objectives into "operational policy." In other words, the statements of purpose, intent, and general direction that convinced funding authorities to provide the revenue for the program must be used in post-budget programming to develop work routines, evaluation and performance standards, and other guidelines necessary to guide and control aspects of the day-to-day agency work world.

Unless one is careful, it is entirely too easy to overstress the "rational" nature of this implementation process. In most instances, rational planning and foresight are only part of the picture. Equally important in many instances are the concomitant processes of management by exception and precedents. The manager should seek to anticipate major problems before they occur. However, to attempt to comprehensively identify all problems and specify policy to cover them would be counter-productive and self-defeating (becoming a problem and disruption, in itself.) In setting up a new program, then, the astute manager will outline to the staff workable management by exception procedures: "If problems with specific clients arise I expect the supervisors to deal with them unless they occur over and over, or involve the agency as a whole."

Similarly, many such exceptions brought to the manager result in "informal" policy precedents. Sometimes these can merely be pointed out to the staff member involved: "After this, when a client refuses to pay the _____ fee, we'll just have to terminate them." In other cases, a memorandum or written statement of policy may be necessary. In either case, however, it is worth remembering that the start-up phase of a new program is often a period of intensive activity with respect to agency policy and procedure, and much of this activity is informal precedent-setting. In this context, some provisions need to be made for instructing the staff in the implementation of the precedents involved.

There are, in addition, numerous aspects of start-up programming that have not been gone into here. In general, however, sensitive application of the approaches discussed should resolve many of the problems that arise. In addition, most of the considerations for existing programs below also apply in the case of new ventures.

Programming in existing programs

Programming in existing programs is one of the more overlooked topics in human service administration literature. The typical assumption in the literature seems to be that one strives to come within five degrees of perfection in the initial set-up, and thereafter the only concerns are operational. Such an assumption in practice may be as pregnant with possibilities for explanation as the more customary explanations of bureaucratic conservatism and the like. It is, for example, always easier to point to intransigence in others than to see it in oneself, and yet one's own programs seem to be as impervious to change as those of other agencies. Are we, then, all secret reactionaries—even those of us who think that we are not? A far more likely explanation, it seems to me, is to be found in our unwillingness to examine our assumptions, habits, routines, and policies, once they have been set.

Some new thinking is emerging on this topic. For example, the so-called "sunset laws" and proposals for a five-year life span for public policies seem to assume that vitality is followed by intransigence in periodic, inevitable cycles. Although it is not a popular position today, I wish to suggest that organizational intransigence need not be an inevitability and that, indeed, one of the principal management responsibilities in human service organizations involves periodic "reprogramming" ventures designed to instill a new sense of purpose, vitality, and enthusiasm in agency efforts.

Although organizational renewal activities are likely to be predominantly psychological in character, the most successful efforts of this type will be integrated with the financial management process in certain key respects. Some agencies, for example, have found that mounting an extensive fund-raising campaign of the type discussed in Chapter 5 generates enthusiasm among workers, brings new volunteers, and in other ways "stirs up" the agency in subtle and important ways.

While it is unlikely that one would successfully tie an organizational renewal effort to the annual budgetary cycle, certain other organizational renewal activities could be so tied. For example, an agency might, as part of the internal budget process, spend some time in staff meetings reviewing policy manuals and making suggestions for revisions. Or, the kinds of "bonus" and "incentive" schemes used successfully in business might be employed: workers could be rewarded for proposing budget, policy, or related modifications that result in substantial savings for the agency. (The argument that because social agencies are "doing the good" they ought to be immune from such petty concerns as cost-cutting is neither very convincing nor very original. Opponents of welfare services should not be allowed to corner the market on the virtues of cost-effectiveness that easily!)

Whether it is labeled an "internal audit," "management survey," or "self-study," every human service agency periodically should be subjected to careful scrutiny from within. And, potential reprogramming should be the explicit intention of such an examination. "What are we doing at present which we could do more effectively, at lower cost, or in a more satisfactory manner?" is a question that should be on the minds of all agency employees at least occasionally. In the financial area, such self-examination may require the assistance of an outside consultant, a volunteer, or board member with the appropriate professional skills and credentials.

The agency should reexamine the full range of practices, procedures, and policies regarding the raising of funds, their allocation within the agency to various sub-units, expenditure practices, inventory procedures, rental and purchase policies, and so forth—preferably in the context of agency service delivery goals. Does the way we collect fees discourage some clients? Could we collect them differently? Is the low-cost of our second-story office rental really worth the inconvenience it causes elderly and handicapped clients, who must climb the stairs? Such questions are typically on the minds of staff members and administrators in most agencies, and the purpose of this collective self-examination is to convert at least some of them into realities—the very conception of programming with which we started this chapter.

Funding sources may either mandate such periodic reviews or make them highly desirable. Particularly in the financial management area, changes may be considered "mundane" or "technical," and consequently, are not even discussed in the negotiations or formal legal agreements. Renewal of existing grants and contracts, however, should be routinely accompanied by a reassessment of the possible changes specified by the funding source in guidelines or other requirements.

Changes in the external environment are likely to create a need for such periodic reexaminations. Payroll practices built on a staggered system of short-term borrowing in a period of low-interest loans will be less advisable as interest rates rise. Likewise, increases in food prices and other major purchase items subject to inflationary pressures are likely to force periodic review, while transportation, heating, and other rising energy costs have forced near-crisis re-examinations in many agencies in the past few years.

Post-budget conferences

In a number of instances, the necessary follow-up information regarding approved budgets, accompanying restrictions, requirements, and other information will be communicated to human service agencies in the form of a memorandum. In other instances, information about budget approvals and the like will be communicated in a series of post-budget conferences, of which three types can be singled out for discussion. One important conference form is the meeting with the funding source representatives. A second is the informational meeting with governing or advisory board members, and the third is the informational meeting with staff members. The salient features of each of these topics will be discussed here.

The novice may be tempted to view such meetings either as a courtesy or a possibility only in cases of locally funded programs. Such views are unfortunate and misdirected. Taking the money and running is seldom wise or prudent strategy. Many who espouse the perspective called grantsmanship fall into a pattern of budget negotiations that calls for what is in essence a "flim-flam" style. In this case one would expect that once a grant has been approved or other budget negotiation completed, the "sharp" grantsman is likely to do one of two things. If he is crude or inept in his artform he will simply "take the money and run." If, on the other hand, he has learned well "the big con," he will stick around and, in Goffman's apt phrase, "cool the mark out." To some degree, post-budget conferences with funding sources may serve such purposes in some instances. In the vast majority of cases, however, such conferences serve the far more pedestrian purpose of information dissemination. That is, once the grant is approved, it may be appropriate for the funding source to supply previously unimportant information on financial requirements for accounting, banking practices, and payroll. Likewise, the recipient agency may use this opportunity to begin firming up the relationship with the funding agency, and shifting it to a less suppliant posture.

Likewise, it would be misleading to expect that such conferences are a reality only when funding source and agency are located in the same city. Telecommunications, air travel, and the like make it possible for all but the most remote agencies to be contacted regularly. While I am personally unfamiliar with any research on the telephone usage patterns of social service agencies, my experience suggests that most agencies are in regular contact with the various federal, state, and local funding sources from which they receive assistance. The post-budget conference is likely to be useful in "getting started" on the tasks of programming, but it is also likely to be just one in a series of on-going communications with funding sources.

Boards of directors are difficult to generalize about, but at least some tentative statements can be made about post-budget conferences with them. The first and most tentative statement is that it can't hurt to inform such groups about the outcome of budget negotiations. In some instances, "strong" boards will insist that they be kept informed at all stages of the process, and indeed, may need to ratify agreements negotiated before they become official. The financial administrator who fails to keep this board informed is simply looking for trouble. Even in the case of "weak" boards with small or non-existent expectations in this area, however, a simple, brief synopsis of the major points of agreement reached on the budget seems appropriate. One common problem in such cases, however, is that unless board members have had prior experience in dealing with the "facts and figures" of budgeting, the explanations may be unclear to them. Lay board members who very quickly become adept at tossing about the jargon of treatment and service delivery often struggle for years, or simply ignore completely the bizarre terminology they encounter in a budget discussion. Special attention might be paid to communicating with these people.

Finally, many agencies simply overlook the task of informing the staff of the outcome of budgeting. The director of a service agency, for example, may simply assume that because she knows the results, and sees staff members every day, they must know also. Staff members, like boards, often do not wish to become mired in the details of agreements, figures, percentages, and ratios. This does not mean, however, that they don't want to know things about the budget.

Policy and procedures review

In addition to the post-budget conferences with board members and key staff members, a second major type of programming activity that is often undertaken is a review of policies and procedures affecting previously existing programs. The purposes of such review are several: to determine whether existing policy and procedures are consistent with agreements made during budget negotiations, or whether such agreements necessitate changes; to "test" existing policy and procedures against new guidelines or requirements issued by the funding source during the negotiations; and to identify those specific areas of program policy or procedure that are problematic because of changes in the "rules of the game."

It is important to note that not all changes will be an active part of budget considerations. Grant-funded agencies, for example, may make changes in their requirements for handling cash assets, dates, formats for filing reports, or other "technical" matters without any notification other than minor revisions of the "boiler plate" standard printed forms that accompany grant acceptance notifications. Indeed, in some large federal agencies such changes may be made by legal or accounting staff, while the program staff with whom an agency is negotiating remain as unaware as the agency that changes have taken place. Such lack of awareness, however, does not relieve the agency of responsibility for implementation. It is always wise to read over the "fine print" of a new grant looking for such changes—or if you have staff for such purposes, better yet, delegate the job!

In the case of changes that did form a part of budget negotiations, the agency (or at least the negotiator of the agency) has some forewarning. Programming requirements usually can then be anticipated, or perhaps the allocation and programming tasks merged to some extent. In any event, a forewarning should, of course, mean that agencies will not be caught completely unawares. Perhaps the city council will only continue channeling revenue-sharing money to a Community Mental Health agency if the outreach program in the inner city is "depoliticized." In working out the budget, then, the agency is faced with a major policy choice: to keep the controversial outreach program and tone it down, or to scrap the entire venture. By the time the budget is completed and programming begins, this issue will have been resolved, one way or the other, and the immediate problem will be one of programming: if the program is to be saved in altered form, what changes are to be made?

Programming and phase-out of activities

Most writers on financial management, like most administrators, are inveterate optimists. Consequently, the topic of programming has been approached from an optimistic "growth" perspective, in which the focus is always on new programs, bigger and better programs, and expanded programs. While the growth of human services has made this quite clearly a legitimate, accurate, and timely topic, it should be pointed out that it is not the only side to programming.

In relatively fewer instances, the concept of programming can also be extended to cover the phased withdrawal, elimination, or "scrapping" of programs, and even in some cases, agencies. In general, program and agency decline and "death," while justifiable, have been of considerably less interest to writers in this area than growth processes. Yet, in an era of rising fiscal conservatism, human service managers can ill-afford to ignore these topics.

Two cases of programming growing out of the budget activity deserve our attention: the case in which fiscal support for a program is simply lost and the case in which the "terms" offered an agency in negotiations make continuation of a program unfeasible. In both instances, the first "fall back" is the same (at least for the independent agency): locate a new funding source. Public agencies that get their funds through public appropriations seldom have this option, however.

Let us assume for the moment that this option does not work and that for one reason or another the decision has been made to discontinue the program. A special set of programming activities comes into being. Three of these have specific financial management significance: the discontinuation of continuous liabilities, the scheduling of "closing out" efforts, and the legitimation of the discontinuation. In the first category, the most important activity is the dismissal of staff. Other activities may include the termination of leases on rented office space or rented equipment, the termination of service contracts for consultants and janitorial services, and the cancellation of insurance coverage or automatic reordering procedures for replacement of inventory. Most of the activities included under this category of concerns are premised, initially, on the assumption that the agency or program is an "on-going concern" and, therefore, certain economic transactions can be routinized on a regularly scheduled basis. Termination of the program upsets this scheduling, and unless the termination is carefully programmed, any number of unpleasant, unsafe, or unsatisfactory discontinuities can occur. A day care center that is to be terminated, for example, cannot afford to have its liability insurance terminated or food supplies exhausted before the last day the children are in attendance.

Just as with start-up activities, certain events in the termination of a program may require careful enough scheduling to necessitate the use of PERT charts, GANTT Charts, or other scheduling techniques. In such cases, all of the points previously made about start-up activities can be applied.

It is important to remember that there are a whole class of human service programs that are, by their very nature, episodic, of short duration, and subject to "close outs" of the type discussed here on an annual basis. Annual camps, annual conferences, summer recreational, employment, educational, or training programs such as Head Start, Neighborhood Youth Corps, and Upward Bound are just some of the many programs of this type.

Profile of a program developer

We can close this discussion of the post-budget task of programming in respect to financial management by discussing some of the peculiar demands and prerequisites of those who are assigned the programming tasks discussed in this chapter. First of all, it would be nice to believe that the program development process approximated the mechanistic model discussed at the beginning of this chapter: just picture an agency full of people thinking up good ideas, discussing them with others, and implementing the worthy ones and setting aside the unworthy. We would all like to work in such a setting, but this is seldom a reality for most of us.

Program development is often conducted in a situation involving false starts, scheduling delays, foul-ups, and assorted other complications, and the program developer must be able to work under such conditions. Above all, in program development of this sort "keeping one's head" is an occupational necessity.

Also, program development—whether it involves new programs or the modification of existing ones—often requires a high tolerance for and ability to deal with the inevitable emotional upsets. New programs often upset the balance of status and influence in agencies, and those who are affected negatively seldom take the matter lightly. In many instances, even slight modifications in staff routines can be the occasion for emotional outbursts by those who liked the way things were done in the past. In all these cases those charged with program development responsibilities may have to confront, manage, and resolve a variety of conflicts as a normal, routine part of their task.

Finally, there is the all important matter of foresight. There are those who would argue that as a rule of thumb, it takes two or three years to "iron out the bugs" of any new program activity or major change, and until then one cannot expect that things will go altogether smoothly. (There are also those who suggest that in the human services one ought never expect things to go smoothly at all, but we can safely discard their opinions for the time being!) Once sufficient time has passed, however, the same "bugs" may be interpreted as indications of structural or design weaknesses in the program, rather than implementation problems. The knack of knowing when to look for the day of smooth operations and when to assume that that day has passed is one of the more valuable skills of the program developer.

Conclusion: Wednesday's problem

By way of summary, it is useful to see the problems of programming from the vantage point of the metaphor of a week: Monday's problem is the identification of goals and objectives, purposes, and functions.

Tuesday's problem is the implementation of what was worked out on Monday: to elaborate policies, establish work routines, and delegate authority and responsibility. Wednesday's problem, then, is the continuation of the agency as an on-going concern. Unlike the mechanistic model of programming identified at the beginning of this chapter, however, the human service administrator should never make the mistake of assuming that on Wednesday he's got it made. Instead, in the on-going operation of most human service organizations, Monday's problems (purposes and goals) and Tuesday's problem (implementation) keep re-emerging. When they do, the human service administrator must be prepared to deal with them, not as examples of agency failures and inadequacies, but as evidence of the need for, and, indeed, the opportunity for organizational renewal.

Part IV

Control
and
Planning Issues

Even after funds are located and secured, allocations made through the budget system, and appropriate programming steps have been taken, a number of additional financial management tasks remain. As in other sections of this work, we may divide these tasks roughly into two major groups: control problems and planning problems. Once this level of the financial management process of human service agencies is reached, a new set of concerns takes on increasing significance: the questions of evaluation and accountability. These three topics—control, planning, and evaluation—will be taken up in turn in the next three chapters.

Chapter 9 is devoted to discussions of six major control topics. These are: the requirements of financial control; supervision as a control device; procedures for "focussing" on control questions; dissemination of financial and other reports, purchasing and inventory control, and the establishment of cost control policies and procedures.

Seven principal topics are discussed in Chapter 10. These are: feasibility studies and projections; capital budgeting, debt management; project scheduling, cash flow management, accounts receivable management; and accounts payable management.

The final chapter of this unit addresses three focal points in the treatment of the evaluation and accountability questions. These are: the linkages between fiscal and program indicators, the use of ratio analysis schemes in human service organizations, and the development and utilization of output and outcome measures (primarily efficiency, productivity, and effectiveness measures).

Some of the matters that are dealt with in these three chapters are already part of the standard practice of some human service organizations. Other items can readily be adapted to human services usage. Wherever possible, examples have been included to clarify and elaborate the discussion.

CHAPTER 9

FISCAL CONTROL
ISSUES

In the early chapters of this book, the point was made that human service organizations, whether they are public or private, have traditionally been viewed as "stewards" granted the use of certain community resources for the pursuit of certain community ends. The entire contemporary accountability movement is derived from the relationship between various human service agencies and the public. From this vantage point, the minimum requirement for the handling of all finances is that adequate management and policy control be exercised by the accountable agencies. Adequate accounting systems meeting the requirements laid out in Chapter 2 are the essential elements in such management and policy control systems. In most instances, however, accounting controls alone are insufficient to adequately respond to the spirit as well as the letter of community accountability. The principal task of this chapter, therefore, is to set forth additional management perspectives relating to the establishment of adequate financial control procedures. The major topics to be addressed in this chapter include: the requirements of financial control, supervision as the critical control factor in human services, procedures for "focusing" control questions for management, and control procedures in three specific contexts—

information dissemination, purchasing and inventory control, and cost-control procedures.

The requirements of financial control

The "existential dilemma" facing every human service administrator at one time or another is how to balance the legitimate demands for fiscal control with conflicting, equally legitimate demands. Cost control may dictate that clerical supplies and materials be kept under lock and key to keep utilization low, but such a policy has a series of side effects like employees' complaints, selective distribution by the keeper of the keys, and other minor but bothersome effects. At a somewhat more profound level cost-control procedures may require extensive documentation from employees for mileage, meal, and travel expense claims, while the exigencies of such travel (and, particularly, of professional habits) may keep employees from collecting for certain expenses (such as cabfare) for which they were unable to get receipts. Clearly, then, the human service administrator responsible for financial management is faced with difficult problems for which some guidance is necessary.

While there are no hard and fast rules or very clear "principles" that can be invoked to aid in the solution of problems of integrating the demands of fiscal controls with other aspects of agency practice, certain generalizations can be made. For one thing, some "value" or standard of fairness seems essential. One may be willing, for example, to allow agency employees to simply "absorb" certain incidental costs of employment, such as an occasional meal, parking fee, or even a conference registration fee. Inevitably, however, the question will arise of how much is too much in such cases: $5? $10? $25? $100? At what point do such costs cease to be an incidental inconvenience for employees and become serious (and unfair) financial burdens? Two questions actually are involved here. One is the management-planning question of whether or not existing reimbursement procedures are adequate. The other involves the dispensing of "administrative justice" in cases in which agency policies clearly have dealt unfairly with an employee. The first question is, in important respects, a pragmatic one: are agency staff members currently satisfied with procedures, or do strong sentiments of unfair treatment exist? If everyone is satisfied, it may simply be prudent to leave well enough alone. If, on the otherhand, there is widespread discontent, some revision of policies may be necessary. Meanwhile, it appears prudent to deal with the adjudication of unfair cases on a management-by-exceptions basis: if the number of such exceptional cases becomes large, it may simply be necessary to revise the rules or "tighten down" on claims approved in this way.

While the case of employee reimbursement for work-related expenses demonstrates the necessity for some standards of fairness in the administration of fiscal controls, it is not the most critical control problem likely to be encountered by the human service administrator. The single most important area of concern is likely to be salary increases.

In general, the questions of the assessment of employee performance and the development of compensation plans, promotion schedules, and the like are more properly topics in personnel management than in financial management. However, certain critical financial aspects can be addressed here.

In dealing with the financial questions of employee compensation, the human service administrator is likely to be faced with four different pieces of information: employee expectations regarding salary increases, budgetary constraints imposed by funding sources, general salary levels in the agency's labor market area, and information on employee performance. These pieces of information must be fitted together to resolve the major financial questions.

The first major question is the break-even issue: does the pattern of proposed expenditures for salaries "fit" with the patterns of available resources? If salary expectations, when combined, exceed available revenues, clearly some cutbacks will be necessary. At this point the question of "fit" enters the arena of fairness. If all employees cannot receive a cost of living increment because of inadequate revenues, for example, is it better to give the same (percentage) increment to everyone, to stratify increments (e.g., giving low-salary employees higher increases) or to distribute increases strictly on a merit basis?

One of the toughest problems encountered in this "fitting" procedure involves the reallocation of funds "freed up" by unfilled positions. In some instances, grant requirements or agency policies may preclude the use of such funds for other purposes, so that the funds are, in effect, lost to the agency. In such cases administrators typically seek to keep positions as full as possible, so that such positions are not lost to the agency. In other instances, formal procedures may exist within the agency or in a grantee agency, to formally reallocate unused personnel funds. For example, the financial handbook for Community Action Agencies issued by the now defunct Office of Economic Opportunity spells out procedures by which grantee agencies can request the reallocation of funds to other functional expenditure categories.[1] Such provisions may differentiate between "within category" transfers (from one personnel use to another) and "between category" transfers (from personnel to travel). In still other cases, administrators may be relatively free to reallocate unused personnel funds to other purposes. It would seem highly desirable that some "contingency planning" take place so that the opportunities for action created by this "freed up" money will not be lost. For example, this may be a perfect time to implement that short-term staff training project that has never quite been feasible, or to underwrite an evaluation study of key programs.

The second major question raised by these bits of information is the "hierarchical balance" issue. Is the present (pre-salary increase) distribution of salaries fair and equitable, in terms of the consistency of salaries for comparable positions and financial recognition of outstanding achievement?[2] To deal with these questions, large public agencies have almost universally incorporated the use of a "salary schedule" such as that shown in Figure 36. In such instances, the establishment and revision of the schedule, and information on the number of incumbents at eah step are critically important in the budget.

FIGURE 36

Salary Schedule

Classification	No. of Positions	Salary Range
Clerical		
Clerk-typist	2	$500–$600
Secretary	3	$500–$650
Clerical supervisor	1	$650 (starting)
Paraprofessional		
Teacher's aide	5	$2.50–$3.50
Case aide	10	$2.50–$3.50
Community liaison	8	$2.50–$3.50
Professional		
Executive director	1	$15,000–$30,000
Assistant director—budget	1	$12,000–$21,000
Assistant director—personnel	1	$12,000–$21,000
Caseworker I	25	$ 8,000–$11,000
Caseworker II	8	$ 9,500–$13,000
Supervisors	4	$10,500–$15,000
Planner–evaluators	4	$ 9,500–$12,000

Even in smaller agencies where the establishment of a formal salary schedule may seem presumptuous, redundant or pedantic, many of the same issues can be dealt with on an informal basis. In addition, in both large and small agencies, the kind of salary schedule shown in Figure 36, because it also yields an estimate of total salary costs, provides important data for the resolution of the break-even problem noted above.

The third major problem faced by the financial manager in allocating salaries involves the adjustment of salary levels in light of "what the market will bear." It would be nice if there were Platonic ideal standards by which one might determine the appropriate levels of employee compensation. In the absence of such standards, however, the principle of supply and demand is but one of several factors that financial managers must take into account. Such factors are likely to be most critical in cases where the market is glutted with employees, which may provide managers with the incentive to reduce salaries (or, more likely, to reduce the amount of salary increases). Similarly, supply and demand questions are likely to be most critical for managers in those cases in which employees with particular sets of skills are relatively rare and, therefore, effectively able to demand higher salaries.

Supply and demand do not prevail in the public sector of human services. It is not at all uncommon, for example, to run across positions in public agencies for which "classified" salary levels are so in-appropriate to the demands or the educational requirements of the position that it is unfillable. Wherever possible, the human service administrator who has the option should seek to reallocate such underutilized funds to some other legitimate agency concerns. Before proceding to consider other types of problems let us pause at this point and introduce, based upon the above discussion, some "principles" of fiscal control.

Principles of fiscal control

In considering the topic of fiscal control, the human service manager is faced with a convergence of three very different approaches toward the control of human behavior. There is a strong tradition of "rational control" perspectives in management science that is principally derived from economics. In this view, the sources of management control are seen as two-fold: on the one hand, employees and others are expected to behave properly and, to that extent, be controlled by their responses to a set of rules. The essence of the management problem of fiscal control, then, involves the adequate specification of a set of fiscal rules. The second element in the rational control perspective arises out of economic behavior as well, and can be termed the "incentives" approach. In this view, the regularity, predictability, and consequent control of employees arises from their patterns of responding to certain incentives. Here the essence of the management problem is the identification of critical incentives and the "design" of incentive systems that will produce the desired results. (This view is sometimes known as the "M and M approach.")

In addition to the management control approach, there is also the psychological approach common in the human services. In this view, the problem of fiscal control is essentially a problem in motivation. Thus, the human service manager must decide what needs to be done (or not done!) in the area of finance, and develop appropriate motivations for workers. Despite some obvious differences in vocabulary and style this approach is highly congruent with the incentives approach.

The most drastic approach one is likely to encounter to the problem of fiscal control is the "social control" argument advanced by sociologists. In this view, all human behavior is "controlled" to greater or lesser extents by group influences, common values and norms, and prior experiences. In devising fiscal control procedures, according to this view, one needs to attend not only to the specification of formal rules, but also to group influences and a host of other situational and social fators. While this approach does not necessarily argue against the development of rules or the isolation of incentives or motives, it does seem to imply that these alone are not sufficient, and that one can expect that other influences will also have an impact on fiscal control procedures. While the social control approach is the most sophisticated, it is also the most difficult to use as a base for developing control procedures. Therefore, in this discussion, we shall use it largely as a backdrop, and concentrate primarily on the other two levels.

The basic elements of any financial control system in a human service agency, therefore, are likely to be four: *rules*, prescribing permissible and prohibited activity; *criteria*, enabling interpretation of the rules, by imposing limits, standards and specific requirements; *understandings*, or interpersonal agreements (whether formal or informal), regarding rules or criteria; and *contracts*, or formally stated and binding agreements, regarding rules or criteria. With these in mind, several basic principles regarding the operation of financial control systems can be outlined:

The principle of individuality. Control systems must be designed for the particular constraints, demands and expectations of a particular agency setting. Rules ("policy") appropriate in one setting may be irrelevant, or even dysfunctional in another context.

The principle of enforcement. Control systems must make some explicit provision for enforcement. Rules that are not enforced are, in their effects, not rules. Similarly, criteria that are not employed in decision-making are not effective. Such "enforcement" is not always a matter of negative sanctions (although in the financial arena this is frequently the case). Enforcement might also include the development of "positive reinforcers" or "incentives" for the pursuit of certain rules through rewards, recognition, or the like. In many cases, anticipation of problems of enforcement can lead to their resolution through such means.

The principle of reportability. Control systems must also make some provision for reporting. Unless instances of abuse are reported in some way, it may be literally impossible to enforce certain rules. Particularly troublesome here are the problems that arise in many large organizations where "everybody knows" that it's all right to informally get around certain reporting requirements.

The principle of exceptions. The general doctrine of management by exceptions, and the principle of individuality noted above coverage, and to some degree, conflict in the area of fiscal controls. The very act of spelling out rules, however, causes the loss of some individualized methods of treating situations. It makes at least some exceptions inevitable. Therefore, the mere act of setting down rules should simultaneously lead the financial administrator to give some thought to the handling of exceptions to the rules.

The principle of amendment. In order for control systems to remain effective for any extended period of time, some provision must be made for their periodic updating. The agency that has no basis, or, a very inadequate basis for revising travel policies, for example, may find itself locked into reimbursing employees at $.05 a mile in an age of high energy costs. Ordinarily, all that is required in this case is an understanding with the staff, governing boards, and so forth of the "amendment process" necessary for making revisions in the control system.

The principle of efficiency. Control procedures, above all, must be low-cost enough to be "affordable." Clearly, the ultimate control system would employ a monitor to control and report on the behavior of each worker. However, the obvious effect of such an approach would be to at

202 | Control and Planning Issues

least double the cost of service delivery with no assurance of a discernible increase in results (except when the manager suspects employees are "doing nothing," in which case such an approach may be a temporary expedient).

The principle of meaning. Rules, criteria, understandings, and contracts must be meaningfully communicated and understood by all concerned if they are to have an effect in control. It is therefore essential that rules be clearly stated, that control documents be readily available, and that procedures for clarification and interpretation of the procedures, themselves, be clearly spelled out. This is particularly important in the case of "irreversible" actions (such as certain types of purchases), for which prior understanding by the employees is vital. The employee who flies first class without justification when the policies clearly prohibit this may have to learn a costly lesson. Likewise, if the same employee purchases five hundred cases of canned peaches retail, when the agency practice is to purchase wholesale, he may have unnecessarily cost the agency large sums of money.

The principle of feedback. Control systems should be "learning systems" in the sense that accumulated experience with rules and standards, understandings, and contracts should contribute to refinements in the control systems of an agency. Such improvements and refinements are likely to fall into several categories: *formalization* of certain rules that emerge through the recurrence of similar exceptions; *abandonment* or neglect of obsolete, irrelevant or unenforcable rules; *routinization,* or the incorporation of formal rules and standards into the understandings and behavior of employees.

The principle of productivity. The final principle necessary in the design of control systems in human services organizations is the recognition that the ultimate purpose of management in human service organizations is not the control of employees and resources. Such control is merely a tool in the cause of service delivery. Therefore, in those instances in which there is a clearcut conflict between the demands of fiscal control and the goals of service, management responsibility falls with the goals of service. For example, prudent financial management may dictate keeping all equipment under lock and key in a juvenile program, because otherwise the "little monsters keep stealing it." In given instances, however, such prudence might be overridden by a concern for the goals of service (such as the development of trust with the boys)—*even if* the result is periodic and recurrent losses due to theft.

The application of these principles in specific human service contexts should contribute to the development of satisfactory, and realistic control procedures. In the remainder of this chapter we shall examine four specific contexts for the application of such principles: supervision, dissemination of financial information, purchasing and inventory control, and cost-control procedures and policies.

Supervision

Probably the key element in the financial control system of any human service organization (as well as a clear reflection of the "social control" perspective introduced above) is the development of adequate employee supervision practices. In the human services, supervision has ordinarily been viewed from a number of fairly standard perspectives, but examination of the fiscal implications of the topic has seldom been one of them. The basis for making this connection, however, should be reasonably clear by now. While expenditure control policies, adequate accounting systems, and all of the other items discussed above are clearly important to adequate fiscal control, they fail to deal in several important respects with the largest bulk of human service expenditures.

The single largest item in the expenditures of most human service agencies and programs is personnel, and the largest category of such costs are for service delivery, as opposed to clerical or administrative workers. It should be clear, therefore, that control procedures are the critical factors in controlling costs in personnel, and by implication, throughout the budget. However, because we are dealing with the care and keeping of human as opposed to material resources, some divergence from ordinary fiscal control procedures is necessary. One does not, after all, expect to employ the same inventory methods with machine tools and people!

How, then, is one to maintain adequate control over personnel costs? In general, the procedures involved are, as already indicated, largely matters of supervision. We may still identify those procedures that are episodic, or periodic, and those that are continuous and on-going.

Foremost among the episodic or periodic procedures related to personnel cost control is the annual review of employee performance. Each employee in the agency should be reviewed annually, and this review should include an assessment of the employee's performance with clients, relationships with colleagues, and similar matters. This information should form the basis for determining the size of his salary increases, and possibly even his access to certain discretionary expenditures (new equipment, travel, and the like). Obviously, in the case of Civil Service or similar personnel systems, the agency administrator may have little or no influence over the actual circumstances and timing of a salary increase. Even in such cases, however, in-house recommendations play a role in determining increases, and are, as a result, related to agency expenditures.

A second periodic procedure that may be useful in some agency contexts involves the re-examination of work loads, job and task assignments, rates of performance, efficiency and productivity, and related matters. Through the use of "random moment" sampling procedures, time and motion studies, and other such techniques, one ought to be able to periodically assess such questions as whether workloads are distributed adequately throughout the agency and whether workloads are adequate, too light, or too heavy. Even in those cases in which agencies are too small or administrative staff to undertake such studies is not available, agencies should be able to engage in more informal assessments of these questions or contract with consultants to conduct a study.

The most important category of continuous control processes growing out of the supervisory relationship in human services is the direct monitoring of day-to-day employee performance. In some cases, the agency may elect to use time sheets, time cards, or some other record of presence or absence. In other instances such procedures may be deemed completely unnecessary, or be limited to use with clerical or paraprofessional employees. In either case, however, the responsibility of supervisors is to see that workers show up for work, perform the duties expected of them, and in other ways live up to the worker side of the "employment contract." Agencies that seek to "humanize" the environment for workers may deliberately seek to make supervision informal or nonpunitive, or accentuate the positive rather than negative aspects. In any case, however, the external demands of accountability are unlikely to allow the complete abandonment of managerial and supervisory concern with these questions. Consequently, the thrust of such approaches should be viewed as an effort to render the procedures reasonable, acceptable, and nonpejorative, rather than to seek their elimination. The complete elimination of control procedures is tantamount to an abandonment of legitimate agency concern with fiscal and community accountability.

A major concern for which there are presently no satisfactory answers is the question of the responsibility of "front-line" supervisors (that is, those responsible for direct supervision of service delivery workers) for enforcing agency norms of efficiency and productivity. Particularly important here is the question of whether such supervisors should be "after" workers to be more productive, work harder and be more efficient with their time, or whether such hounding would undermine the worker-supervisor relationship relating to clients and the actual delivery of service. Would the responsibility of a supervisor for "nagging" workers to use their time better lead to a decreased willingness to consult with supervisors in the handling of problem cases? If so, it is questionable whether the demands of fiscal control should be allowed to override the demands of service delivery.

There are probably other aspects of supervision in modern human service settings that are equally important in establishing adequate fiscal control procedures. However, the most essential point here has already been made: that is, that in concerning themselves with the adequacy of fiscal control procedures administrators cannot afford to ignore the area of supervision.

Internal budgets

The peculiar role of budget-making in the negotiation of a human service agency with its environment has already been elaborated in Chapters 3 and 6. One point not covered at that discussion, however, involves the use of budgets as internal control documents in the on-going operation of the agency.

The use of budgets as controls serves two important purposes. First, in conjunction with dividing up the overall work task, internal budgets, which provide for a planned distribution of resources among the units of the agency, are an expedient link between the intentions of planning and the realities of implementation. This linkage is the topic of Chapter 8.

The second use concerns us here. Internal budgets also offer a practical means of linking planning into the operation of the type of fiscal controls discussed elsewhere in this chapter, and of broadening the scope of the day-to-day supervision of worker performance. The supervisor of a large unit who can determine the dollar cost of a day of "released time" for the workers on the unit to attend a workshop or in-service training session may be in a better position to weigh the qualitative and quantitative benefits.

The question of whether such budgets are simply distributed to departments, units, or individual supervisors, or become a part of the negotiation of assignments and workloads is essentially a matter of how participatory the management is. This is not the place to argue either for or against participatory management. The point here is that if the use of internal budgets is keyed into the existing management style of the organization, it can be used to elaborate and enhance the decisions that contribute to work performance in the agency.

Distribution of special studies

Still another technique that occasionally may be useful, if indirectly, in agency control procedures is the distribution of special studies. There is reason to suspect, for example, that at least some employees will be more careful in their use of agency secretarial services after they have been informed of the actual cost of every letter or memo produced. Similarly, total agency telephone bills can sometimes be used to shock employees into more limited use of long-distance telephone calls. The same might be said for copying facilities and other equipment. Care must be taken, however, to see that management does not convey as a covert message, "Don't use this at all!"

Information control

One of the persistent issues of concern in human service organizations is the matter of how much information to release to boards, committees, newspapers, and others. The discussion of this issue here is essentially a bringing together of isolated observations made at various points in this work. The management task of disseminating financial information is a variable one depending upon the types of accountability involved. The purposes of fiscal accountability may be served sufficiently by the presentation of mandated financial reports to various funding sources. Ordinarily, this is an open-and-shut question. The problems of whether or not to disseminate financial information typically arises within the context of either internal management accountability or community accountability. Such questions as whether or not employees should know one another's salaries or whether such information should be known to the general public are typically among the most serious control issues to be faced. Similar questions may arise over such diverse items as the amounts paid by an agency for its office equipment, rental of buildings and office space, and travel costs. Typically, however, concerns expressed either within the agency or in the community relate more to expenditure items than to income or asset items. Also typical is the nearly universal wish among human service administrators to avoid misunderstanding, controversy, or other (from their point of view) unfortunate mishaps by keeping as much financial information under wraps as possible.

The essential management question is relatively simple: does formal or informal withholding information contribute more to helping or to hindering agency objectives? As a general rule, the release of information and an "open awareness context" are preferable to secrecy in this and in other matters. However, it also must be recognized that secrecy in the withholding of information can very readily come into conflict with the stewardship obligations of human service agencies.

Purchasing control

Some level of purchasing activity is an essential aspect of all human service organizations. In the smaller agencies, purchasing may be handled informally by the director or another staff member. In the larger, a special department devoted exclusively to purchases may be created.

Most human service purchases are likely to be at one of three levels. At the lowest level, the agency is likely to have a *petty cash fund* for making small purchases of an emergency or immediate nature. Employees may be reimbursed for expenditures of their own money, or they may withdraw money from the fund to make necessary purchases. In either case, typical practice requires that employees sign purchase vouchers and provide receipts for their purchases. The petty cash fund itself operates, like other funds, on a "balanced" basis. That is, the total cash available plus the face value of all vouchers and receipts should constantly total the fixed amount at which the fund is established. Management personnel do not need to fuss with the operation of a petty cash fund, but may delegate this responsibility to a trusted secretary or some other staff member. Management oversight of the purchase fund operation may be periodically necessary, however, because employees who disagree with prohibitions on particular expenditures may be using the fund to subvert agency policy. In addition, other misuses of the fund, such as the purchase of items that should go through ordinary purchasing channels, may be detected periodically by such review.

The second major category of purchasing activity contains what might be termed "ordinary purchases." Good management practice dictates the use of some level of expenditure control and approval process for this type of purchase. In human service organizations either a standardized form purchase order may be used or employees may be required to submit memoranda detailing the intended purchase. It should be noted here that travel and conferences may be among the major items "purchased" by human service organizations. Along with consulting contracts, purchase of service agreements, and other similar "purchase orders" all major expenditure items of this type should be subject to some kind of centralized approval. Part of the on-going management responsibility for such approvals is to determine whether the requested purchase conforms to agency policies. A second, and equally important concern is whether the requested expenditure is in compliance with approved agency budgets and program guidelines.

One of the areas in which most human service organizations are somewhat faulty is in regard to the feedback of information on purchases to management-level decision makers. Whether this information is included in a specific report or the kind of general expenditure reports detailed previously, it appears important that agency leaders periodically receive information on funds remaining in such areas as travel, consultation, and conferences.

With respect to purchasing, human service agencies tend to fall into two major categories. On the one hand there are the agencies (such as family services, adoptions, community mental health, counseling services, and services for the elderly) in which purchasing is a relatively incidental activity. Purchases during a given year may include travel, conferences, office supplies and materials, and perhaps other "incidental" items. By contrast, a number of human services programs presently (among them, day care, foster care, institutionally based programs, and nutrition programs) are involved in extensive purchasing activities as part of their on-going operation. These require a number of techniques and procedures beyond the scope of this book. Readers concerned with such programs should pursue this matter further in some of the business administration literature on the subject.

The third and final area of purchasing in human service organizations is the periodic purchase of very large, costly, "capital" expenditures. An agency, for example, may decide to purchase its own office building, or it may construct a clinic, residential facility, or some other building to house its operations. Other types of capital expenditures might include equipment such as furnaces, computers, bookkeeping equipment, permanent audio-visual installations, and the like.

The standards of management prudence dictate that such capital expenditures be subjected to advance approval by the governing board or supervising agency. In many instances, large purchases of this type, particularly when public funds are involved, may require public advertisement, formal biding procedures, and similar arrangements. If there is any question about the need for such arrangements, the financial manager would do well to check with legal counsel, funding sources, state law, or other sources of information.

Inventory control

In those human service agencies that do maintain inventories of materials (particularly other than office supplies) the purchase of materials inevitably leads to problems of maintaining inventory as well. In residential institutions, for example, one may need to be concerned with inventories of food, clothing, mattresses, beds, furniture, and other items necessary for the operation of the institution. In non-profit day care programs, there may be the somewhat unique difficulty of maintaining inventories of food and supplies separately from a "host institution" making facilities available (a church, a school). Even in those agencies where the only inventories maintained are writing materials, typewriter ribbons, paper, and other office supplies, some concern must inevitably be addressed to maintaining the inventories in a secure manner. In addition to questions of security, inventory control also involves concern for the proper rotation of perishable stock and the establishment of routine reorder procedures to assure that needed stocks are not depleted.

One of the perennial tensions of maintaining inventories is probably the difficult problem of balancing the demands of efficiency and low investment in inventory with the differential demands of staff for variety. In office supplies, for example, staff members may prefer half-a-dozen shapes, sizes, and colors of paper as well as different grades of pencils and different colors of writing materials. If such employee preferences are allowed to operate unchecked, the agency may find itself maintaining many times the inventory of supplies and materials it needs. In such cases, administrators really need to ask themselves what is most important.

Two methods used for rotating inventory in business may have relevance to the human services. In cases where inventories are not dated, serially numbered, or perishable, it may be possible simply to employ a method known as LIFO (Last In–First Out). In this method, new stocks of inventory are simply placed on the shelf in front of existing stocks. By contrast, if one is dealing with perishable, dated, or serially numbered items, it is more desirable to use a rotating inventory scheme, or FIFO (First In–First Out).[3]

In addition, although it is typically not a pleasant subject to broach, one of the enduring problems of inventories is the theft or misuse of inventory items. Some level of misuse of materials and supplies must simply be tolerated. However, most agency administrators will find that it is necessary to "draw the line" at some point. For example, if it's appropriate for agency staff members to use typewriter ribbons or paper supplies for their own (albeit professional) purposes, would it be similarly useful in a day care setting, for example, for staff members to help themselves to food supplies? One level for dealing with this problem is simply to set forth clear, explicit policies on the subject (complete with stated punishments or punitive measures for more serious offenses). Another step that is often necessary is to take physical security precautions with inventory supplies. Food stuffs can often be kept in a locked room. Office supplies may be kept in a locked cabinet, and so forth.

It is a customary accounting practice to maintain the dollar value of certain inventories at specific points in the financial management process. (See the inventory discussion in Chapter 9.) In addition, it may or may not be significant for specific agencies and programs to keep track of the number of items on hand. If inventories are small, the procedure for reordering exhausted supplies may simply be one of visual inspection and initiating new orders as needed. In cases in which relatively large inventories are maintained, some record of particular stock items on hand may be necessary. In this instance the reader is encouraged to consult standard business management discussions on the subject.

In summary, it should be noted that inventories of goods and materials in the human services are almost never of the raw-materials-of-production character. That is, such materials are seldom basic to the services that are delivered or the purposes of agencies. Except in the cases noted above, such inventories are of a supportive or ancillary nature. As a result, the inventory problems faced by human service agencies tend to be relatively minor. In certain circumstances, however, if adequate inventory control procedures are not established, major administrative headaches can result.

Cost-control policies and procedures

In human service administration, as in many other fields of endeavor, experience in a subject reveals certain underlying patterns that were not previously apparent. While it appears to the fledgling administrator each financial action should be considered on its own merits, exhaustion sets in after a period of time, and the principle of management by exception begins to take on a peculiar charm. One particularly significant approach to dealing with the standardization and routinization of a large number of relatively minor administrative actions is the specification of a set of policies and procedures regarding allowable agency expenditures. In areas like the reimbursement of staff for overtime, existing personnel policies may already cover the issue adequately. It also may be necessary to develop additional policies dealing with purely financial questions, such as reimbursement for personal materials donated to the agency, and the like. In addition, such subjects as travel can easily be clarified through a set of expenditure policies and procedures. Can any employee traveling on agency business expect to be automatically reimbursed? Is prior approval necessary? If so, who must approve the travel request? Likewise, on the subject of disbursements to clients in those agencies (other than public welfare) in which payments to clients are periodically made—are the rules for such payments clearly outlined in a form available to the staff?

Another area of possible development of expenditure policies and procedures is discretionary purchasing. Are employees routinely allowed to order supplies? Can they order furnishings for their offices? In addition, who must approve the contracting of paid consultants and in-service staff trainers who contribute their professional services to agency employees? There are, it seems, literally hundreds of such relatively trivial decisions to be made in the average human service agency. One fairly common approach to handling these decisions, particularly in small agencies, is for every decision to be brought to the attention of a key executive. Regardless of the level of formalization of such policies, a more desirable practice, it would seem, is to attempt to specify and make known to employees the "ground rules" for frequently encountered decision actions. In large agencies, clearly stated and available expenditure policies in some of the areas mentioned seems highly desirable. In smaller agencies, it may simply be sufficient to periodically mention to employees at staff meetings that the chief secretary, or bookkeeper, or some other clerical person "knows the rules" for what is and is not allowable, and will bring the exceptions to the director's attention.

In closing this section, it is perhaps important to note that the cost-control aspects of such policies should not be interpreted as indicating "cost elimination." Obviously, many different types of expenditure of resources are necessary to keep the modern, complex, diversified human service enterprise going. The legitimacy of such expenditures is not under question here. The point with such expenditure control procedure, it should be re-emphasized, is to distinguish between those categories of expenditures determined to be legitimately related to agency goals and objectives from those expenditures that are not.

Establishment of standards

Yet another approach to the subject of fiscal control is through the establishment of standards at certain critical junctures in the agency process of producing services. Koonz and O'Donnell, in the *Essentials of Management*, identify six dimensions of standards: physical, cost, capital, revenue, program, and intangible standards.[4] At first glance, the first two of these would seem to be completely inappropriate, the second two only partly relevant, and the last two most applicable to the human service context. Upon closer examination, however, one finds all six types of standards employed in fiscal control contexts in the human services. They also serve as a basis for the further articulation of standards in various service contexts.

Physical standards, for example, are already in widespread use in setting space requirements for day care programs, public housing, nursing homes, educational facilities, and similar activities. Furthermore, the articulation of physical standards of design, color, floor space, facilities, and so forth could be important in the development of mental health, counseling, health, and other services.

Agencies are likely to be involved with such standards at several levels: as regulation as well as guidance and suggestion, and as externally imposed requirements and internally generated policy. Generally speaking, however, human service agencies have not made extensive use of any of the above types of standards in internal management settings.

Conclusion: Profile of a supervisor

The thrust of the preceding discussion is clear: in a service agency or program, personnel expenditures are likely to be the principal expenditure item, and as a result, the supervision of employees becomes the most critical of several expenditure control responsibilities. In this light, the question of what makes a good supervisor of human service workers is paramount.

Fortunately, the literature on professional supervision in social work is large and growing, and we need not undertake a review of it here. Instead, only a relatively few points with major financial implications need be noted. For example, supervisors charged with financial responsibilities are very frequently faced with some peculiar dilemmas. Nobody likes to work for or with a stickler who is always citing policy, rules, and obligations to guide subordinates' actions, and yet, in the financial area, these same policies, rules, and obligations are often ruthlessly uncompromising. Very few agencies have arrangements whereby the professional staff members can just use their discretion in purchasing, travel, and the like, with the full expectation that they will be reimbursed. Prior approval is far more typical, and when it is not obtained, the employee may be jeopardizing reimbursement.

Such circumstances obviously require supervisors who can "soft-sell" rules, making clear that they are clearcut and will be enforced, without angering or alienating subordinates in the process. At the same time, many supervisors assume a strong advocacy posture in protecting the financial interests of their subordinates in internal budget discussions and at other times. If fuel costs are rising sharply, it may be up to the "middle managers" to press the case with top management and the board that changes in mileage reimbursement rates are necessary.

This raises another major financial issue for supervisors: in recent years budget cuts and other negative financial consequences frequently have been the cause of serious morale problems in human service agencies. To the extent that anyone can realistically be charged with responsibility for shoring up, or improving morale under such conditions, that responsibility falls on first-line supervisors.

Inevitably, under the present conditions of the lack of integration of the fiscal and substantive in human service agencies, some tensions can be expected between supervisory responsibilities for program and for fiscal control. One of the responsibilities that should be assumed by agency managers is the identification, and where possible, the anticipation of tensions, so that supervisors do not become part of the problem rather than the means to its solution.

CHAPTER 10

FINANCIAL PLANNING
ISSUES

As indicated in the previous chapter, the human service manager must establish proper financial control systems for the various resource allocations and financial transactions of an agency or program. Before such controls are established, not only is adequate management of resources impossible, the very act of delivering services may be interrupted or prevented. Many human service agencies at present are content with financial management practices geared primarily toward control processes. Others are not, and this chapter is for them. For once purposeful, intentional, pro-active management of resources has been established in an agency, the conceptual and technical base for financial planning has also been established. Without such a control system, adequate financial planning is virtually impossible, because the data to support such a planning effort is simply not available, and even an adequate basis for estimations is lacking. Fortunately, advances in the past decade in all the areas of knowledge included in this book have improved the prospects for financial planning in human service organizations.

Social planning and financial planning

Planning is one of those terms everyone uses, everyone approves of, and most of us are secretly somewhat confused by. Just about any

214

adjective can be placed in front of the term "planning" and a new idea created. Because there are so many different uses of the term, we need to distinguish carefully what we mean in this context. Planning is generally recognized as the preparation of a set of decisions for action (that is, for deciding) in the future. Human service agencies are involved in many types of planning. Adequately distinguishing among them involves a careful delineation not only of what Dewey calls the end-in-view, but also whose ends they are. The term *social planning* is used to identify planning ventures directed at large-scale social problems or broad objectives, in which the planning entity is planning for or with a society or community. *Social policy planning* denotes similarly broad-scale planning, with a more immediate focus on "policy" in the form of legislation, organizational goals, and the like. *Administrative planning* is planning for a specific entity, and is typically directed at the design or construction of directives, rules, and procedures to carry out agency missions. In this context, *financial planning* is administrative planning focussed explicitly on those questions involving a fiscal issue. In the human service agency financial planning is a two-edged concern: on the one hand, there are those purely fiscal issues, such as the rate of return on investments or cash flow management, that are largely lacking in program or substantive considerations but whose outcome has at least an indirect effect upon service delivery. On the other hand, there are those mixed issues, in which fiscal and substantive concerns are intertwined, such as collection of accounts receivable or feasibility studies. Altogether, nine major topics will be discussed in this chapter: feasibility studies and cost projections; capital budgeting; debt management; project scheduling; "profit planning" or break-even analysis; cash flow management; accounts receivable management; accounts payable management; and planning fiscal mergers. Before this discussion, however, there are several points to be made about the nature of planning as it relates to an agency's management of finances.

Feasibility studies and projections

In another context, Morris and Binstock have eloquently and succinctly stated the case for the assessment of feasibility as an element in social planning: "The components comprising the feasibility of any planning goal vary according to the nature and extent of influence possessed by the planner and the nature of the problem to be solved."[1]

While the principal focus of their work was on the first factor (influence), the principal focus in financial management is on the second. That is, we may properly regard influence, and the related questions of the nature of the goal, the definition of the problem, and so forth as substantive matters that act upon and constrain financial considerations. Feasibility, from a financial management perspective, becomes essentially a matter of the cost of the problem to be solved—assessed in terms of "opportunity costs," that is, alternative uses of financial resources that would have to be foregone if a certain goal were adopted. It is important to keep in mind here that the feasibility of most issues will not be adequately estimated if only outlay costs (i.e., projected expenditures) are taken into account. This point can be made in the context of service delivery issues or in a purely fiscal context such as consideration of a fund-raising campaign. If only outlays are considered, for example, a campaign that will cost the agency $5,000 is clearly superior to one that will cost $50,000. But if one campaign is expected to yield $25,000 in revenues (a 5-to-1 return on investment), while the other will yield $1 million (a 20-to-1 return), considering only the outlay will seriously misrepresent matters. As a general rule, therefore, it is essential that "net costs" (that is, costs and expected returns) be taken into account in feasibility studies.

In the preceding example, a "net costs" computation yields a negative figure, since returns far outweigh costs. This is the result to be expected in fund-raising ventures. (If it is not obtained, some reconsideration is obviously necessary!). This state of affairs, then, might better be termed a "net return" estimate. In programmatic contexts, however, the "net cost" estimate is likely to be more appropriate, since those revenues that will be relevant to include will likely be equal to or less than expenditures.

The methodology of cost analysis is, therefore, largely applicable to the conduct of a financial feasibility study, with certain adaptations arising from the focus on the future: in particular, the greater use of estimates, rather than hard data, and a clearer specification of assumptions. (On this latter point, see the discussion of cost-benefit analysis in Chapter 11.) In essence, the method amounts to the determination of the major cost items, assignment of dollar values to them—either by analogy with similar current expenditures or through some sort of estimating procedure—and organization or categorization of these cost items by functional expenditure categories, "cost centers," or some other classification scheme.

The key issue, however, is not the method of conducting a feasibility study, but when such studies should be utilized. It would appear that there are at least four occasions on which the estimation of financial feasibility would inform and contribute to substantive decision-making by human services management.

Major policy changes. If an agency is thinking of changing its client groups, the types of services offered, the location and circumstances of service delivery, or some other major aspect of agency policy, it would seem both desirable and necessary to estimate, at least in a crude way, the feasibility of the proposed change in terms of its effects upon program revenues and program expenditures. It is also worth asking whether there will be additional impacts, perhaps indirect, on general revenues not tied to the specific program or policy involved, on expenditures of other programs, or on administrative expenditures or overhead. In some cases, it is worth considering whether there will be any significant "lag" effects. If the policy change is to take place on a given date, and one can expect that income generated by the change will not be arriving for sixty to ninety days, the lag in cash flow may itself be a major feasibility consideration (see the discussion of cash flow analysis below).

Major price changes. A second occasion that may require a reconsideration of financial feasibility is when one or more of the major items in the production of a particular service undergoes a significant price increase (or decrease). In recent years, dramatic increases in grocery prices and the costs of energy have forced such reconsideration on most agencies. The kind of feasibility study endorsed here would have been one way of determining the impact of such environmental conditions on agencies and programs. Other conditions that might create the occasion for a feasibility study include a significant new labor contract, new guidelines for a grant or contract, or promotions of a large percentage of the personnel in a program. To take into account annual fluctuations in prices, one might also consider such feasibility studies on an annual basis. In contrast to the previous type of occasion, price changes will ordinarily fit a "fixed benefit" model, in which revenues are assumed to remain constant while expenditures alone change. When compensatory actions to cut expenses are in order, however, one should be careful again to take into account the possible effects on income. Thus, a 15 percent increase in costs will not, by itself, affect income, but if it is passed along to fee-paying clients, will some clients "drop out" rather than pay the higher cost?

Major change in the method of financing. A typical occasion for a feasibility study during the late 1960s and the early 1970s was a change in a major funding item of an agency or program. The loss or addition of a grant funding source, the discovery of a new avenue of third-party funding, the passage of new legislation, and the modification of funding-agency guidelines are all likely to be occasions for feasibility studies in human service agencies and programs. As with a fund-raising campaign, the net return approach is likely to produce more meaningful results than the net-cost approach.

Creation of a new agency or program. When the management of an agency is trying to decide whether or not to undertake a new program, the situation is certainly right for a financial feasibility study. When a governing board has been put together for the purpose of creating a new agency, conditions are also right for a feasibility study. In both instances, equal attention should be paid to "cost" and "income" considerations, as well as to the relationship between them. Certainly, there are also other situations in which the decisions under scrutiny could be focussed and clarified by a feasibility study.

Costing social problems

In recent years the use of financial projections for "costing" social problems, which was once common practice in community health and welfare planning councils, has fallen into disuse. Perhaps we have all been so overwhelmed by the scope and intransigence of social problems that we have simply given up on the idea of resolving them. Since such national estimates ordinarily involve enormous figures well beyond one's ability to comprehend, they may have shock value but seem to have little other use.

However, an agency with a clearly delineated "catchment area," serving a client group that is a major proportion of the client population in that area, could well use such estimates as part of a general planning process for questioning the appropriateness of agency objectives.[2] Two principal methods seem most appropriate for such a study. In the first, one would need to establish a "unit-cost-per-client" figure for services presently delivered, and extend this figure to the total client population.[3] If the difference between client group and client population is great, it may be necessary to take certain "scale effects" into account as well. In the second method, one would seek to establish the characteristics of the client population in comparison with the client group (perhaps through a sample survey) and use this information to determine the "service mix" needed to serve the entire group. Once this mix is determined, the appropriate cost estimates can be made. One should not leap too quickly to the conclusion that such cost estimates are "unrealistic," "impractical," or useless. They may be highly useful, for example, in orienting boards of directors, fund-raisers, and others to the size of the problem the agency seeks to deal with. These estimates could also be usefully employed in the context of budget negotiations to "up the ante" or argue for a large increase in the agency's base. They may also be cited as evidence of the skill and sophistication of agency management under appropriate circumstances!

Capital budgeting

One important management technique widely used in both business and government settings also has limited, but important, applications in the human service agency context. Capital budgeting is a general term referring to fiscal planning for certain types of long-term expenditures, most typically involving the acquisition of buildings or major equipment. Thus, a business seeking to acquire a new plant and a state government considering the construction of new highways are both involved in capital budget decisions. So too is a human service agency considering the purchase or construction of an office building, or the purchase of a major piece of equipment, such as a copying machine or a micro-computer.

One of the factors ordinarily used to differentiate capital from other expenditures is the consideration of large sums of money. A second is time. Clearly, a decision that will result in the expenditure of $29 of agency resources is of a different order of magnitude from one that will expend $450,000. Not only is much more money involved in the latter case, except in rare instances the larger sum will represent a long-term liability against the agency, in the form of a loan, mortgage, or other arrangement.

Central to most applications of capital budgeting is the concept of present value and its corollaries, interest and discount. Most people are familiar with simple interest, which is a type of "use charge" levied for borrowing other people's money, and compound interest, which is a method of computing interest in which changes in the principle are taken into account in computing the interest charge. Few persons in human service settings, however, are likely to be familiar with discounting, which is a common practice in the issuance of bonds.

Generally, discounting may be identified as interest paid in advance. Examples of such a procedure are not at all difficult to locate. The "face value" of a U.S. Savings Bond is $25. Yet, at the time of purchase, it only costs $18.75. Thus, at the time of purchase the Federal Government is "paying" the purchaser $6.25 interest on the bond, and one has only to wait the appropriate time to be assured of collecting the full face value.

By contrast, if the bond is held beyond maturity it will yield full face value plus an appropriate interest charge for the period beyond maturity.

Both the concepts of interest and discount are essential to an understanding of "present value," which in turn is basic to an understanding of capital budgeting, as well as the following discussion of cost-benefit analysis. In the above instance, what is the "present value" of a $25 savings bond? At the time of purchase, it is $18.75, and the "discount" represents the difference between present value and face value. After holding the bond for the designated six years, the "present value" of the bond is the same as its face value—$25. These "present value" figures are especially important in aiding one in sorting out the immediate and long-term consequences of the kinds of investment decisions we identified above.

Let us follow up the savings bond example. If I wish to buy a savings bond, and two persons offer to sell me one for $20—one is six months from maturity and the other fours years, an intuitive sense of present value tells me that the first is clearly the better buy since the price is well below the present discounted value of the bond, while the other is somewhat above its discounted value. In both cases, by focussing on the present value rather than the ultimate face value of the bond at maturity, attention has been shifted from the ultimate benefits I can expect to gain to the present cost. This shift is fundamental to an understanding of capital budgeting in an agency context.

Using these kinds of calculations, experts in capital budgeting techniques have worked out a number of methods for assessing the desirability of capital proposals. One of the most common of these is called "payback" and involves the determination of the period of time required for the return on an investment to equal the investment. By discounting the present value of future returns at the appropriate cost of capital, less the cost of investment, one can apply the *net present value* method. The *internal rate of return* method involves the determination of the interest rate that equates the present value of future returns to the investment outlay. Finally, the *benefit/cost ratio* involves the present value of future returns divided by the present value of the investment outlay. (This last method is discussed below under cost benefit analysis.)

Because the kinds of investment decisions identified above are relatively rare in human service settings, the applicability of capital budgeting is an infrequent occurrence. Detailed understandings of capital budget computations appear unnecessary for most human service administrators. Those who find themselves faced with such calculations should employ appropriate consultation, or refer to any of the many standard works on the subject, some of which are listed in the Additional Readings for this chapter.

Despite its limited applicability in agency management, capital budgeting theory is presently of interest to the human services. Because the benefit/cost method of analysing investment decisions is a basic element in cost-benefit analysis, capital budgeting represents an important conceptual link between existing public finance perspectives on the subject, which are concerned principally with the investment decisions of units of government and agency management perspectives.

Capital budgeting provides this important linkage by providing a normative criterion by which to assess capital decisions: a firm (or in this case, an entity) should operate at the point at which its marginal revenue is just equal to its marginal cost. As applied in the case of capital budgeting, marginal revenue is defined as the percentage rate of the return on investments, while marginal cost is the firm's cost of capital.[4]

Debt management

It should be clear to the reader by this point why human service organizations ordinarily ought not to be concerned with short- or long-term borrowing to finance operations. For those who feel the need of some explanation, suffice it to say that, except in those instances where there is a certainty of future income to meet the obligations created by borrowing, deficit financing of human service operations is merely a disguised form of agency suicide. If your agency were to fail to recognize this fact, rest assured that even the friendliest of loan officers in your bank would notice![5]

In some instances, however, the failure to receive a scheduled grant payment or a similar exigency interrupting the normal cash flow pattern may force short-term borrowing. Under such circumstances, two points should be noted. First, the dictates of fiscal and community accountability suggest that the human service manager should attempt to get the most favorable terms for the agency, just as if the money were her own. Second, an extra dose of prudence may be required in such circumstances: wherever possible, approval of the board or executive committee should be sought before action is taken. In even the direst emergencies, at least the Chairman of the board, or the treasurer, or both should be consulted.

"Speculative" borrowing, in which an agency borrows funds for reinvestment purposes as a means of generating new revenues, is generally unwise practice. In the case of federal funds, for example, the Office of Management and Budget requires that income made by investing federal funds be reported, and that it be deducted from the total amount of a grant. Other funding sources may follow similar practices. Even in instances in which there are no legal impediments to this practice, however, it is unsound. First, it represents a breach of trust with those from whom the original money was borrowed—unless one can find an unusual person willing to lend money for reinvestment purposes of this type. Second, there is almost always an element of risk involved in investing money, and for the human service administrator the risk is simply not worth the possibility of return. On the other hand, the circumstance of investing funds which are "surplus" as a natural result of operating programs are substantially different, and under such circumstances, investment should be encouraged.

Project scheduling

The topic of project scheduling has been taken up already under the general heading of programming. The purpose here is to examine three planning techniques that have been developed for use in scheduling: Gantt Charts, PERT-CPM, and PERT-Cost. In order for us to examine these topics more fully, we need to take a brief look at the role of time and money in human services.

It goes without saying that time is a critical factor in human services. The time of professionals is one measure of their fundamental contributions, and is widely used to compute the value of services. In the context of project scheduling, we are concerned with three time-related dimensions: duration, sequence, and time-cost. In the best of all possible worlds, one could assume that staff members in human service agencies would know how to make the best use of their time. In this world, however, concern for how people use their time is one of the most important management responsibilities. Ordinarily, the use of time is a matter for first-line supervisors. In the context of planning, however, the issue also arises with some frequency. It is this latter concern that we are addressing in this section.

A basic understanding of time in planning can be derived from the initial conception of "time lines." Like the number line in the new math, it is possible to visualize time as a line of moments. This is basically what we do in referring to the calendar or clock. We know, for example, that there are sixty minutes in this hour, one "after" another, and that another hour comes in sequence after this one. The efficient use

Figure 37

Time Line of the Work Week

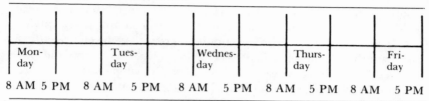

of time from this standpoint, is a matter of "filling" the time line with productive activity.

In planning a "full line" of time, the human service manager must be concerned both with the duration and the sequence of events. One approach to this problem, built up from the time line notion, is simply to divide the time line into segments, as in Figure 37. In this way, we can visually display both the order and the approximate proportion of time to be consumed by each activity. Furthermore, if we were to "break" each of these segments, and display them vertically as in Figure 38, we would still be able to determine their sequence, by reading down the column. In addition, we would be able to compare more directly the duration of each event, and determine which will take the most and which the least time. Figure 38 is, in fact, a very old management tool, known as a Gantt chart, after its inventer. Deceptively simple in context and design, the virtues of the Gantt chart are easily overlooked. However, as a means of visualizing a schedule of events, examining planning assumptions in detail, presenting materials in a document, report, or committee meeting or even as a visual aid to hang on the wall, the Gantt chart has much to offer. In these circumstances, it can also be used for recording

FIGURE 38

*Gantt Chart of the Length of Coffee Breaks***

	0	5	10	15
Monday	▬▬▬			
Tuesday	▬▬▬▬▬▬▬			
Wednesday	▬▬▬▬▬▬▬▬▬▬			
Thursday	▬▬▬▬▬▬▬▬			
Friday	▬▬▬			

*In minutes.

the progress in achieving the plan, simply by coloring, cross-hatching, and the like. (See Figure 39.)

Both the time line and the Gantt chart are, however, essentially linear in character. That is, they assume a single, universal time line applying equally and consistently to all events and persons. As the complexity of tasks, number of persons involved, or costs, increases, and the possibilities that persons in discrete tasks will be phased in and out increase, the assumptions of the Gantt chart become more and more simplistic and unrealistic.

In such instances, many human service managers, like those in other fields, have come to make use of a technique known as PERT-CPM (Program Evaluation and Review Technique–Critical Path Method). Developed by the U.S. Navy in conjunction with the Polaris submarine program, PERT, as it has become known, is basically a method of projecting multiple time lines and their relationships together with a technique for probabilistically determining the most likely "critical path." The critical path is defined as the sequence of events (portrayed by circles) and activities (portrayed by lines) involving the least elapsed time. Efficient time scheduling, it is assumed by the technique, can be worked out by constructing a PERT diagram, determining the critical path, and then restructuring the schedule for maximum efficiency. Thus, in building a submarine, if the electrical equipment cannot be installed until after the superstructure is completed, it would be most effective to bring the electricians in after the metal workers. Exactly how long after is a matter to be determined by examination of the critical path. Figure 40 shows a simple PERT chart based on a hypothetical interview. The times and probabilities shown are approximate. The use of PERT involves the identification of major events and activities in a

FIGURE 39
*Progress in Staff Conferences (3rd week)**

	0	5	10	15	20	25	30	35

Clerical

Paraprofessional

Professional

///// = 1st week
/XXX/ = 2nd week

*In number of half-hour conferences.

FIGURE 40

PERT Chart of Interview Process (alternative views)*

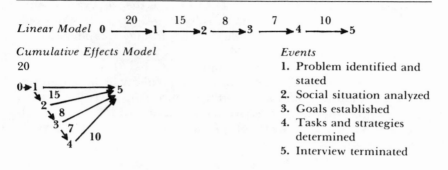

Linear Model

Events

1. Problem identified and stated
2. Social situation analyzed
3. Goals established
4. Tasks and strategies determined
5. Interview terminated

*In minutes (assume one hour).

project, the determination of time values and probabilities of various alternative events occurring, and finally the construction of a PERT-chart and determination of the critical path. It should be noted that several major computer soft-ware producers have readily available computer programs for assisting the analyst with PERT-charts.

The value of using PERT in financial planning is three-fold. First, it is highly useful as an orienting device for illustrating the assumptions and sequences of a given proposal. Second, it is useful for examining the implications of different courses of action in terms of their effects on the timing of projects. Finally, it is a concise informational tool—a way of "keeping everyone informed" about what is to happen and when. A well-constructed PERT chart on a single sheet might easily replace a ten-to-twenty page memo to staff, for example, detailing the events and activities proposed for the next program year. Furthermore, either a PERT chart, or the related decision table-flow chart is a good way to introduce new staff members to standard operating procedures in the agency, as well as to orient them to the intricacies of how their job relates to the jobs of others.

PERT-Cost. A more recent method that is coming into increased use in settings with adequate cost-accounting schemes is "PERT-Cost," in which the elapsed time and computations of the basic PERT chart are replaced by cost estimates. In the context of human services, use of this approach is entirely dependent on the existence of the kind of cost-accounting and program budgeting systems already discussed, since without such basic information systems, no basis for accurately determining cost estimates of this type exists. Given the close relationship between personnel costs and total costs in the human services, it is very likely that use of PERT-Cost would, in many instances, produce results similar to the basic PERT-CPM. However, some variance is to be expected, not only due to non-personnel costs, but also because some personnel costs are fixed, whereas others (particularly in large agencies, and those employing part-time staff and consultants) may be variable. Consequently, the human service administrator will have to weigh these factors in determining whether PERT-Cost is applicable in a given planning context.

Break-even analysis

One of the normative assumptions made in most budgetary contexts is the simple observation that revenues will equal expenditures for a given period. If such a state of balance is not immediately forthcoming, several actions are necessary to bring things into line: reducing revenues by diverting them to some other activity, increasing or decreasing projected expenditures to match anticipated revenues, or increasing revenues to match expenditures by diverting them from some other activity. Once the balanced budget is set, it is often assumed that no further problems are to be anticipated. And yet, seldom is it the case that as the end of the year approaches, available revenues and total expenditures will be closely in line. Such a situation is dangerous for the agency on several accounts. First of all, such unspent funds represent the evidence for a potential case of "inefficiency" or "mismanagement" against it. Second, such funds could be diverted away from one agency to another, cutting the agency's base on the grounds that they didn't need the funds anyway.

The method most commonly employed to deal with this problem in many agencies might be termed the "annual fling." For example, some time before the end of the budget year, officials in an agency may determine that funds will be left over at the end of the budget period. They then engage in a "spending fling" seeking to identify items the agency could use, and get them purchased as quickly as possible. If the review comes near enough to the end this fling can take on truly phrenetic overtones! While it could be argued that such an approach results in acquisitions that would not otherwise get made, at least two criticisms of this approach are worth making. First, because of the urgency involved, it is inevitable that ordinary agency decision-making processes will be short-circuited, and it is likely that at least some poor choices will be made or obvious needs overlooked. Second, the urgency of this procedure probably creates a certain "hardware" mentality—favoring purchases of equipment or supplies over services. After all, it may be easier to purchase $1,500 of paper than to figure out a way to get that much additional clerical service.

A substantial case can be made, therefore, for more adequate planning of the "fit" between revenues and expenditures, so that anticipated surpluses can be predicted well enough in advance for more suitable contingency plans. Fortunately, a method from business practice can readily be adapted to deal with this problem. The method is called "break-even analysis," or sometimes profit planning, and is concerned with methods for accurately projecting the assumptions of "balanced" budgets over a given period of time.

In applying break-even analysis to the human service context, we must make only one major adaptation from the for-profit context in which it is ordinarily applied. Typical business applications of the technique work like the solution of algebra problems: solving for one or more unknowns among several factors, including income from sales, expenditure, and profit/loss. The basic formula is that income from sales equals expenditure plus profit/loss. In the human service context, income is likely to come from any of the sources noted in Part II, and the fundamental legal-accounting assumption of both not-for-profit and governmental entities is that they will "break even" with no profit or loss involved. In other words, revenues will equal expenditures, in the normal, and desired state of affairs.

When this is not the case, the terms "surplus" or "deficit" are employed in place of profit or loss. Unlike the business situation in which profit reflects positively on management, both surplus and deficit conditions in human service organizations reflect negatively on management (witness the annual fling discussed above). Consequently, the need for accurate break-even projections is, if anything, more important in human services than in business. Even the amount of the variance becomes a critical factor in human service settings. The businessman who projects a 5 percent profit and experiences a 15 percent profit, due to increased efficiency in operations, will probably be elated. The human service manager with the same circumstances is faced with a new problem at budget time.

Cash flow management

One of the most universal financial planning problems facing human service agencies, and fortunately, one of the simplest problems to resolve is the problem of cash flow management. It should be abundantly clear by now that the assets of a human service organization are not always synonymous with its "liquid assets." The agency may have been approved with a budget or grant of $500,000 but only have $10,000 cash on hand, or it may have $20,000 in outstanding accounts receivable from fees. In such instances, the differences between the assets that are owned and those that are immediately accessible can be a critical one when it is time to pay the bills or meet the payroll.

Consequently, as the first step in cash flow management, the human service manager should have a pretty good idea, at all times of the approximate balances of cash on hand for each of the various fund accounts maintained by the agency. Such a present-oriented focus, however, is only a first step in adequate cash flow management. It is also essential that the same awareness be projected into the future. What will the cash flow situation be in two weeks? The first of next month? At the end of the quarter?

Several simple steps make such projections a relatively routine matter. First, when a new funding source is secured, one of the steps following implementation should be to determine the anticipated cash flow pattern from this source. Will they pay all at once in a lump sum? Or monthly? Quarterly? Will the funds be advanced to the agency or paid as reimbursements for prior expenditures by the agency? If the latter, where will the cash to make such expenditures come from?

Once this pattern of cash flow has been determined, it should be examined closely for its implications for the agency. Part of this task involves the questions noted above. It also involves questions regarding the "fit" between cash from this source and others. Is "comingling" of funds allowed—in which cash from various sources can be mixed in a single checking account, or is separation of funds required by the terms of the funding source?

The most important step in cash flow management involves the projection of cash flow requirements and expected cash on hand. Ordinarily, such patterns can readily be projected for the agency over the entire program year, with quarterly or monthly revisions of the projections as appropriate. Two basic steps are involved in such projections. The first is the projection of the sequence of fixed and variable expenditures on a month-by-month basis. In many instances, when the

FIGURE 41

Monthly Cash Flow Projection with Fixed Expenses

Jan. Feb. March April May June July Aug. Sept. Oct. Nov. Dec.

AA = Expenses
BA = Cash on hand

major expenditures are on-going, regular, fixed expenditures, and variable expenditures are a very minor consideration (for incidentals, etc.), it may be sufficient to project expenditures as fixed throughout the year, as in Figure 41. In such cases, the only question is whether the timing of cash receipts will consistently keep ahead of expenditures. In other instances, both revenues and expenditures must be projected as variable, as in Figure 42, and in such cases, the matter of timing the receipt of cash is even more critical.

Usually, it will be appropriate to prepare a separate cash flow chart for each separate fund or checking account from which expenditures are made. In those cases in which the agency has the added flexibility of making internal transfers between funds as needed, it is also desirable

FIGURE 42

Quarterly Cash Flow Projection with Variable Revenues and Expenditures

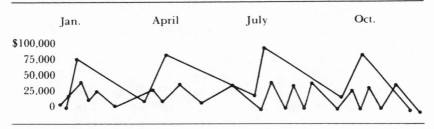

to prepare an overall cash flow chart, since the question then is not only whether sufficient cash exists in a single account, but whether the total cash available in all accounts is sufficient.

Several points should be noted by the reader who has never worked with this kind of cash flow consideration. First, cash flow assumptions should be as realistic as possible. Reference should be made to project scheduling documents, such as those discussed in this chapter, as well as basic agency procedures such as the handling of payrolls, accounts payable, and accounts receivable. Second, in constructing a cash flow diagram, the analyst in an accrual accounting system should not make the mistake of projecting expenditures, but rather project cash disbursements (increases or decreases in accounts payable during a period will reflect the difference between the two). Likewise, total assets should not be included, but only "cash on hand and in bank." Finally, cash flow assumptions should be "dovetailed" with other planning assumptions as noted above, to the maximum extent possible. It is for this reason that the cash flow item is included, for example, in the consolidated budget worksheet (Figure 36) discussed in Chapter 7.

Accounts receivable management

In a full accrual accounting setup, both outstanding or uncollected fees and other income from grants, budget authorities will be carried on the agency books as "Accounts Receivable." In many modified accrual setups, this category is not reflected until actual payments are received. In either instance, the management stance is roughly the same. The astute financial manager in a human service organization cannot afford to assume that outstanding revenues will automatically come to the agency, but rather should assume a "pro-active" stance with regard to the collection of funds.

In the case of grants from federal or state agencies, for example, care should be taken to determine the payment schedule, as noted in the cash flow management discussion. Wherever necessary, due to late payments or a reimbursement method, the manager may need to arrange for short-term loans, using the outstanding balance of the grant as security.

The most problematic aspect of accounts receivable management in the human services, however, is likely to occur in the agency that is partially dependent on fee collections. Two expectations can be assumed to apply nearly universally in such cases. As in any other situation of this type, the agency can expect to write off a certain proportion of fees as uncollectable. The active pursuit of such un-collected fees also appears to be a necessary management responsibility, which may clash with service delivery objectives, and give rise to concern that management is undercutting treatment of clients. After all, some staff may argue, how can the agency appear caring and assume a helping posture, when clients are constantly being harassed about their unpaid bills?

Ultimately, of course, this problem poses a major dilemma for the fee based service agency. In most instances, however, the problem need not reach serious proportions, if the agency has a clearly spelled-out policy regarding collection of accounts receivable which is familiar to all concerned and administered fairly and evenhandedly. In most respects, a realistic fee structure based on ability to pay should resolve most problems. If clients are charged on such a fair basis, failure to settle their account should be met with a fairly firm agency response—possibly including the suspension of service.

In all instances, even when staff are convinced of the fairness of a fee schedule and collections policy, some provision for the appeal and suspension of fees should be tied to the agency's provisions for writing off accounts receivable. The decision to eliminate, or write off an account as no longer considered collectable should be documented with one of two kinds of evidence: an indication from the person in charge of collections that appropriate efforts to collect the account have been made without success, or in rare instances, a declaration from the client or the worker that the fee charge places an undue burden on the client and should therefore be waived.

The active management of accounts receivable in many agencies may include a procedure for "aging" them: clients may be billed at the end of each month with payment due by the tenth, the fifteenth or the end of the following month. A notation might be made on an overdue bill the following month, with a form letter indicating the bill is overdue after sixty days, and perhaps a phone call, or a note to the appropriate worker after ninety days, with a provision for the sus-pension of service to the client after that. Special notes, stickers, and similar items are commercially available to facilitate this process (or "humor" the client into paying). The use of such devices to facilitate the basic process will depend upon particular agency circumstances.

Special mention should be made of the problem of collecting partic-ipation fees. Such fees ordinarily are set so low that clients will have no problems paying them. This makes them a special problem for the agency since the costs of collecting such fees may easily outstrip the revenue they bring in. For this reason, agencies using participation fees may seek to incorporate their collection into the routines of service delivery. For example, clients can be informed that they are expected to "leave a dollar with the receptionist" each time they check in, or "passing the hat" can be a regular part of group experience. Certainly, however, there will be instances in which such collection procedures will be awkward or impossible. The human service administrator should anticipate this problem, expect that it will occur at least occasionally, and be prepared to deal with it in whatever manner is deemed suitable.

Accounts payable management

Payment of accounts payable is the simplist of all management responsibilities. Right? You just pay the bills as they come in, and that's all there is to it. Wrong. The agency which engages in this practice is doing so at its own expense, and its creditor's profit. Even when only small sums of money are paid out, overly prompt payment can be to the agency's disadvantage. By the time monthly cash disbursements reach into the thousands, the losses involved to the agency can become considerable. The reasons for this are actually quite simple: paying a bill ten days before it is due simply gives the creditor ten extra days to use the money paid. If it is a small amount, this may be a matter of indifference to you. However, if it is a large sum, you may be able to make use of that money during the period. Even for the smallest agencies, such funds can be "invested" in reducing the bank charges for maintaining a checking account. In the case of very large sums of money, even short-term investments might be advisable. Thus, large municipal or state governments may invest funds overnight—between business hours—since with very large sums, even hourly interest income can be substantial. Few, if any, human service agencies can be expected to go to such lengths. However, the prudent agency can ordinarily derive some benefits by a well-conceived accounts payable policy that pays bills when they are due, and not weeks or months before—and makes effective use of the cash assets until then.

To illustrate we shall take the case of a small agency making disbursements of roughly $3,000 a month. At 6 percent interest, it would cost this agency roughly $15 a month to pay all of its bills as received, rather than within thirty days. During a year, this totals $180 of unnecessary cost—not a princely sum, perhaps, but unnecessary. Furthermore, increases in disbursements can be expected to yield corresponding savings.

How can such additional costs be avoided? Essentially, three steps are involved. The first is adequate cash flow management as already discussed. It is essential that the manager have a clear understanding of cash available at all times. Second, cash on hand should be working for the agency rather than lying around. If the bank where the agency checking account is maintained has a minimum balance or interest-paying checking account, this itself may work the appropriate savings. Benefits accrue to the agency in the form of saved checking charges or interest income. If such arrangements are not adequate, however, it may be possible to invest unused funds in a savings account, certificates of deposit, or other short-term investments (always keeping the possibility of risk in mind).

Finally, when using this method, it will be necessary to "age" accounts payable, so that they are paid on time, but not before. One very simple method of doing this in the small agency is to write all checks on the first of the month, dating them for the date due, or a day or two before by making a notation on the front of the envelope when the bill should be mailed or paid, and storing them in a safe place, with a secretary or bookkeeper assigned to pay them on the appropriate day. Figure 43 is based on a actual case in which this method was employed, and shows the additional cash on hand over a three month period.

Care should be taken, however, to see that this method is not applied over-zealously. In most cases, business practice allows accounts to be

FIGURE 43
Cash Disbursements: $1,560, $1,820, $1,350*

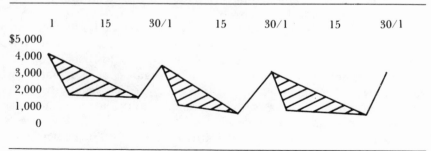

*By day. Shaded area represents extra time/money available.

due for thirty or even sixty days before they are overdue. Even when an invoice is marked "due upon receipt" the thirty-day limit may be assumed. Some prudence should be employed by the agency, however, in "feeling out" creditors, since the line between the legitimate use of the technique of aging accounts payable and being, or becoming a bad credit risk can be very fine, even for a non-profit human service agency.

Planned fiscal reorganization

One of the most popular topics in social work literature in recent years has been the attention devoted to organizational change. Yet, one of the most unrecognized aspects of this focus on reorganization, integration of service delivery systems, and so forth has been systematic attention to the financial implications of such changes. While it is currently impossible to present any comprehensive treatment of this subject in the present context, several comments of a tentative nature can be made. We shall be concerned here with two principal forms of reorganization: dissolution and merger. In the first, the primary concern for human service managers is with the distribution of the assets and the setting of claims against the entity being dissolved. In the latter case, the focus is on merging the assets and liabilities of the fiscal entities involved.

"Organizational death" is a relatively uncharted subject, with one or two notable exceptions. For the most part, both legally and operationally, we have tended to treat organizations as immortal. Yet, the simple fact is that, occasionally, an agency does "die." More important, many organizational relics exist at the present time, only because no one has taken the time and interest to dispose of them. It appears that the role of "executor" increasingly will be appropriate for the "estates" of organizations as well as persons.

In general, the concerns of an agency executor are both legal and practical. Legally, adequate provisions must be made to settle the outstanding claims against the organization, and to dispose of the remaining assets in accordance with the corporate charter or statutory law. As with persons, such dispositions may include legal advertisements notifying creditors of the pending action, and other actions deemed appropriate by legal counsel.

In addition, the unique legal status of a non-profit agency may require additional notifications. Memberships in federated funding schemes may need to be terminated, state officials may need to be notified of the dissolution of corporation, and so forth. Such actions usually will require official action by the board of directors, with the executor advising them. One of the reasons that many people believe that "organizations never die" is the high likelihood of resistance from board members and other supporters. In such cases, the executor may need to assume a pro-active role, pointing out to resisters the necessity of the posed action.

In the practical vein, provisions will need to be made for the transfer, storage, or destruction of agency files, furniture and equipment, and the like. In the case of federally funded programs, all of the equipment and furniture purchased with federal funds legally may be remanded to the closest federal surplus property officials of the General Services Administration. Some provision should also be made for mail service: perhaps the board president can be asked to receive and screen mail in the year or two until mail ceases. If the agency owns its building, not only will provisions have to be made for the sale of the property, but also for the disposal of any additional assets involved.

It is more likely that an organization will be merged with another than that it will die. In this case, the essential actions of the executor are to arrange for the transfer of assets to the "host" agency, the working out of agreements for assuming the liabilities of the old agency, and the like. One of the principal issues in such cases is the transfer of legal authority from an agency's original board of directors and management to its new officials. In such cases, legal counsel should be sought to avoid difficulties.

In the case of a merger most of the practical provisions involve transfer of files, equipment, furniture, mail service, and the like from the old location to the new. In the case of federal contracts, some problems may arise, however, about whether the federally purchased property goes to GSA or to the host agency. In such cases consultation with the regional GSA office is advisable.

As a general rule of thumb remember that organizations are not people. Dissolution and merger will not simply happen naturally. They must be planned and executed, with continual attention not only to the legal, but also the psychological implications involved.

Conclusion: Profile of a financial planner

Very few human service agencies, now or in the forseeable future, will likely have the necessary resources to create a special full-time position for financial planning. As a result, one can expect to find persons performing the financial planning tasks discussed above in one of three places. In the smallest agencies one can expect that in the future, as in the past, responsibility for financial planning, indeed, for all planning will fall to the director or chief administrator. This suggests that in educational settings concerned with preparing administrators for these roles, a place should be devoted to this topic in the curriculum. It also suggests that students seeking to direct small agencies should take pains to prepare themselves in financial planning. Second, in the medium-range agencies responsibility for financial planning may fall to either the chief fiscal officer responsible for all staff work in finance or the staff person charged with program planning. Depending on personalities, the division of the workload, agency history, and other factors, a reasonable case for either practice can be made.

In either case, there are some broad skills and traits that can be identified for this responsibility. Perhaps the greatest requirement is mathematical skill beyond the level of high school alegbra—and, if possible, familiarity with bookkeeping, and the mathematics of prediction equations. It is not clear that either general planning theory or general management theory is especially useful for this particular function, although it is definitely the case that neither should prove harmful.

It should also prove helpful if the persons responsible for financial planning were assertive in general management decision-making, since frequently in the human service context the usefulness of such planning data is less dependent on routines, standard procedures, and policies than it is on the assertiveness of the planners in "spreading the word." Another highly important character trait is the ability to be wrong strategically and gracefully. It should be clear from the preceding discussion that planners seldom can expect the luxury of always anticipating the future correctly, and that adjustments, revisions and corrections of past predictions are standard procedure. Being able to explain inevitable errors without undermining the credibility of future planning often requires considerable skill.

CHAPTER 11

EVALUATION ISSUES

Ours has been described as the "Age of Accountability." In fact, the related concepts of the accountability of agencies and officials and of program evaluation have, during the past few years, become clichés. Thus, they are equivalent to earlier and equally fundamental insights like "communication is the essense of human relations," "man is not merely a rational, but also a socio-emotional being," and the ever-popular "everything is a system." Two things appear to happen to concepts when such distortions occur—both of which endanger the value of terms. First, use of the term becomes nearly indiscriminant, with the result that many of the subtleties and nuances are lost, ignored, or glossed over. Second, the original insight of the concept is dwarfed as the term is applied to ever-broader topics.

Both trends were already well in motion by the early 1970s, and it is not too difficult to predict that—as so often in the past—the trends they stimulated will soon result in frustration and the abandonment of accountability and evaluation. To some extent, an ignominious end to the "accountability movement" will be well deserved. From the very beginning it has been relatively clear that many ideological opponents of human services saw in what has come to be called accountability an effective weapon to serve their cause. There is little question in anyone's mind, for example, that such considerations motivated the interests of the Nixon administration in "greater efficiency," "less fraud," and other putative legal and economic approaches to public welfare reform.

In far too many instances accountability questions have been posed as though there were only two possible positions: either one was "for" human services, in which case unquestioning loyalty was expected, or one was "against" human services, in which case one ought to be "for" the assessment of program effectiveness and evaluation research as a way of pointing up the weaknesses and inadequacies of service ventures. Such simplistic responses to phenomena as complex and multifaceted as the human services in the United States simply fly in the face of evidence to the contrary. (A second, related set of concerns involve the issue—also taken up in Chapter 2—of whether the answers to questions of accountability are "political" or "scientific.")

"Accountability," as that term is used here, refers to the assignment of responsibility for the individual and collective actions of human service delivery. In a very real sense, the contemporary calcification of accountability matches to some degree the more limited calcification of the concept of administrative responsibility among administrative scientists two decades ago. As noted in Chapter 2, from the standpoint of financial management, we are concerned principly with three forms of accountability: fiscal, program, and community. In each instance, those responsible for the delivery of human services are accountable to a different audience (community, if you will) and on slightly different questions. It is our purpose in this chapter to examine what some of the different questions are.

"Evaluation," as that term is used here, refers principally to the process of determining value, a major aspect of which involves assigning responsibility in administered contexts. In the context of financial management, we are concerned with three separate levels of evaluation—the monitoring of administrative actions (of the type demonstrated in Chapter 2); process evaluation, concerned with establishing appropriate procedures and determining the effectiveness of established procedures; and impact assessment.

It so far should be clear to the reader that as defined, both accountability and evaluation overlap or "interface" with virtually all aspects of the topic of financial management as outlined in this book. The principal focus in this chapter, therefore, will be explicit attention to impact assessment, which is the major area that has been least attended to in previous chapters.

In the following discussion, therefore, we shall direct our attention to the matter of fiscal impact. We shall not be concerned, except in a very minor way, with the kinds of attention to program impact considerations that so interest evaluation researchers. Such concerns will be limited to a very brief consideration of the "problem-free interval" as a representative of the type of program-impact measure that might be usefully employed in the fiscal context. Other matters to be taken up in this chapter include the use of efficiency, effectiveness, and productivity as fiscal impact measures; the possible use of a system of ratios; and the general phenomenon of cost-benefit technology.

Problem-free interval

Much attention is being devoted today to the subject of evaluation in human services. Publishing in this area has become a minor industry, and enormous amounts of time and effort are being expended in debates and discussions of methodology, findings, and policy impli-cations. Relatively little management effort, however, has yet been expended in efforts to link program impact assessment approaches to ordinary day-to-day management decision-making. Researchers, for their part, have developed sophisticated models of policy-making and methods to minimize the inherent abrasiveness of social inquiry. Even so, however, great areas of doubt and uncertainty remain, and it is questionable that evaluation studies will at any time in the near future exert much influence on financial decisions in fund-raising, allocations, or other areas. The major reason for this is that the logical "pathways" from an evaluation finding of "impact" or "non-impact" to program-ming decisions are often truly torturous. In particular, evaluation measures have not yet attained a level of precision and reliability that enables direct comparisons with expenditure and income data in a management context. A major aspect of the deficit is the absence of higher level, interval or ratio data on impact assessment. Such data would allow more refined assessments, not only of the presence or absence of effects, but also the degree or "amount" of impact, and would be highly useful in making at least modest cross-program com-parisons.

One modest approach to cross-program comparisons can be built up from the use of "problem-free interval" measures, using client counts of groups affected together with standard ("universal") time units (minutes, days) to construct interval-level impact measures. One unit of measure, for example, is the number of days per month of relative income security provided by public assistance payments. Although far from ideal, such measures appear to have certain advantages from a management perspective. For example, if the "problem" attacked by a program is alcoholism, and it can be determined that Program A produces six "dry days" per client per $100 expended, and Program B produces eight "dry days" per client per $100 (or six dry days per client per $75), certain limited judgements about the effectiveness of the two programs in comparative dollar terms become possible. However, several major problems with trying to compare incompatible objectives, and so forth remain. The most important point, however, is that such judgements appear to be "in line" from a program standpoint. That is, a measure such as "dry days" is a basic operational definition of the purpose of many, if not all, alcohol and chemical dependency programs. If such a measure fails to capture all of the subtleties and nuances of the program objectives, the failure must be seen in terms of the fact that this approach does less violence overall in incorporating program and fiscal concerns together than do many past approaches.[1]

A concept such as the problem-free interval is also applicable in a wide variety of contexts—child abuse, hunger (food stamps, mission work), psychotic episodes, housing, and other fields. In all cases, preventing and "relieving" problems are major formal objectives. Similar proximal objectives, which are directed toward lengthening the elapsed time between problem-crises, are in themselves desirable interim objectives.

The problem-free interval does not, and cannot resolve the basic value dilemmas involved in choices about the allocation of scarce resources. (E.g. which is "better"—spending to decrease child abuse, or to decrease hunger, or partially decreasing both?) However, such an approach appears to have great potential for sharpening and focussing the consideration of difficult issues, if combined with an adequate system of cost analysis.

In addition the context of human services leads to the bifurcation of fiscal and program concerns, and measures such as the problem-free interval cannot alone be expected to overcome the gulfs involved. As a practical matter, dual evaluation systems—fiscal and substantive—can be expected to continue in most agencies. As a result, in many instances agencies will simply be unable to deal with policy and fiscal issues in common. This circumstance is abetted by the tendency in recent years toward the application of certain evaluative concepts from economics in human service fiscal evaluation. Most of these concepts are taken directly from the private sector where such bifurcation is overcome by

the "profit motive." In particular, the concepts of efficiency, effectiveness (that is, fiscal effectiveness), productivity, and perhaps fiscal impact
must be noted. In the following discussion, each of these terms is defined
and elaborated in the context of the evaluation research terminology of
variable analysis (rather than economic terms), and related to human
service administration.

Efficiency can be defined in purely formal terms as the rate of the
expenditure of inputs to outputs. In research terms, both are variables
and the assumed constant is the quality of output. Thus, in abstract
terms the service unit that handles through to termination five hundred
cases with twenty workers (an efficiency ratio of 1 to 25) is said to be more
efficient than one in which four hundred cases are similarly handled by
forty workers (a ratio of 1 to 10). For such comparisons to be meaningful
it is absolutely essential to assume uniform service quality overall (that
is, that the five hundred received treatment comparable to the four
hundred, and were not merely sacrificed to the numbers). In reality, such
assumptions turn out to be very difficult, if not impossible to make
about the human services, which are highly ideosyncratic by nature. As a
result, there is no evidence of any consistent measurement of the
efficiency of human services being pursued by any agencies in the field
over long periods of time. The ideal of efficiency measurement, however,
is still periodically put forth as a desirable fiscal objective.

If, rather than assuming the consistent quality of service units
produced, we turn our attention directly to them, we may be said to be
concerned with *effectiveness*, or impact. If, in addition, we seek to link
such measures with resource-input measures, we have the basic elements
of cost-effectiveness analysis. We have already noted the attention given
in recent years to program effectiveness in evaluation research.
Comparable attention has been devoted to a range of fiscal effectiveness
criteria, as well. (Cost-benefit measurement, for example, is discussed in
a separate section below). Also of interest in the context of federal grants
to states and communities is "fiscal-impact" assessment, wherein the
effort is to assess in purely economic terms the consequences of an
infusion of dollars into a particular economic unit. Such assessment is
largely in terms of the stimulation of production, demand, consumption
of goods and services, and similar concerns.[2]

Productivity is essentially the opposite of efficiency: our concern is
with the amount of resources necessary to produce a single unit of
service. More efficient services may also be more productive, but this is
not necessarily the case. The most notable example in which this is not
the case involves the failure of the "consistent quality" assumption

discussed previously. What are usually pointed to as excessive concerns with "efficiency" in human services are really concerns for unbridled productivity. Efficiency, it bears repeating, must assume consistent quality, or else the rationale for measurement of this concept is destroyed. Interest in productivity measurement in government goes back at least to the post-war period, and several provocative approaches to the matter can be found in the literature. However, as with efficiency, effectiveness, and fiscal impact, the realistic measurement of productivity has seldom become an operational reality in the human services.

Overall, then, it can be seen that fiscal evaluation in human services is, like program evaluation, an infant enterprise. Whether anything will come of it (or program evaluation) in terms of management routines and procedures remains to be seen.

Cost-benefit analysis

Much has been said and written on the subject of the applications of cost-benefit technology to human service settings. Readers interested in this literature should consult the extensive list of articles in the Additional Readings for this chapter. The purpose of this discussion is not to teach the unitiated how to do cost benefit analysis. Rather, following an initial discussion outlining the main points of cost-benefit technology, two essential points will be made and discussed. The first is that following more than a decade of efforts at applications and ballyhooing of the potential gains, cost-benefit analysis remains essentially an intellectual toy in human services. Second, with a few relatively narrow exceptions—most notably in income-assistance programs—it is unlikely that cost-benefit analysis will ever be fully applied in human service evaluation and decision-making, primarily because the cost-benefit paradigm fails to fit closely with essential features of human service decision problems.

The basics

Perhaps one of the principal reasons that there has been such great ballyhooing about cost-benefit analysis in the human services over the past decade is that the cost-benefit paradigm appears to represent an operationalization of the "exchange principle" articulated by Homans as part of "exchange theory" that has enjoyed some popularity in human services during the same period.[3] If one is to engage only in those actions whose "costs" are outweighed by their "benefits," as Homans argues, then clearly some procedure for assessment of both these variables is an essential aspect of rational action. In the context of ordinary social life, such assessments can be made using primarily seat-of-the-pants judgements. However, in the administered context, in which consequences may arise months, or even years later, and in which the assignment of costs requires considerable information processing cost, a more clearly articulated methodology seems in order. For many persons, cost-benefit analysis appears to offer such methodological aid and rigor.

Unforseen difficulties

Unfortunately, cost-benefit technology is built on a comprehensive set of assumptions thoroughly integrated into contemporary economic theory, but somewhat contrary to the warp and woof of various practice theories employed in the human services. Economists, for example, can ordinarily justify to themselves the assumption that the "true meanings" of most activity can be measured quite well by the ebb and flow of income among producing and consuming entities.[4] Activity not adequately measured in this way can hardly be thought of as meaningful. Unfortunately, this assumption is hardly in keeping with the human service view of income as one of a number of variables having an effect on the well-being of individual persons and families (social entities identified as of central importance). In a very fundamental sense, one that has systematic implications in all uses of this technique, cost-benefit analysis makes basic assumptions at variance with the human-service view of life. This fact alone has made many suspicious of its usefulness.

For others, however, the lorelei-call of accountability, true believer-ship in the theosophy of systems analysis, or membership in the priesthood of systems analysts have been sufficient causes to overlook, or argue through the problems with assumptions, and to see cost-benefit analysis as a highly useful technique. In general, those persuaded by this view have tended to fall into two groups: the "pragmatists," who argue that there is much which is useful in cost-benefit thinking (in this group, I would include myself), and the "true believers" who see cost-benefit analysis as the way to bring a Puritan revolution of orderliness, efficiency, clearer purpose, and rationalism to what they perceive as the disorderly, chaotic, and "political" environment of human service decision-making. In some respects cost-benefit analysis has been the crucible for the contending forces of "science" and "politics" in the making of human service policy during much of the past decade.[5]

Terminology revisited

Like many other nascent areas of social science interest, cost-benefit technology has been characterized in recent years by a knot of terms, most of which are seldom used consistently or clearly. Cost-benefit analysis is also called cost-utility analysis, benefit-cost analysis, and several other things. In general, what is meant by all these terms is the systematic inquiry into the relationship (measured by a ratio) between the "costs" of an activity (measured in either sense of the term cost discussed above) and its "benefits" (measured in dollar terms). Thus, if the training of a master's level social worker costs $50,000, and his professional lifetime earnings will approach $100,000 more than those of a bachelor's level worker, the cost-benefit ratio will be 2 to 1. The questions of costs-for-whom and benefits-to-whom are important ones, and were recognized early in the literature on cost-benefit technology, but often overlooked in practice. The income benefit to the master of social work accrues largely to the individual while the major burden of the costs is born publicly.

An even more important consideration for the human services, however, has been the commonplace observation that not all significant benefits of human service activity are measurable in dollar terms, and many of the most significant questions are clearly misleading when converted into purely economic terms. Can the treatment of depression be measured in dollars? Suicide prevention? Early childhood development? Institutional care, or deinstitutionalization? Child abuse? In some cases, the conversion of policy questions into purely economic terms seems simply a diversion. In other cases it seems to border on perversion. Consequently, some effort among cost-benefit analysts has been devoted to the development of models of "cost-effectiveness analysis" in which costs are measured in dollar terms, while benefits are measured in other, generally ordinal terms.[6] The articulation of a fully non-economic cost-effectiveness analysis, in which costs are measured as non-economic opportunity costs and benefits as either individual or group increments, has yet to be successfully accomplished.[7]

In a certain sense, all correlation studies of the "burdens" and "benefits" of human services constitute a type of this study, except that while a correlation coefficient measures the degree of association between cost and benefit, the cost effectiveness approach seeks to measure the magnitude of the association. In other words, while the correlation paradigm establishes the probability of a relationship between two variables, a cost-effectiveness study determines the interactive effects of that relationship: if the "benefit" is increased, in what way is the "cost" simultaneously diminished or depleated? Social analysis in the correlation paradigm seldom approaches such questions—assuming always that "independent variables" are non-scarce resources. However, in certain cases in the human services, such conclusions may not be warranted. We know power, status, and prestige to be consumable, for example, yet our analyses seldom take these dimensions into account.[8]

This digression points up the little-recognized fact that, at heart, cost-benefit analysis is simply conventional analytic research applied to a particular set of problems. Gene Fisher's enlightening definition of cost-utility analysis highlights this important finding.[9] Two aspects of the operationalization of cost-utility problems, however, have posed particular barriers to understanding in the human services. The first of these is the differential use of the term "value" in human service and economic contexts. The second is the equilibrium assumption of utility theory.

Problems with the conception of value are central to the purposes of this chapter. "Evaluation" is, in at least one sense, the process of assigning values. Yet, what, in fact, are values? On this point, contemporary economics and human services are, to some degree, involved in two quite different traditions. Economists, along with other positivists, are often inclined to write off the more subjective aspects of evaluation as hopelessly muddy and "unscientific," preferring instead the more objective definition of economic value in the behavioral terms of "price." Thus, it is very easy to reach the conclusion that what an item costs (its price) is a satisfactory measure of its value.

By contrast, the "humanistic" tradition in human services has been less concerned with the product than with the process of valuation, so that "value" is more likely to be used to refer to the attitudes, preferences, or predilictions of persons that favor certain actions and discourage others. In contrast to the market-mechanism for setting values, humanists have generally abandoned economics for ethics and the setting of values according to some absolute standard. Consequently, it requires a considerable act of will for many in the human services to deal with the literature on economic subjects such as cost-benefit analysis without "reading in" unintended philosophical and ethical overtones.

At the same time, the concept of equilibrium analysis fundamental to all economic theory is largely unknown in the other social sciences.[10] The essential difference here is between "determinant" and "probabilistic" analysis—which might also be termed "closed" and "open" systems analysis. Cost-benefit analysis is as definitely posited on such equilibrious assumptions as classical mechanics: every "cost" has a "benefit." Cost-benefit analysis is largely a matter of determining the mathematical function that brings equilibrium to the cost-benefit equation. Furthermore, that function is a measure of the "drawing power" of costs to attract dollar benefits from other aspects of the economy. (The increased income "benefit" to a Neighborhood Youth Corps trainee must come from somewhere else in the economy. The principle of scarcity demands it!)

Fisher identifies two basic forms of cost-benefit analysis. One is the fixed-utility (or full-benefit) approach, in which the analyst begins by assuming a certain desired level of utility—benefits to be derived—and compares alternative methods for achieving this level most efficiently, that is, with the least outlay of cost. The second approach is the fixed-budget, or fixed-cost method, in which it is assumed that there are certain levels of resources available for spending, and the problem is to determine which alternative yields the greatest benefit.

The most difficult problem in using cost-benefit analysis for planning questions is that of dealing with the future. We simply cannot say anything definite about the future. Part of this is, Fisher says, a statistical problem, relating to the likelihood of certain occurrences within a known range. There is also the problem, however, of being uncertain of the ranges that may occur. Cost-benefit analysis generally seeks to deal with these problems in one of four ways. *Sensitivity analysis* involves creating alternatives for analysis across an expected or possible range from "high" to "low," and comparing the fluctuation of cost-benefit ratios across the range. Thus, a fixed-utility analysis of a manpower training program might incorporate a sensitivity analysis in which increases of $5,000, $3,000, $1,000, and $500 in annual income are the projected benefit. *Contingency analysis* involves a systematic shifting of the assessment criteria for measuring benefits or costs in order to determine whether there is any impact on the rank ordering of alternatives. Thus, the definition of the cost of a service program offered in a blue-collar neighborhood might be altered to include a write off for uncollectable accounts receivable as part of the "program cost" in order to determine its impact on the ranking of alternatives. *A Fortiori Analysis* involves a prior assessment that, of two alternatives, X and Y, one is definitely favored over the other. The assumptions are then biased in favor of the less desirable alternative, and the ranking is re-evaluated. Thus, if the institutional and non-institutional care of the unemployed are being compared, and the institutional care approach appears initially more favorable, *a fortiori analysis* involves a change such as the inclusion of the social costs of the dysfunctional consequences of institutionalization in diminishing desirable employee traits, and a recomparison of the results. Finally, as with all such planning ventures, the synthesis of new alternatives is a clearly applicable approach. When it is unclear whether it is more appropriate (in cost-benefit terms) to offer psychological or social work counseling, it may be appropriate to consider the "new alternative" of a team approach.

A tentative judgement

As one who was originally among the converted—a true believer, as it were, in the beauty, wisdom, and grace of systems analysis and, in particular, cost-benefit technology—I wish to offer a tentative contrary opinion: following more than a decade of highly inflated rhetoric regarding the coming revolution in decision-making in human services resulting from the application of cost-benefit methods, there is scant evidence to support even the most reasonable claims. True, several exemplory analysis have been done, but these alone are not sufficient justification. In the hands of the best minds, even an ordinary analysis can be transformed into an extraordinary theory. There is scant evidence, however, that the proximate decision-makers dealing in those issue areas have paid more than mild attention to the results of their analyses. More important, there is no evidence whatsoever that even if they did pay attention, the results of current cost-benefit output would be of much use to them. Like the other forms of evaluation discussed in this chapter, cost-benefit results are, by their very nature, comparative in nature. To treat them otherwise is either to engage in a massive self-deception or to set oneself up as an arbiter of absolute standards. Yet, by their very nature, cost-benefit analyses are costly and require esoteric skills not widely possessed. Because of this, they are unlikely ever to be incorporated into daily management routines. They will instead, remain, like opinion surveys and other techniques, for occasional use— a use hardly conducive to generating the kinds of data necessary for truly comparative purposes. By contrast, funding the completion of large numbers of cost-benefit analyses requires relatively large sums of money from within a sector of the economy that is already underfunded.

Tentatively, at least, the case for the eventual demise of cost-benefit analysis as just another costly intellectual toy is quite strong. This judgement is, however, tentative for the simple reason that unforseen events could override it. Of particular importance here would be the development of methods for measuring benefits of human service efforts in non-dollar ratio-measurement terms (that is, measuring benefit variables having equal intervals and a common zero-point, like dollars or the thermometer). Using the terms discussed above, this would, however, still constitute an abandonment of cost-benefit analysis in favor of cost-effectiveness analysis. Short of this it seems unlikely that there is much of a future for cost-benefit technology in the human services, regardless of its applications in watershed management or defense studies.

Ratio analysis

Various "systems approaches" to the management of human services set forth in recent years have made much of the interrelatedness of various aspects of the administrative task and administered organizations. However, they have generally not been especially successful in setting forth practical programs for management strategies designed to enhance control and planning within the identified systems. Consequently, today, as in the past, management's handling of the consequent or simultaneous effects of a decision that directly affects one component of the "administrative system" on other parts continues to be largely a hit-or-miss proposition, dependent in large measure on the intuitive skill and experience of the administrator. Although this problem is a general one in human service management, it is especially critical in the fiscal area—where there is the successful example of the use of cost accounting and related techniques in business settings to constantly remind us of the possibilities and our own shortcomings.

In this section, we shall explore the possible application to human service settings of a single administrative technique currently in widespread use in business. The technique is called "ratio analysis," and can be defined as the use of certain standardized mathematical indicators to assess the performance and impact of decisions on the financial structure of an entity. In business the entity is the firm. In the application developed here either the agency or the program, as outlined in Chapter 2, may be the basis for the development of a set of indicators.

For those already imbued with the currently popular conceptions of Management Information Systems (MIS), the type of Ratio Analysis System (RAS) outlined in this section can be seen as but one practical application of MIS principles in a rather narrow field. Using the business analogy, we might also suggest that the properly developed RAS should yield evaluative data on agency or program performance that are useful to outside funding sources and the community, and also useful for internal management and planning purposes. In other words, if the kind of ratio analysis used in business can be translated to the human service context, it should yield data relevant to all three forms of accountability already identified.

Several assumptions are fundamental to the adaptation of ratio analysis for the human services. The first of these is that the "fiscal structure" of an agency or program parallels, matches, or "measures" performance in the program structure in several respects. Thus, expenditures are assumed to reflect activity on the part of the program, and conversely, the lack of expenditures means a lack of activity. Obviously, a number of serious problems arise from such an assumption in the human service setting. For one thing, there are often long and variable delays between expenditure and action, and it is difficult to attach "action meanings" that are significant rather than trivial to expenditures. The purchase of a new desk or the payment of salaries may indicate that something (a desk) has been bought, and employees have been paid, but what do these transactions mean in program terms? Whether the resulting ratio-analysis system measures the most trivial actions of the agency or its more far-reaching meanings is largely a function of how the ratios are devised and implemented.

A second important assumption is that there are certain key points (of the type analogous to what are identified in the decision-theory literature as "decision-points") that can be used essentially as observation or monitoring points from which to assess the full range of interrelated activities characteristic of the administrative system. Since complete knowledge of the full range of activities and events occurring in the organization and delivery of services is an obvious impossibility, the argument holds, carefully selected and continuously monitored observation points offer the next best alternative.

Third, the essential thrust of measurement in the ratio-analysis approach is to select observation points that can be measured in terms of numerical ratios, using data from the agency's accounting system and additional supplementation from management information data, when available. In the business context the "current ratio" is a widely used measure of the liquidity of a firm. The ratio consists of the relationship of current liabilities to current assets expressed as a decimal fraction, and is an excellent measure of how prudent it would be for a firm to go further into debt. This particular ratio also has approximately similar uses in debt-related decisions in human service organizations. Care should be taken in interpreting the results, however, since debt has a very different meaning for profit and not-for-profit enterprises. (See the discussion of debt in Chapter 10.)

A fourth major assumption is the fact that there is no inherent meaning or significance to ratios. Rather, meaning must be developed in an essentially comparative context. Two principal forms of comparison are most feasible in the human services: *trend analysis,* involving the comparison of ratio indicators for the present period with prior measurements; and *unit comparison,* in which ratios for one agency or program are compared with those of a comparable equity, or with publicly available averages for similar industries, programs, or entities. Human services of many types are hampered in the latter type of ratio analysis by the general lack of readily available "industry averages" comparable to those available to most types of business. Such data, however, may be more readily available than one at first assumes. Head Start-types of day care programs, for example, have made use of "cost-per-child-per-month" figures for at least the past ten years. With only minor adaptation most of these figures should be generally applicable to other types of day care settings in a given community. In many parts of the country youth employment programs, such as NYC and Title XX programs, are developing extensive, but largely unanalysed data on the "unit cost" of services. Similarly, since 1972 many United Way operations using the UWASIS system have been building a similar data source.

Unit cost information, however, is likely to be only one component of a complete ratio-analysis system—specifically, a measure of the "costs of production" for a unit of service. Other ratios will have to be devised for specific entities in question, and in some instances new data collection routines may have to be worked out.

The question facing the financial manager in human service organizations, then, is how does one go about developing a ratio-analysis system suited to the needs of his particular setting? Starting completely from scratch, the process will ordinarily entail five cumulative steps. First, a reasonably comprehensive "working model" of the entire procedure should be worked out. It may not be necessary to express the entire model in graphic or narrative form, in which case the "working model" consists principally of a detailed working knowledge of the entire operation. From this model, a set of key decision points and observation points must be identified. Third, the relationships between the decision points and observation points should be worked out, and the nature of the relationships clearly understood. For example, in an agency in which borrowing must be approved by the board of directors, which meets monthly, the decision points would occur at monthly intervals. The related observation points for computation of the "current ratio" that would monitor the impact of such borrowing on the organization's operations, however, could be interpreted as only occurring annually, when the audited financial statements in the annual report is produced. One should not overlook the fact that essentially the same information can be gotten on a more current monthly basis from the trial balance. Despite possible inaccuracies arising from the lack of adjusting entries, which are made in the year-end closing process, the figures from the trial balance will ordinarily yield reasonably good approximations from which to compute the "current ratio" identified above. Generally speaking, therefore, ratio analysis is a post–trial balance procedure. Fourth, after decision points and related observation points are identified, the relevant ratios thought to best measure the effects of the decision being observed are selected. Fifth, one should not automatically assume that the decision and observation points and ratios initially selected will be immediately and permanently useful. Some trial and error may be necessary before the right combination of indices is devised. Furthermore, because of the comparative quality of such measures, a period of time will be required before meaningful comparative data can be accumulated, and, equally important, before experience among managers, supervisors, board members, and others involved in the use of indices can be built up.

To further clarify the use of ratio analysis in human services, two exemplary sets of possible indices will be set forth in the following discussion. The first of these is a set of nineteen indicators, all derivable from the financial statements of a business concern, divided into six major categories, shown in Figure 44. The second is a set of twenty-four indicators, either wholly or partly derived from financial statements of a human service organization using the AICPA Standards (Figure 45). (Definitions of all of the terms used in Figure 44 can be found in the Glossary.)

The indicators in Figure 44 that can also be drawn from the human service financial statement and appear to have some meaning in that context are marked with an asterisk. Because this discussion is general in nature, and not directed for a single type of human service program, the ratios listed in Figure 45 are suggestive only, and it is very unlikely that all would be applicable or useful in a single program. It is, therefore,

FIGURE 44

A System of Financial Ratios for Business

Inventory
Inventory ($)/working capital
Sales/inventory

Accounts receivable
*Average collection during period

Fixed assets
Fixed assets/net worth
Sales/fixed assets

Financing
*Adjusted current assets/adjusted liabilities
*Acid test
  Current liabilities/net worth
  Long term debt/working capital
  Total debt/net worth
  Common equity/capital funds

Sales
Sales/capital funds
Sales/net worth
Sales/working capital

Profit
Net profit/net worth
Net profit/capital funds
Net profits/sales
Operating profits/capital funds
Operating profits/sales

essentially a "crib sheet" useful for the financial manager embarking on the analytical protocol identified above. Financial managers with a background in statistical analysis may also be able to use this type of ratio system for planning purposes and for conducting more sophisticated analyses of operational information. The standard deviation for example, is the tool used to measure the variability of ratios over time or in a comparative context. Furthermore, it is possible to develop predictions useful in a planning context by developing

FIGURE 45

A System of Ratios for the Human Services

Demand / need ratios
Needs analysis cost estimates
Needed revenues projections
"Shortfall" projections

Capitalization ratios
Circulating capital
Revenue sources (%)
"Hard money" (%)
Fees / total revenue (%)
Public revenue / total revenue (%)
Third-party payments / total revenue (%)
Return on "seed money"

Conversion ratios
Program expenditures / total revenues (%)
Individual program expenditures / total program expenditures (%)
Program expenditures / total expenditures (%)
Supporting services / total expenditures (%)
Personnel costs / total expenditures (%)

Primary production ratios
Total expenditure / hours total service
Program expenditure / hour program service
Expenditure / service or benefit unit
Expenditure / beneficiary
Productivity ratios

Impact ratios
Growth increments (revenue or expenditure)
Cost/benefit ratios
Fiscal impact assessment
Cost / effectiveness ratios

---

multivariate regression equations using selected rations and a predetermined "dependent variable," such as unit-cost or other "output" measures.

The listing of ratios shown in Figure 45 was devised using a modified version of the procedure listed above. First, a general model of the "fiscal flow" of human services containing five phases was devised. Second, through a combination of "guesstimation" and logical permutations, possible ratio indicators in each category were identified. Although the list is primarily for illustrative purposes, sources that further support the efficacy or use of many of the ratios are cited for further reference. The five "periods" of the model are: (1) recognition of the need or demand for a service, (2) the capitalization process of gathering together enough resources to mount a program, (3) the process of conversion of revenue-inputs into expenditure-outputs, (4) the primary production process creation of the intended service or benefit, and (5) the impact of the delivery of the primary service on the relevant environment. Some of the ratios employed are already in limited-to-widespread use in the human services. Others are logical permutations from known indicators. The most common permutation employed is to take the numerator of a ratio and make it the denominator of at least one other ratio. A completely "closed" system of indicators would be one in which each numerator and each denominator is the denominator or numerator in one and only one other ratio. The system shown here is an open system.

This figure assumes the "dual track" organization of fiscal flow outlined in Chapter 9. In devising indicators, reference is either made to some other point of fiscal flow or to a nearby reference point in program flow.

Profile of an evaluator

Anyone taking up the task of evaluation in a human service setting can expect to confront an ever-present dilemma. On the one hand, various publics expect either definitive assurances that their money is being spent well or equally definitive evidence of malfeasance. On the other hand, generating such unequivocal results, in which one can place high confidence, is extremely difficult and in many stances, impossible. Consequently, the contemporary evaluator must be both a person with strong professional ethics and the ability to cast issues in strictly black-and-white terms to please various audiences. Because experience with the demanding context of human service evaluation is an important element in the handling of the problems one can expect to encounter, those planning to work in this area would do well to "apprentice" themselves before attempting independent work on their own.

There are a number of existing areas of knowledge that seem especially valuable to evaluation. Of greatest importance, perhaps, is social science research methodology—with particular emphasis on research design, data collection techniques, measurement and scaling techniques, and statistics. Because many evaluative problems in the human services must be approached from the standpoint of non-parametric, multivariate, or other statistical techniques not offered in introductory social statistics, the student expecting to work on this topic should seriously consider study of statistics beyond the first course.

Special mention should also be made here that some of the materials discussed in this chapter are not part of the standard vocabulary of evaluation research, but are found instead in areas of "applied economics," public administration, business management, and operations research. At present there is little, if any, fit between these procedures and the behavioral science techniques of evaluation research. About all that can be said is that the student expecting to work on the evaluation of fiscal problems and issues should expect to be prepared in both orientations.

Finally, some working knowledge (possibly from organizational studies) of the day-to-day operations of human service agencies is also highly desirable for the evaluator working on fiscal matters. Trial and error is a very poor teacher in the politicized environments that frequently surround critical fiscal questions in the human services.

Conclusion

We might summarize the basic themes of this chapter by suggesting that the concept of cost is a central one in any consideration of accountability from a management perspective. While contemporary concerns for program evaluation seldom explicitly incorporate cost considerations into their measurements, meaningful management consideration of the results of such studies will almost certainly do so. A general evaluation indicator such as the problem-free interval discussed in this chapter points up the possibility for the future integration of cost and program measures in management level evaluation.

For management purposes, three levels of concern for costs appear particularly noteworthy in the evaluation context. First, there is a long history of concern for cost-analysis, per se. This involves the sheer determination of total outlays associated with the particular consumption or production activities of an agency. Second, there has been growing interest in recent years in the application of cost-benefit or cost-effectiveness technology to human service financial management problems. Although the judgements reached about cost-benefit analysis in this chapter are, on the whole, negative, it should be recognized that the approach speaks to very real evaluation issues and problems that will remain whether or not any particular approach to solving them survives. The final section of this chapter takes an entirely different approach to the use of cost-data in evaluation. While most approaches concentrate only on the evaluation of output or results, ratio analysis, as used in business, devotes attention to various aspects of the management and production process. A brief argument is sketched as to why this approach might similarly be applied to the human services, and a hypothetical set of ratios that might be employed in the human service context is identified.

CHAPTER 12

CONCLUSION:
BEYOND ACCOUNTABILITY
TO MANAGEMENT

The materials collected in this book are intended as a "state of the art" report on the craft of financial management in non-profit human service organizations. The preceding chapters unfold a substantial record of collective achievement in this area, as well as numerous problem areas where much additional work remains to be done. All together, however, the level of financial management practice that is reflected is considerably more sophisticated and advanced than is sometimes assumed. As has been indicated at several points, what is offered here might be interpreted as the middle-ground: a number of agencies are currently not making full use of the potential present in the tools discussed here, while perhaps as many or more are working at levels well beyond that offered here. The principal remaining task of this final chapter, however, is to set forth some overall interpretations and implications for future development. This task will be undertaken in three parts: a number of summary, interpretive, and integrating comments on the financial management process model, breaking even, and other topics introduced in Chapter 1; discussion of a number of the theoretical implications of the organization of this body of work; and some suggestions for organizing future work on the subject of financial management in the human services.

Summary comments on the state of the art

In general, what can one say about this body of materials and its implications for the task of handling agency finances?

First, it appears that fund accounting is the most clearly established and authoritative aspect of the entire financial management setting. In the near future, agencies and auditors can be expected to continue to experience-test the national AICPA guidelines, gradually refining and clarifying their uses. Likewise, the types of financial statements offered by the United Way UWASIS design will probably become increasingly standard in agencies outside the United Way system simply on the strength of their practicality. Beyond this, fund accounting for non-profit human services should remain the fixed, stable core around which the whole of financial practice in this area will be built. If there is any genuine innovation in this area, it is most likely to occur in the convergence between cost accounting and program budgeting. Before any genuine innovations result, however, some major theoretical, conceptual, and measurement problems must be overcome.

Second, success in the area of financial planning is likely to be dependent to some degree on external conditions. If the turbulent political environment of recent years continues, the task of projecting income, for example, will remain difficult to impossible. If, on the other hand, some greater stability is achieved with respect to political support for human services, predicting the short-range trends for agency finances can be expected to become correspondingly easier.

Interest in fund-raising in the human services is truly like an old and precious wine: fund-raising campaigns have been experience-tested virtually since before most of us were born! And there is relatively little evidence to suggest that any new innovations or insights will arise for many years, although it may certainly be the case that each new generation of fund-raisers discovers this body of information and theory anew. Both the interest in appropriations politics and the interest in grantsmanship are more recent. However, as noted previously, both subjects complement and supplement existing knowledge of fund-raising more than they challenge any of its fundamental insights. While it might be said that grantsmanship is truly old wine in new bottles, certainly it should also be noted that no matter how new or interestingly blown, the glass does not affect the quality of old wine. Underneath the hyperbole and showmanship many of the trumpeted new insights of grantsmanship remain sound—each time they are rediscovered.

Contemporary interest in budget-making has clearly focussed the issue of the substantive and technical relationships in financial management. The old theoretical question of how choices should be made is answered by some authorities in a substantive manner: budget choices are essentially moral and political expressions of individual and group preferences in combination with the power to enforce those choices. Other authorities answer the question in a technical manner: budget choices are constrained by the inefficiency and irrationality of obsolete budget systems, and should be freed from such irrational constraints by reorganizing budget systems and procedures. The question of which of these perspectives will prevail will not be settled for some time to come. There are reasonable grounds, however, for some accommodation of these perspectives. It has never been convincingly shown that rationalized budget procedures and the use of analytical technology must be antithetical to the full expression of political choice. The evidence only suggests that, under existing circumstances, such opposition can occur. From an agency perspective, there is still a large unexplored reserve of potential for budgetary practice that is both technically sophisticated and politically astute.

A further conclusion that can be drawn from the materials presented in preceding chapters is that there is a major role for interpersonal skill in a number of financial topics. The ability to communicate, persuade, or negotiate appears to be particularly critical in various facets of fund-raising and budget-making, and is a major component in fiscal control activities in the human services by virtue of the critical supervisory responsibilities of fiscal control.

With respect to our knowledge and capabilities in the area of fiscal and program evaluation, there is a major gap existing at present between the "social science" perspectives of program evaluation, which plays out the substantive concerns of the goals of service programs, and the fiscal perspectives of cost-benefit technology and measurements of efficiency and productivity. This problem is increased by the disciplinary and professional boundaries separating proponents of the two points of view. Indeed, so rigorously are these boundaries maintained that one can easily find defenders of the claim that program evaluation and program productivity are mutually exclusive, unrelated topics.

Finally, it is clear from the contents of this volume that the capacity currently exists, and should continue to grow, for agencies to make the transition from accountability to true management of financial resources. Accountability, as it traditionally has been interpreted, is a passive phenomenon from the agency standpoint: communities and various groups who provide funds for human service programs expect, and often demand, assurance from the agencies that the funds are needed, well-utilized, and make a real impact on problems. As often as not, human service agencies have been able to respond to such demands for accountability with little beyond rhetoric, promises, and empty generalizations. In essence, donors make only a "good faith" donation, with no way of assuring themselves that their contribution was well-placed. By contrast, full utilization of the range of management technology discussed in preceding chapters seems likely to produce much clearer and more useful information to insure that promises to funding sources are kept, and that that fact is demonstrated to donors. This capability could, conceivably modify the entire process of the accountability of agencies to their funding sources, as well as the ability of agencies to use the resources at their command.

Future directions and implications

It would not do, however, to conclude that the financial management revolution in the human services is complete—only that it is well-begun. Before capabilities comparable to those employed in business settings can become operational, a number of additional practical and theoretical developments must occur.

For one thing, there is considerable room for improvement in the pattern of disseminating new techniques and approaches among areas of service. Most of the new developments that come along occur as immediate responses to problems. The track records of universities and research and development centers in developing innovations in this area is hardly an impressive one. Because of this, the diffusion of new ideas tends to take place along service and program lines. Children's services almost universally employ techniques of cost analysis that are almost unknown to mental health services, aging agencies, or other settings in which they might be equally applicable. Academicians and professional associations have done little to undermine or overcome this dominant pattern of dissemination. Consequently, there is a continuing need for conferences, symposia, short-courses, and similar educational forums specifically directed at spreading financial perspectives across program, disciplinary, and professional lines.

In addition, there are certain problems remaining to be solved that are not particularly suited to practical solutions like field testing and trial and error, but would likely respond to research-and-development or applied research strategies. The problems of improved cost-analysis procedures, cost-accounting strategies, refined capital-budgeting approaches, and a generally applicable ratio-analysis scheme for the human services should all be approached in this manner.

Until better patterns for organizing, disseminating, and presenting knowledge are developed, managers can expect to remain largely "indentured" to a given field of service or type of agency whose financial practices they know and have worked with. Unfortunately, such an apprenticeship system makes widespread adoption of innovations a hit-or-miss business, as it has been in the past. Indeed, were it not for the emerging role of federal fiscal influence in the 1960s (and other trends cited in Chapter 1 that overcame some of this tendency), it is truly doubtful that the state of the art today would have progressed as well as it has.

Along with the continuing need for disseminating knowledge is a need for some basic theoretical work on the state of the art. Chapter 1 introduced and briefly discussed a number of theoretical issues and concerns of importance to the non-profit human service agency. In general it was suggested that the concept of balancing revenues and expenditures, or breaking even, can be utilized as the starting point for elaboration of what is a kind of micro-economics of the agency. However, the kinds of suggestions directed toward the theoretical unity found in this volume are no substitute for a full-scale theoretical statement on this subject. The latter is very much needed, and given the state of the art, substantially more possible today than ever before. Until the time such a theoretical statement is made, one will always be tempted to view the fiscal rationality of the human services from the standpoint that an agency is just a looser form of firm, and the human services are simply another form of commodity. In the past this approach (never itself formalized in monograph form) has brought a number of results. While those who have tried have been unable to produce non-trivial results, or have simply obscured well-understood problems, human service workers have been highly skeptical, or downright suspicious of efforts to measure or study their work— regardless of where such studies originate.

Finally, in addition to organized knowledge, there is also great need for baseline information, or "data" to allow the comparison of different types of service within communities, similar services in different communities, and other comparisons. Data on human service programs are universally minimal, and in some cases non-existent nationally.

National center for non-profit human service finance

What all of this suggests is that there is need for a clearing house to gather, collate and, disseminate information on funding patterns, cost patterns, and other financial aspects of human service programs, as well as to organize and sponsor conferences for the dissemination of new approaches, to sponsor research and development projects, and engage in other activities intended to further work in this area. Either the federal government or a major national organization such as United Way of America would be appropriate to undertake sponsorship of such a center. Some type of "certification"—indicating that agency practices conform to those endorsed by the center and that agency financial statements are submitted to the center—could be used to encourage agency membership.

All in all, human service agencies have come a very long way in their quest for adequate financial management. Furthermore, there is every reason to believe that progress in this area will continue as it has— slowly, haltingly, but gradually achieving a substantial record of accomplishment.

APPENDIXES

A PROGRAMMING
CHECKLIST

I. INTERNAL ALLOCATION PROCESSES
   A. *Departmental Budgets*
      1. Are there existing departments or sub-program units?
      2. If not, can program expenditures be divided to correspond with meaningful subsets of activities?
      3. Can these departmental budgets be related to on-going activities for planning and control?

   B. *Lines of Credit*
      1. If departmental budgets are impractical, what budgeted variable expenditures are most relevant to which staff members?
      2. Can lines of credit or expenditure limits be extended in these areas?

   C. *Post-Budget Conferences*
      1. What budget decisions, precedents, priorities, or restrictions should be communicated to program staff?
      2. What is the best way to disseminate this information?

II.
   A. *Policy*
      1. Have policy statements been converted to work standards or behaviorally specific objectives?
      2. Have job descriptions been developed?
      3. Have work assignments been made?
      4. Has a personnel policy been adopted?

5. Has a plan for resolving emergent problems been devised (management by exceptions, etc.)?
6. Who must act on what kinds of new policy (director, dept. heads, etc.)?
7. Is the program in compliance with affirmative action guidelines?
8. Is the program in compliance with the "work program" accompanying the approved budget?

B. *Supervision*
1. Have adequate and clear delegations of authority been made to first-line supervisors?
2. Does every employee have a suitable supervisor?
3. Does the personnel plan specify grievance procedures?
4. What criteria, standards and objectives are supervisors to employ in directing and evaluating workers?
5. How are the supervision and evaluation of employees linked to salary increases?

C. *Scheduling*
1. Who is responsible for the overall coordination of events and activities in the program?
2. Has a master schedule for the first program year been identified (budget, reporting dates, cash flow, etc.)?
3. Are anticipated cash flow levels adequate?
4. Will workers be available as clients begin coming in?
5. Do workers schedule their own appointments or will there be a central schedule?
6. What are the procedures for billing fees with respect to missed appointments?
7. Will regular time be set aside for staff meetings?
8. How much? When?

D. *Reporting*
1. What reports are required by the funding source and when?
2. Have procedures been established to collect the information necessary in advance of the deadline?

III. OFFICE SET-UP
1. Does the agency have existing purchase orders and procurement policies?
2. Is the new program head aware of these?
3. How (and by whom) are budget limits and actual purchase requests coordinated?
4. Are any equipment and supplies essential for initial start-up of the program?

5. Can they be acquired in time for start-up?
6. What procedures exist for monitoring inventories?
7. Will these procedures alert the staff before supplies are exhausted?
8. Is there to be a petty cash fund?
9. Who will manage it?

IV. LEGAL
   A. *Incorporation*
      1. Is the agency incorporated as a not-for-profit corporation?
      2. Does the new program fall within this incorporation? Or, does it involve political activity, as defined by the law? Does it involve disposition of assets to private persons?
      3. What reporting and representational requirements are specified by this charter? Is an annual meeting required? An annual report? Must copies be sent to the state?

   B. *Tax Liability*
      1. Does the agency have a tax exemption certification from the IRS?
      2. Does this exemption apply to the new program activity?
      3. If not, should a separate application be filed?
      4. Does the agency have adequate procedures for completion of W-2 forms, withholding of payroll deductions, and the like?
      5. Are there any city, county, or state tax waiver procedures that must be honored?

   C. *Personal Liability Insurance*
      1. Are those officials of the program who will be handling funds for the program covered by a fiduciary bond?
      2. Are those employees of the program who will be traveling for official purposes covered by automobile liability insurance?
      3. Will employees of the program be engaging in any activity dangerous in any way to themselves, clients, or members of the general public? If so, should they be covered by some form of liability or malpractice insurance?
      4. Should this insurance coverage be paid for by the agency or the employees themselves?

   D. *Fringe Benefits*
      1. Are employees of the agency regularly covered by any fringe benefits? Will these benefits be extended to employees of the new program?
      2. Is someone responsible for making payments to governments, insurance carriers, and so forth from withheld funds?

   E. Have appropriate arrangements for banking and checking been made?

NOTES

CHAPTER 1

1. See, for example, Henry Fayol, "General Principles of Management," *Classics of Organization Theory* (Oak Park, Ill.: Moore Publishing, 1978), pp. 23-26; and Luther Gulick, "Notes on the Theory of Organization," op. cit., pp. 52-61. Difficulties with this division have been chronicled in various publications of Melville Dalton and others.

2. Although the "neither-fish-nor-fowl" character of non-profit services (as neither government nor proprietary) is generally recognized, literature dealing with this important "third sector" is scanty.

3. Sheila Kamerman and Alfred Kahn, *Social Services in the United States*, (Philadelphia: Temple University Press, 1976), pp. 1-21 and 503-19.

4. Ibid. pp. 504-05.

5. For example, studies of organizational behavior done in recent years have seldom paid much attention to differences between non-profit and other organizational forms.

6. James P. Culley, Barbara H. Suttles, and Judith B. Van Name, *Understanding and Measuring the Cost of Foster Care* (Newark, Del.: University of Delaware, 1975), has an extensive bibliography of this literature.

7. Anthony Downs, *Inside Bureaucracy* (Boston: Little, Brown, 1967), is the most explicit theoretical treatment of this perspective.

8. Carl S. Shoup, *Public Finance* (Chicago: Aldine, 1969), p. 57.

9. The evaluative literature has grown too voluminous to include here. The reader is referred to *Evaluation Quarterly*, a periodical devoted exclusively to evaluative studies.

CHAPTER 2

1. American Institute of Certified Public Accountants, "Review and Resume," (New York: The Institute, *Accounting Research and Terminology Bulletins* 1961), p. 9.

2. In order to develop linkages between accounting and planning in human service administration one must understand the "interface" of these two processes represented by agency financial statements. "Baseline" data in planning is one of several uses of such statements, and financial statements are one of a number of possible sources for data collection and analysis in planning.

3. Two quite distinct uses of the term "social accounting" are apparent in the literature. In accounting, the term is used to refer to adjustments of corporate financial statements reflecting (in economic terms) the environmental or ecological impact of corporate actions. This usage is almost entirely unknown in human services. The other usage involves what is essentially a link between evaluative research and social indicators—that is, assessing agency or program performance in terms of changes in aggregate statistical indicators.

4. The basic source for accounting standards in the non-profit sector is the Committee on Voluntary Health and Welfare Organizations, *Audits of Voluntary Health and Welfare Organizations*, New York: American Institute of Certified Public Accountants, 1974. Federally-funded projects should refer to the Comptroller General, U.S. General Accounting Office, *Standards for Audit of Governmental Organizations, Program Activities and Functions* (Washington, D.C.: G.P.O., 1974). An earlier publication by the National Health Council and National Social Welfare Assembly (1966) is largely supplanted by the 1974 publications, while United Way of America, *Accounting and Financial Reporting* (Alexandria, Va.: United Way, 1974), is written in light of the 1974 standards. Published prior to the latest standards, but nonetheless helpful in many ways are *An Accounting Manual for Voluntary Social Welfare Organizations* (New York: Child Welfare League of America, Family Service Associations, and Travelers Aid Associations of America, 1971) and National Institute of Mental Health, *Accounting Guidelines for Mental Health Centers and Related Facilities* (Washington, D.C.: G.P.O., 1972).

5. The approach adopted here is for the inclusion of up-to-date, and preferably audited, statements (including at least a balance sheet, statement of functional expenditures, and statement of support, revenue and expenses and changes in fund balance) in the annual report of the agency required by law in most states. In this way, a minimal link between fiscal and community accountability is established.

6. Malvern J. Gross, *Financial and Accounting Guide for Non-Profit Organizations* (New York: Ronald Press, 1972), p. 29.

7. It should be noted that the revised formats for financial statements prepared by AICPA and the United Way financial reporting system outlined in United Way of America, *Accounting and Financial Reporting* (Alexandria, Va.: United Way, 1974) ideally should resolve this problem. However, when at least one of the funding sources is a government agency that mandates the use of its own list of accounts and reporting formats, the practical problem still remains for the agency.

8. AICPA, *Audits*, p. 32.

9. United Way, *Accounting and Financial Reporting*, p. 8.

10. AICPA, *Audits*, pp. 24–7.

11. AICPA, *Audits*, p. 26. AICPA usage incorporates "Management and General Costs" into a single category.

12. AICPA, *Audits*, p. 26.

13. Federal regulations prohibit, in particular, the use of federal funds to solicit other federal funds.

14. Eric J. Kohler, *A Dictionary for Accounting*, 4th ed. (Englewood Cliffs, N.J.: Prentice-Hall, 1970), p. 115.

15. United Way, *Accounting and Financial Reporting*, p. 8.

16. United Way, *Accounting and Financial Reporting*, pp. 8–9.

17. See also United Way, *Accounting and Financial Reporting*, pp. 39–43, and discussions of financial statements in Gross, *Financial and Accounting Guide*.

18. See, for example, John G. Hill and Ralph Ormsby, *Cost Analysis Method for Casework Agencies* (Philadelphia: Family Service Agency of Philadelphia, 1953); John G. Hill, Ralph Ormsby, and William McCurdy, *Time Study Manual*, 4 vols. (New York: Family Service Association of America, 1962); John G. Hill, "Cost Analysis in Social Work Service," *Social Work Service*, ed. Norman Polansky, (Chicago: University of Chicago Press, 1960), pp. 223–46; Ralph Ormsby, "Cost Analysis in the Family Field," *Planning Social Services for Urban Needs* (New York: Columbia University Press, 1951), pp. 102–11; American Public Welfare Association, *Standard Classification of Public Assistance Costs* (Chicago: The Association, 1942); Norman L. Bonney and Lawrence H. Streicher, "Time-Cost Data in Agency Administration: Efficiency Controls in Family and Children's Service," *Social Work* 15 (1970): 23–31; James P. Culley, Barbara H. Suttles, and Judith B. Van Name, *Understanding and Measuring the Cost of Foster Care* (Newark, Del.: University of Delaware, 1975); Robert Elkin, *A Conceptual Base for Defining Health and Welfare Services: An Application to Family and Child Welfare* (New York: Child Welfare League, Family Service, and Travelers Aid Associations 1967); National Institute of Mental Health, *Cost Finding for Community Mental Health Centers: An Annotated Bibliography* (Washington, D.C.: G.P.O., 1970); D. W. Young, "Case Costing in Child Care: Critical Step Toward Increased Accountability in Social Services," *Child Welfare* 52 (1973): 229.

19. The elaborate and detailed typology of United Way of America's: *A Taxonomy of Social Goals and Human Service Programs* (Alexandria, Va.:

United Way, 1976) *UWASIS II* offers a starting point for programmatically oriented cost accounting.

20. Incredibly, there is no clearinghouse or archive in human services that collects, much less disseminates, even rudimentary data on service costs on a regular basis. For further discussion see the conclusion.

CHAPTER 3

1. Jill Ammon-Wexler and Catherine Carmel, *How to Create a Winning Proposal* (Salt Lake City: Mercury, 1978); Kenneth Boulding, *The Economics of Love and Fear: A Preface to Grants Economics* (Belmont, Calif.: Wadsworth, 1973); Daniel Conrad et al., *The Grants Planner* (the Institute for Fund-Raising, 1976); Martha Derthick, *The Influence of Federal Grants: Public Assistance in Massachusetts* (Cambridge, Mass.: Harvard University Press, 1970); Paul Dommel, *The Politics of Revenue Sharing* (Indianapolis, Ind.: Indiana University Press, 1974); Robert Fogelson, et. al., *Federal Aid to the Cities: An Original Anthology* (New York: Arno Press, 1978); Anita S. Harbert, *Federal Grants In Aid: Maximizing Benefits to the States* (New York: Praeger, 1976); Howard Hillman and Karin Abarbanel, *The Art of Winning Foundation Grants* (New York: Vanguard, 1975); Armand Lauffer, *Grantsmanship* (Beverly Hills, Calif.; Sage, 1977); Robert Lefferts, *Getting A Grant: How to Write Grant Proposals That Get Results* (New York: Prentice-Hall, 1978); Judith Margolin, *About Foundations: How to Get the Facts You Need to Get a Grant* (New York: Foundation Center, 1977); Virginia P. White, *Grants: How to Find Out About Them and What To Do Next* (Riverside, N.J.: Library of Science, 1977).

2. Aaron Wildavsky, *The Politics of the Budgetary Process*, 2nd ed. (Boston: Little, Brown, 1974); Harold J. Seymour, *Designs for Fund Raising: Principles, Patterns and Techniques* (New York: McGraw-Hill, 1966); Irving R. Warner, *The Art of Fund Raising* (New York: Harper and Row, 1975); and Michael MacIntyre, *How to Write a Proposal* (Washington, D.C.: Training and Research Services Corp., 1971).

3. Wildavsky, *Politics of the Budgetary Process*, pp. 63–126.

4. MacIntyre, *How to Write a Proposal*, p. 39.

5. Ibid., pp. 39–40.

6. Ibid., pp. 47–53.

7. Ibid., p. 50.

8. Ibid., p. 51.

9. Ibid., pp. 52–53.

10. Wildavsky, *Politics of the Budgetary Process*, p. 64.

11. Ibid., pp. 64–65.

12. Ibid., p. 65.

13. Ibid., p. 66.

14. Ibid., pp. 63–126.

15. Ibid., p. 70.

16. Ibid., p. 70.

17. Ibid., p. 72.

18. Ibid., p. 72.

19. Nixon aide John Ehrlichman's advice to social workers to seek honest work is, for many, the archetypical comment of this era.

20. Aaron Wildavsky's term, "The Political Economy of Efficiency," coined in a 1962 study of the effectiveness of program budgeting in the Department of Agriculture, is perhaps the best summary term for the entire set of attitudes and practices.

21. Wildavsky, *Politics of the Budgetary Process*, p. 74.

22. This point touches upon a major theoretical issue in the social sciences: the blend of "conflict" and "consensus" in social relations. The Hegelian "War of each against all" and sociological "cooperation" seem to be the opposite poles in this discussion.

23. Wildavsky, *Politics of the Budgetary Process*, pp. 74–75.

24. Ibid., p. 77.

25. Warner, *The Art of Fund Raising*, p. 86.

26. Ibid., p. 104.

27. Seymour, *Designs for Fund Raising*, p. 79.

28. Ibid., pp. 42–43.

29. Gerald Soroker, *Fund Raising for Philanthropy* (Pittsburgh: Jewish Publication and Education Foundation, 1974), p. 45.

CHAPTER 4

1. Two classic—and opposing—treatments which integrate this issue of the assignment of costs into the larger fabric of social justice are John Rawls, *A Theory of Justice* (Cambridge, Mass.: Harvard University Press, 1971), and Robert Nozick, *Anarchy, State, and Utopia* (New York: Basic Books, 1975).

2. The "dual-class structure" of service refers to the presence of free public social services (of lower quality?) alongside fee-based services, which are often assumed to be of higher quality, but beyond the reach of those with low incomes.

3. One of the strongest arguments for this approach is to be found in the vendor-payment approach. Such an intervention strategy is seriously undermined, however, when it results in essentially similar "dual-class" service-delivery systems with subsidized vendors specializing in services to lower income clients. The much publicized "Medicaid Mills" represents a specific instance of this phenomenon.

4. Nozick, *Anarchy, State, and Utopia* (pp. 26–53) employs the concept of "side constraint" in this sense to point up situational emergents or qualifiers that tend to modify or neutralize a rule. In this case, the argument is that the allocation of costs via fees is fair and just except in those instances when some specific situational or client characteristic enters in. (Thus, a fee would only be appropriate from an agency viewpoint in those instances when need for the service does not exceed the client's ability to pay a proportionate share of costs.)

5. These estimates are based upon hearsay and the author's personal

knowledge of such fees. In general, information on general patterns of fee collections is very scarce, even within specific communities. Suggestions for remedying such informational deficits are discussed in the concluding chapter of this volume.

6. Nathaniel Goodman, "Fee Charging," *Encyclopedia of Social Work*, 16th ed., ed. Robert Morris (New York: National Association of Social Workers, 1971). pp. 413–15.

7. One such explanation identifies fee payments as an indicator or measure of client willingness to assume responsibility or make a commitment to counseling. It is relatively easy to take an extreme posture either for or against such a view. A more reasonable approach, however, might be to seek some accommodation of clinical and managerial perspectives. Either the human-relations approach to organizational morale or the behaviorist fascination with token economies appears to offer a neutral theoretical ground for sorting out this issue.

8. Of particular use here is the multi-volume national study of family income and expenditures done by James Morgan, et. al., *Five Thousand American Families* (Ann Arbor, Mich.: Survey Research Center, 1974). See also, James Morgan, et al., *Income and Wealth in the United States* (New York: McGraw-Hill, 1963), for some related issues.

9. The key term here is "inappropriate" (see note 7). It seems naive to deny or ignore the possibility of such misuse of fees. Here as elsewhere, the manager who anticipates problems may be able to prevent their occurrence. For example, all "fee-waiver" discretions granted to staff members could be subject to peer or management review.

10. Such uncollectable accounts may well represent a true test of the altruistic goals of fee-based service programs. The knowledge that even the most hard-nosed commercial organizations have to write off some accounts as uncollectable may also be of interest here.

11. August Hollingshead and Frederick Redlich, *Social Class and Mental Illness* (New York: John Wiley, 1958).

CHAPTER 5

1. Different perspectives on this division of social work are found in Philip Klein, *Fron Philanthropy to Social Welfare* (San Francisco: Jossey Bass, 1968); Roy Lubove, *The Professional Altruist* (New York: Atheneum, 1969); and Steven J. Diner, "Scholarship in Quest of Social Welfare: A Fifty-Year History of the *Social Service Review*," *Social Service Review*, 51 (1977): 1–66.

2. The term "fund-raising" is frequently used in the voluntary sector only to refer to the particular form of fund-raising discussed in this chapter, that is as contributory campaigns or fund drives. This restricted usage is logically and theoretically unsupported today, when funds are "raised" in several different ways through fees, as well as drives, grants, and special events. The more generic usage employed here is to be preferred.

3. The third component of the standard trilogy of organizing such a federated

funding mechanism is a "planning committee." Since about the turn of the century, planning directed at both defining problems and rationalizing allocations has been a correlate of fund-raising and allocation in this type of operation.

4. Charles S. Levy, *Education and Training for the Fund Raising Function* (New York: Bureau for Careers in Jewish Service, 1973). Levy notes that "not a single article appeared on this subject in *Social Work* between January, 1966. . . and December, 1971. Neither has any article on the subject of fund-raising been included in the *Journal of Education for Social Work*, the publication of the Council on Social Work Education, since it first appeared in Spring, 1965."

5. See six articles on this topic in "Symposium on Management in the Third Sector," *Public Administration Review*, 35 (1975): 443–77. Michael McGill and Leland Wooten, "Management in the Third Sector," *Public Administration Review* 35 [1975]: (444–55) presents a detailed review of the problems alluded to here.

6. "Special Events" is used here to refer to two distinct sets of activities: direct appeals for funds, such as benefits, in which the major concern is the funds raised; and other events, in which other purposes, such as rewarding volunteers for their efforts, may be uppermost in importance.

7. Many economists would no doubt assume that such activity is economic exchange in a theoretically meaningful sense. See, however, Kenneth Boulding, *The Economics of Love and Fear* (Belmont, Calif.: Wadsworth, 1973).

8. For an account of this "movement" see Lubove, *The Professional Altruist*, pp. 157–224.

9. Those who doubt this statement should read, for example, John Dawson, "Community Chests and War Chests," *Social Work Yearbook* (New York: National Association of Social Workers, 1945), pp. 84–92.

10. United Way of America, national representative for the community-level United Way organizations, estimates that there were over 2000 such local funds in 1979.

11. Irving R. Warner, *The Art of Fund Raising* (New York: Harper and Row, 1975), pp. 24–25.

12. Warner, *Art of Fund Raising*, p. 25; Gerald Soroker, *Fund Raising for Philanthropy* (Pittsburgh: Jewish Publication and Education Foundation, 1974), p. 178; Harold J. Seymour, *Designs for Fund Raising: Principles, Patterns and Techniques* (New York: McGraw-Hill, 1966), pp. 42–43.

13. See, for example, Warner, *Art of Fund Raising*; Soroker, *Fund Raising for Philanthropy*; or Seymour, *Designs for Fund-Raising*.

14. See the sources in note 12, as well as Levy, *Education and Training for the Fund Raising Function*, for extensive suggestions for training volunteers.

15. Levy, *Education and Training for the Fund Raising Function*, p. 77.

16. In this he follows Herbert Simon, *Administrative Behavior* 3rd ed. (New York: Free Press, 1976), who noted the tendency of such "principles" to be mutually contradictory (see esp. Chapter 2, "Some Problems of Administrative Theory," pp. 20–44.)

17. Levy, *Education and Training for the Fund Raising Function*, pp. 24, 25, 24, 39.

18. Ibid., pp. 33, 26, 29, 39.

19. Ibid., pp. 34, 40, 39, 28.

20. Ibid., pp. 29, 43, 31, 39, 44, 34, 33.

21. Ibid., p. 66.

22. For example, a national organization, the National Association of Fund-Raising Counsels, speaks for fund raisers, and has produced a code of ethics for fund-raising.

23. This practice seems to be the most explicit and operationally defined in fund-raising ethics.

24. David M. Church, Foreword to Edwin Liebert and Bernice Sheldon, *Handbook of Special Events for Non Profit Organizations* (New York: Association Press, 1972), p. 5.

25. Liebert, *Handbook of Special Events*, p. 26.

26. National Health Association and National Social Welfare Assembly, *Standards of Accounting and Financial Reporting for Voluntary Health and Welfare Organizations* (New York: The Association, 1964), p. 32.

27. Ibid., p. 34.

28. Newspaper exposés of such charlatanry have become somewhat less common in recent years—perhaps because of increased scrutiny of fund-raising by the Internal Revenue Service and other federal, state, and local government agencies.

CHAPTER 6

1. The approach taken here that resources which are in short supply create a logical necessity for choosing among alternative courses of action is a familiar one in contemporaty economics. It is also receiving new consideration in social welfare following a long series of arguments (from Simon Patten to Gunnar Myrdal and beyond) that the age of abundance has replaced the age of scarcity. The key point here, however, is that fund-raising techniques—from taxation to fees—seldom generate unlimited revenues, and thus administrative decisions allocating those revenues are, ordinarily, made under conditions of scarcity.

2. The "lack of fit" between fiscal and program units is one of the most basic problems in human service finance from an agency point of view.

3. This emphasis on balanced budgets is consistent with the dynamics of fund accounting outlined in Chapter 2. It places great conceptual importance on the break-even point where revenue and expenditure assumptions meet.

4. A somewhat dated but still understandable introduction to this topic is Walter Heller, "Modern Economic Policy," in his *New Dimensions of Political Economy* (New York: Norton, 1967), pp. 58–116.

5. In Chapter 2, two types of financial statements—statements of position and statements of activity—are discussed. The former are cross-sectional reports of financial condition on a given date, while the latter are reports of activity during a given period of time.

6. There are no satisfactory general discussions of the adaptation of capital-budgeting techniques to the human service context. The subject is introduced in Chapter 10.

7. Roger A. Lohmann, *Variations in the Adequacy of Old Age Assistance in the United States* (Ann Arbor, Mich.: University of Microfilms, 1974), pp. 99–109.

8. Such summary budgets often serve legal, as well as fiscal, purposes, and constitute in some respects a "contractual" agreement with agencies to fund them at agreed-upon levels.

9. For a schematic presentation of the full federal budget cycle, see Aaron Wildavsky, *The Politics of the Budgetary Process*, 2nd ed. (Boston: Little, Brown, 1974), pp. 241–50.

10. On the significance of the increment, see Wildavsky, *Politics of the Budgetary Process*, pp. 13–18. See also David Braybrooke and Charles Lindblom, *A Strategy of Decision* (New York: Free Press, 1963) for a basic discussion of this issue.

11. See, for example, the articles in Fremont Lyden and Ernest Miller, *Programming, Planning, and Budgeting: A Systems Approach to Management* (Chicago: Markham, 1967), or David Novick, *Program Budgeting* (Cambridge, Mass.: Harvard University Press, 1965). Categorical grants represent (from the recipient's perspective) examples of the problems of zero-sum approaches to allocations.

12. For a brief history of the emergence of budgets in American government see Allen Schick, "The Road to PPB: The Stages of Budget Reform" (reprinted in Lyden, *Programming, Planning, and Budgeting*, pp. 26–52).

13. In states with particularly weak governorships, effective control of the state budget may still rest with a legislative budget commission. See G. Theodore Mitau, *State and Local Government, Politics and Processes* (New York: Charles Scribner's Sons, 1966), pp. 612–15 for discussion of this point. See also Ira Sharkansky, "Taxing and Spending in State and Local Governments," *The Politics of Taxing and Spending* (Indianapolis: Bobbs Merrill, 1969), pp. 83–142.

14. Francis E. Rourke, *Bureaucratic Power in National Politics*, 2nd ed. (Boston: Little, Brown, 1974).

15. A high percentage of non-social insurance trust fund expenditures by HEW are "intergovernmental transfers" to the states and localities.

16. Indeed, most analyses of revenue sharing have found remarkably little effect upon local human services.

17. In a number of accidental sample surveys I conducted among social work students at the University of Tennessee, for example, I found that the vast majority were unaware of the state role in passing through and contributing to Title XX in 1974–77.

18. Those who are not familiar with this distinction should see Philip Selznick, *TVA and the Grassroots* (New York: Harper and Row, 1966), pp. 251–52; and J. M. Pfiffner and Frank Sherwood, *Administrative Organization* (Englewood Cliffs, N.J.: Prentice-Hall, 1960). For an approach that virtually

eliminates the formal organization, see Anselm Strauss, et al., "The Hospital and Its Negotiated Order," in *The Hospital in Modern Society*, ed. Eliot Friedson (New York: Free Press, 1963), pp. 147-69.

19. Wildavsky, "Strategies," *Politics of the Budgetary Process*, pp. 63-123.

20. The term "distribution" is chosen here to accentuate the difference between the activites of legislative bodies and the subsequent actions of administrative agencies whose allocational efforts are conditioned both by legislative mandates and by the demand for funds from their constituencies.

21. See, for example, Albert Hyde and Jay Shafritz, *Government Budgeting: Theory, Process, Politics* (Oak Park, Ill.: Moore Publishing, 1978).

22. Theodore Lowi, *The End of Liberalism* (New York: Norton, 1969).

23. Wildavsky, *Politics of the Budgetary Process*, p. 37.

24. For a brief review of the development of community health and welfare councils see John Tropman, "Community Welfare Councils," *Encyclopedia of Social Work*, 16th ed., ed. Robert Morris (New York: National Association of Social Workers, 1970), pp. 150-56.

25. The United Way of America has produced a number of publications in financial management. See especially the United Way of America, *Accounting and Financial Reporting* (Alexandria, Va.: United Way, 1974): and United Way of America, *Budgeting* (Alexandria, Va.: United Way, 1975).

26. The rush toward public funding among voluntary agencies raises serious questions about the future of the voluntary sector. A "law" that states that the freedom and effectiveness of social action or advocacy are in inverse proportion to the amount of public fun ls received has even been proposed, by Gordon Masner, "Further Thoughts on the Purchase of Services," *Social Casework* 55 (1974), pp. 421-24.

27. Notably, the index of the 1967 publication of the American Academy of Arts and Sciences on this subject contains no references to social welfare or human services. See Warren Weaver, ed. U.S. Philanthropic Foundations: Their History, Structure, Management and Record (New York: Harper and Row, 1967).

28. See "Budgeting: Legislative Dimensions," in Hyde, *Government Budgeting*, pp. 324-412.

29. In such cases, the problem of budget-making corresponds more closely to that found in business than to the kinds of budget systems discussed previously. However, non-profit sources appear genuinely reticent to acknowledge this similarity.

30. V. O. Key Jr., "The Lack of a Budgetary Theory," *American Political Science Review* 34 (1940): pp. 1137-40.

31. The earliest contribution to the theory base is Robert Dahl and Charles Lindblom, *Politics, Economics, and Welfare* (New York: Harper and Row, 1953); Its most elegant expression is to be found in Lindblom, *A Strategy of Decision. In The Intelligence of Democracy* (New York: Free Press, 1965), Charles Lindblom fits the incremental model to national policy-making in American history. Most students of human services organizations are only

familiar with Lindblom's widely reprinted, "The Science of Muddling Through," *Public Administration Review* 19 (1959), pp. 79–88. The title of this essay, together with its somewhat convoluted style, may have contributed to part of the general lack of clarity on this subject.

32. Criticisms of incrementalism abound. Two of the most informed and thought-provoking are to be found in Amitai Etzioni, *The Active Society* (New York: Free Press, 1968), pp. 282–304; and Yehezekel Dror, *Public Policy-Making Revisited* (San Francisco: Chandler, 1968).

33. A ready distinction can be made between incrementalism as a theory of *choice* (or decision theory) in which the primary issue is how one approaches evaluative issues of judgement in a rational manner, and incrementalism as a theory of *change* in which the primary issue involves the degree, type, and circumstances of change. The central focus of incrementalism in *The Strategy of Decision* is on the choice issue, and the Braybrooke-Lindbloom argument presented there blends with certain major themes in pragmatic, existential and phenomenological philosophic traditions, as well as contemporary social psychology. By contrast, the tie made by these authors between choice and change (see pp. 66–71) is less than completely convincing. However, if Dror and Etzioni are setting themselves up as proponents of "revolutionary" or thorough-going change, their own positions are equally unclear. One likely explanation, it would appear, is that most ordinary social relations, including those occurring in administered organizations, do indeed fall into the incremental model when viewed from a participant perspective. One is hard pressed, for example, even in the case of the Russian, French, or Chinese Revolutions, to identify the one all-or-nothing decision that by itself brought the changes. Instead, what one sees among revolutionary leaders, as among other leaders, is the kind of partial, remedial, cumulative decision-style set forth by Braybrooke and Lindblom.

34. In some respects, Wildavsky's position and the reactions to it are more directly related to the debate between "rationalist" and "behaviorist" positions among political scientists than they are to the incrementalism debate in the policy sciences generally.

35. The "satisficing" approach of Herbert Simon (*Administrative Behavior*, 3rd ed. [New York: Free Press,] pp. 240–44) covers some of the same ground as incrementalism but is a much less general position. In particular, "satisficing" is genuinely unclear in its descriptive and prescriptive elements: granted, some decision makers do opt for the first acceptable alternative. In so doing, are they demonstrating desirable or undesirable behavior patterns? In other words, does this observation translate into any moral prescriptions applicable to all decisions? Many of Braybrooke's contributions to *A Strategy of Decision* address this very issue.

36. See, for example, Everett Rogers and F. Floyd Shoemaker, *Communication of Innovations* (New York: Free Press, 1971), pp. 320–46.

37. An unexamined issue in this area involves the implications of traditional "nature-nurture" debates in psychology for decision-making. Is incrementalism

a natural human response to conditions of uncertainty, a cultural product of the deterioration of traditional western rationalism, or a learned response to situations that are in some way strange, perplexing, and confusing?

38. W. I. Thomas, "Situational Analysis," *Thomas on Social Organization and Personality* (Chicago: University of Chicago Press, 1966), pp. 154–67.

39. The critical point here is that "success" in budget making is partly dependent upon those making the determination, as well as the convergence between the perspectives of observers and actors.

40. A partial history of federal experience with performance budgeting is "The Road to PBB."

41. John F. Due, *Government Finance: An Economic Analysis*, 3rd ed. (Homewood, Ill.: Richard D. Irwin, 1963), p. 62.

42. Carl S. Shoup, *Public Finance* (Chicago: Aldine, 1969), p. 62.

43. Due, *Government Finance*, p. 62.

44. Shoup, *Public Finance*, p. 62.

45. Due, *Government Finance*, p. 62.

47. An especially problematic aspect of this issue is the reconciling of similar (and different) goals and objectives in "programs" that transcend organizational units.

47. This may also be due to increased general awareness of "resource allocation" as an important facet of planning. See, for example, John Friedmann, *Retracking America: A Theory of Transactive Planning* (New York: Doubleday, 1972).

48. United Way of America, "Introduction to UWASIS II," *UWASIS II: A Taxonomy of Social Goals and Human Service Programs* (Alexandria, Va.: United Way, 1976), pp. 5–13.

49. Graeme M. Taylor, "Introduction to Zero-Base Budgeting," *The Bureaucrat* 6, no. 1 (1977): 33–55; U.S. Office of Management and Budget, "Zero Base Budgeting," *OMB Bulletin* 77–9 (April 19, 1977): 77–79. Robert N. Anthony, "Zero Base Budgeting is a Fraud," *Wall Street Journal* (April 27, 1977): U.S., Congress, House, Committee of the Budget, *Testimony on Zero Base Budgeting*, prepared for the Task Force on the Budget Process by Peter A. Phyrr, 93rd Cong., 2nd sess. July 27, 1976. All of these sources, as well as articles on applications of ZBB in New Mexico, New Jersey, and Wilmington, Del., are reprinted in *Government Budgeting*, pp. 218–324. See also Peter A. Phyrr, *Zero Base Budgeting* (New York: John Wiley, 1973).

50. Peter Phyrr, "The Zero-Base Approach to Governmental Budgeting," *Public Administration Review* 37 (1977), p. 2.

CHAPTER 7

1. Generally, the issues raised in this chapter are concerned with "rhetoric," or the relationship between the formats and organization of information in budgetary documents and the effectiveness of negotiations and outcomes. This topic has often been ignored or treated as self-evident in the literature.

2. It is suggested here that the principal reason this topic has been ignored in the human services literature is that no professional or paraprofessional group, special interest or other entity, has assumed responsibility for it (in the way accountants assume professional responsibility for the format of financial statements).

3. In one of the earliest efforts to provide management information in the human services, the Office of Economic Opportunity in 1967 began collecting quarterly data from all community action agencies. The format used often meant agency submissions of dozens of pages of forms—many with a single entry (or no entry at all) per page.

4. Federal grants typically specify starting and ending points. Management problems arise, however, when these dates are inconsistent with the planning assumptions or contractual obligations of the agency.

5. The exact point at which such adjustments become advisable in human services budget making is largely a matter of managerial judgement. A major factor in such judgements is the "time horizon" of consequences deriving from a decision. If all allocations are for current liabilities and are to be expended in the present fiscal period, there is less reason for concern about long-term indebtedness.

6. Unit-cost budgets, where they are available, considerably simplify this task. Unfortunately, unit-cost approaches are used in only a very few human service contexts at present. Most "needs-assessment" approaches in setting up client budgets in public welfare, for example, are in reality unit-cost budgets, with fixed amounts of allowable expenditures in given categories. Some federal day care funds are allocated to agencies on a unit-cost basis of dollars per child per month.

7. The principal limitation on the use of this approach in human services has been the selection of non-comparable units of analysis. For example, cost-per-client contact is a notoriously variable measure, since needs may vary with the individual client, and the length of contact (and as a result, the resources devoted to the client) may also vary from a few minutes to entire days. In this context, the Hill-Ormsby Time Study method, essentially an historical-comparative approach to examining the previous pattern of actual performance in order to establish norms or standards for the present and future, is subject to sudden (and unnoticed) obsolescence as changes occur in the way the agency delivers service. Periodic repetition of the time study, therefore, is essential to the validity of this approach. By contrast, the usual approach in business has been simply to define "objective" units of analysis (linked to production outputs) and rely upon face value. No similiar approaches, which appear on their face to be valid, have been put forth for the human services. (Nearly universal acceptance is critical to this approach).

CHAPTER 8

1. Shiela Kamerman, "A Paradigm for Programming," *Social Service Review* 49 (1975), pp. 412–20.

CHAPTER 9

1. Office of Economic Opportunity, *Financial Handbook for Community Action Agencies* (Washington, D.C.: G.P.O., 1966).
2. See, for example, the "Affirmative Action Budget" discussion in Chapter 7.
3. FIFO (First In-First Out) and LIFO (Last In-First Out) are standard inventory procedures also discussed later in this chapter. The point here is that "inventorying" human beings is neither possible nor morally acceptable.
4. Harold Koonz and Cyril O'Donnell, *Essentials of Management* (New York: McGraw Hill, 1974), pp. 367–69.

CHAPTER 10

1. Robert Morris and Robert Binstock, *Feasible Planning for Social Change* (New York: Columbia University Press, 1967), p. 28.
2. "Costing out" social problems here refers to efforts to determine the total outlays necessary to adequately resolve a social problem. A "net-cost" method of this type would involve subtracting appropriate current "problem-maintenance" outlays from the total figure to reach an adjusted amount of additional expenditures necessary.
3. For the ramifications of the distinction between "client group" and client population" see Janel Reiner, Everett Reimer, and Thomas Reiner, "Client Analysis in Social Planning," *Urban Planning and Social Policy*, ed. Robert Morris and Bernard Friedan (New York: Basic Books, 1970).
4. J. Fred Weston and Eugene Brigham, *Managerial Finance*, 4th ed. (Homewood, Ill.: Dryden, 1972), p. 139.
5. At a more technical level, long-term debt in not-for-profit organizations is unjustified in that it cannot in principle be secured. The agency, unlike a firm, has no capital base, and security is a year-to-year arrangement, grounded in current assets only. This is a subject which warrants further investigation by those interested in the management of human services. Several "decision rules," however, are likely: (1) funds should be available for relatively long periods of time (thirty days or more). (2) Great care should go into the investigation of sources of investment. Ordinarily, federally-insured deposits (FDIC or FSLIC) are the most evident. (3) Such actions should be "open," and, certainly, board officers should be kept informed. The most obvious rule of all is that all income generated in this way reverts to the agency and not to private persons.

CHAPTER 11

1. From an evaluation research standpoint, the merger of fiscal and program measurement, it should be noted, has aroused almost no interest. One might conclude from this that management perspectives on evaluation have not yet been fully accommodated in evaluation research.
2. By taking a skeptical stance toward economic measurement as unduly

concerned with efficiency, many in human services have simply failed to perceive that other fiscal objectives are also involved in such questions.

3. George Homans, *Social Behavior: Elementary Forms*, 2nd ed. (New York: Harcourt, 1974).

4. By contrast, most practitioners in the human services take for granted that the "true meaning" of human activity is to be found in its socio-emotional contents—a stance conspicuously lacking in fiscal and economic referents.

5. Roland McKean, "Costs and Benefits from Different Viewpoints," *Planning, Programming, Budgeting: A Systems Approach to Management*, ed. Fremont Lyden and Ernest Miller (Chicago: Markham, 1967), pp. 199-220, accommodates both perspectives.

6. Gene Fisher, "The Role of Cost-Utility Analysis in Program Budgeting," *Program Budgeting*, ed. David Novick (Cambridge, Mass.: Harvard University Press, 1965), pp. 61-78.

7. One of the most formidable problems is reaching a consensus on terms and definitions. In principle, however, measurement of both costs (in the sense of opportunity costs) and benefits (in the sense of advantages gained) outside an economic context is conceivable. Sociological exchange theory represents one approach to this subject.

8. See, for example, Roger Lohmann, "The Measurement of Influence in Organizations and Communities," *Sociology and Social Welfare* 5 (1978), pp. 66-90.

9. "The Role of Cost-Utility Analysis," pp. 61-78.

10. Equilibrium, for example, is far more often assumed than measured in social theory. The same might be said for personality theory.

GLOSSARY

ACCOUNTABILITY: In NON-PROFIT organizations, a legal and ethical responsibility of management to report upon and justify program performance and achievements.

ACCOUNTABILITY, COMMUNITY: That aspect of general ACCOUNTABILITY most concerned with the effectiveness and legitimacy of an agency and its programs from the viewpoint of the community.

ACCOUNTABILITY, FISCAL: Direct legal and ethical obligations for the appropriate use of FUNDS by an agency to those from whom it receives funds.

ACCOUNTABILITY, INTERNAL: Responsibility for the appropriate use of shared resources by members of an agency.

ACCOUNTING: The American Institute of Certified Public Accountants defines accounting as "the art of recording, classifying, and summarizing in a significant manner in terms of money, transactions and events which are, in part at least, of a financial character, and interpreting the results thereof."

ACCOUNTING CYCLE: The regular fiscal period of a NON-PROFIT CORPORATION between closings. Usually one year. (See also BUDGET CYCLE.)

ACCOUNTS PAYABLE: A LIABILITY account reflecting total amounts owed by the FUND to others.

ACCOUNTS PAYABLE BUDGET: A SUB-FUND BUDGET showing balance payable at the beginning of a fiscal period, expected purchases and payments during the period, and closing balance of payables.

285

ACCOUNTS PAYABLE MANAGEMENT: Explicit development of a management strategy for processing payable accounts.

ACCOUNTS RECEIVABLE: An ASSET account reflecting the total amounts owed to the FUND.

ACCOUNTS RECEIVABLE BUDGET: A SUB-FUND BUDGET reflecting beginning balances of a FISCAL PERIOD, expected new receivables and collections, and expected closing balances.

ACCOUNTS RECEIVABLE MANAGEMENT: Explicit development of a management strategy for processing payable accounts.

ACCRUAL ACCOUNTING: An ACCOUNTING system increasingly common among human service agencies. Transactions are entered as they are made, which necessitates distinguishing EXPENDITURE and cash disbursements. Accrual accounting generally results in more accurate statements of an agency's financial position than does CASH ACCOUNTING.

ADMINISTRATIVE COST BUDGET: A SUB-FUND BUDGET showing ADMINISTRATIVE COSTS. (See also OVERHEAD BUDGET.)

ADMINISTRATIVE COSTS: COSTS that are incurred from the overall direction of the organization, general record-keeping, business management, budgeting, general board activities, and related purposes (accepted definition, AICPA's *Audit*).

AFFIRMATIVE ACTION BUDGET: A type of PROFESSIONAL AND PARAPROFESSIONAL SERVICES BUDGET in which entries are categorized into Affirmative Action groupings (such as "Minorities and Women" and "Male" employees). A SUB-FUND BUDGET.

AGENCY: Non-profit organization of paid employees together with one or more FUNDS and PROGRAMS.

ALLOCATION: The act of assigning resources to an ENTITY (agency, department, program) or group of entities. In complex situations, allocation decisions can be distinguished from distribution.

APPRECIATION: An increase in the value of an ASSET over time. For example, real estate owned by an agency may appreciate steadily over the years. The opposite of depreciation.

APPROPRIATION: A term used for the public (congressional or legislative) allocation of funds to various ENTITIES. It is essentially synonymous with "budget-making" in this context, since anticipated expenditures are frequently the basis on which appropriations are made (although this need not be so).

APPROPRIATIONS SYSTEMS: PUBLIC BUDGET SYSTEMS in which membership is established by law and participation of members is assumed. (See also BASE, INCREMENT, BUDGET SYSTEMS.)

ARENA: An inter-organizational decision system. (See also BUDGET SYSTEM).

ASSETS: An ACCOUNTING term for what is owned or held by an organization and that has a money value.

AUDIT: A periodic (usually annual) investigation of the financial statements of an agency to determine the accuracy, fairness and the degree to which they adhere to standard practices of reporting and recording. An audit may be internal or external, independent or staff-directed.

AUDIT EXCEPTION: This term is used for items identified in an AUDIT report as violations of standard accounting practice. These may be technical problems only, or more serious matters of malfeasance, embezzlement, or other illegalities.

AUDIT REPORT: A written statement, following a prescribed format, and signed by an authorized accountant (A CPA or LPA) to indicate that s/he has examined the records of a particular ENTITY and finds that the accompanying financial statements are a true reflection of its financial position.

BALANCE SHEET: A financial statement designed to show the overall financial position of an agency or firm at a given moment. In commercial firms the standard format of the balance sheet is total assets = total liabilities plus total capital.

BALANCED BUDGET: A BUDGET in which the total revenues equal or are "in balance with" total expenditures.

BASE: (1) that portion of a BUDGET request to which an AGENCY is assumed by others to have a presumed or privileged claim; (2) operationally, an amount equal to last year's APPROPRIATION.

BENEFIT: That which is gained or increased by an action or transaction. An addition of something valuable or of resources.

BOND: A form of security issued by various levels of government to generate revenue over and above that raised by taxes. Bonds typically are used to finance capital construction, or other long-range, durable operating expenditures.

BONDED INDEBTEDNESS: The degree and amount of an agency's debt (liabilities) covered by BONDS. Ordinarily, in bankruptcy cases, or other liquidation proceedings, bonded indebtedness is honored prior to all other claims.

BOOKKEEPING: The task of making entries in accounting records, or "books." A paraprofessional task usually performed by clerks.

BREAK-EVEN ANALYSIS: A set of techniques for determining or projecting the fit between expenditures and revenues over time, or under various hypothetical conditions.

BREAK-EVEN POINT: Point at which INCOME or REVENUE equals EXPENDITURES.

BREAKING EVEN: The primary fiscal objective of non-profit organizations. The process of matching revenues and expenditures in a budget or in operations.

BUDGET: (1) a plan of future or anticipated activities, stated predominantly in fiscal terms; (2) a document listing words and numbers in paired sequences to reflect anticipated expenditures by category (and anticipated income, either implicitly or explicitly) for a given period of time.

BUDGET, ACCOUNTS PAYABLE: See ACCOUNTS PAYABLE BUDGET.

BUDGET, ACCOUNTS RECEIVABLE: See ACCOUNTS RECEIVABLE BUDGET.

BUDGET, ADMINISTRATIVE COST: See ADMINISTRATIVE COST BUDGET.

BUDGET, CAPITAL IMPROVEMENTS. See CAPITAL IMPROVEMENTS BUDGET.

BUDGET, COSTS OF DEBT: See COSTS OF DEBT BUDGET.

BUDGET, DEPARTMENTAL: See DEPARTMENTAL BUDGET.

BUDGET, DIRECT LABOR: See DIRECT LABOR BUDGET.

BUDGET, FUNCTIONAL: See FUNCTIONAL BUDGET.

BUDGET, INCREMENTAL: See INCREMENTAL BUDGET.

BUDGET, INTERNAL: See INTERNAL BUDGET.

BUDGET, LINE-ITEM: See LINE-ITEM BUDGET.

BUDGET, MARGINAL: See MARGINAL BUDGET.

BUDGET, OLD YEAR / NEW YEAR: See OLD YEAR / NEW YEAR TABLES.

BUDGET, PRODUCTION: PRODUCTION BUDGET.

BUDGET, PROFESSIONAL AND PARAPROFESSIONAL SERVICES: See PROFESSIONAL AND PARAPRO-
FESSIONAL SERVICES BUDGET.

BUDGET, PROGRAM: See PROGRAM BUDGET.

BUDGET, PROGRAM MATRIX: See PROGRAM MATRIX BUDGET.

BUDGET, PROJECT: See PROJECT BUDGET.

BUDGET, SOURCES OF REVENUE: See SOURCES OF REVENUE BUDGET.

BUDGET, SUPPLIES: See SUPPLIES BUDGET.

BUDGET, UNIT COST: See UNIT COST BUDGET.

BUDGET, ZERO-BASED: See ZERO-BASED BUDGET.

BUDGET ANALYSIS: Process of examining items in a budget, and constructing or reconstructing BUDGET documents. (See also BUDGET MAKING.)

BUDGET CYCLE: A sequence of events usually incorporating a request, publication, or circulation of criteria or guidelines; deadlines; formal presentations; BUDGET ANALYSIS; and decisions. (See also ACCOUNTING CYCLE.)

BUDGET ENTITY: FUND for which a budget is prepared and organized. May or may not be a meaningful PROGRAM unit.

BUDGET FORMAT: Rules for organizing the information contained in BUDGETS. (See also FUND BUDGETS, SUB-FUND BUDGETS, and SUPRA-FUND BUDGETS.)

BUDGET MAKING: Interpersonal negotiations and decision-making that convert BUDGET documents and decisions into authoritative controls over agency operations and staff performances.

BUDGET SYSTEM: ARENA in which the primary focus of decision-making is on BUDGET MAKING.

BUDGET WORKSHEET: See CONSOLIDATED BUDGET WORKSHEET.

BUDGETARY PROCESS: See BUDGET CYCLE.

BUDGETING: The phase of financial management concerned with preparing a detailed plan for the future expenditure of organizational funds in a manner designed to coordinate effort, maximize efficient use of resources, and attain goals. Incorporates BUDGET ANALYSIS, BUDGET MAKING.

BUDGETING, CAPITAL: See CAPITAL BUDGETING.

BUDGETING, PROGRAMMING, PLANNING SYSTEM: See PROGRAMMING PLANNING BUDGETING SYSTEM.

CAPITAL BUDGETING: A plan for the future generation and expenditure of capital (land, labor, and buildings). It is most likely to be used in human service agencies in the context of a major construction project—building or purchasing a new building, constructing a summer camp, etc.—or in the purchase of expensive equipment.

CAPITALIZATION: In non-profit settings, a term used loosely for the process of acquiring assets necessary to begin a program or service. See also SEED MONEY or FRONT MONEY.

CASH ACCOUNTING: An accounting system once prevalent among AGENCIES in the voluntary sector. Transactions are entered in JOURNALS only when cash is actually paid out or taken in. The principal virtue of cash accounting is its simplicity, although it can badly misstate an agency's financial position.

CASH FLOW: The actual movement of money payments to, through, and from an agency. This is not to be confused with income and expenditure flow, which, in an accrual based system, records not only cash but also credit transactions.

CASH FLOW ANALYSIS: A set of procedures for plotting the patterns of fluctuation in cash ASSETS at fixed intervals over an ACCOUNTING CYCLE or part of a cycle.

CATEGORICAL GRANTS: Transfer payments in consideration of some specific objectives or purposes agreed to by the grantor and the recipients (grantees). Public assistance, and most other federal programs, are categorical grants.

CONSOLIDATED BUDGET WORKSHEET: A BUDGET FORMAT for consolidating a number of BUDGETS for different FUNDS into a single, unified AGENCY perspective.

CONSTITUENCY: Aggregate of persons and organizations whose support can be depended upon or mobilized when needed, for example, at key times in the BUDGET CYCLE.

CONTRACT: Legally, an offer and an acceptance. In social work, it is a general term for an agreement between a worker and client, and in economic terms, an agreement affecting exchanges of goods and services. In recent years, the federal government has placed less emphasis on grants and more on PERFORMANCE CONTRACTS.

COST: A term with many nuances of meaning in accounting and economics. Usually, that which is given up in order to gain an objective. For most purposes, measured by EXPENDITURES or OUTLAYS. But see also OPPORTUNITY COSTS and SOCIAL COSTS.

COST ACCOUNTING: An ACCOUNTING system in which the EXPENDITURE of an AGENCY or firm is systematically related to units of production output.

COST ANALYSIS: An analytic method used in planning and evaluation in which COSTS are identified and systematically associated with line items, cost centers, or other significant or meaningful categories.

COST-BENEFIT ANALYSIS: A set of analytical procedures for determining the ratio of COSTS to BENEFITS, both measured in monetary units. See also COST-EFFECTIVENESS ANALYSIS.

COST-EFFECTIVENESS ANALYSIS: Procedures for determining the COST of a unit of effective service delivery or other output.

COST CONTROL POLICIES AND PROCEDURES: Usually, rules intended to reduce or constrict the volume of total EXPENDITURES.

COSTING SOCIAL PROBLEMS: Estimating the total COST of a program or strategy necessary to fully resolve or handle a set of problems.

COST-OF-DEBT BUDGET: Estimates of the current EXPENDITURES to be incurred in the present BUDGET PERIOD for long-term obligations. (SUB-FUND BUDGET.)

COST-PLUS: A method of contracting sometimes used by governments (particularly the federal) in PERFORMANCE CONTRACTS. It usually allows the contractor to charge for the actual cost of goods or services supplied, plus a fixed percentage or agreed-upon amount for services rendered.

COST, BUDGET UNIT: See UNIT-COST BUDGET.

COST, FUND-RAISING: See FUND-RAISING COST.

COSTS, OPPORTUNITY: See OPPORTUNITY COSTS.

COSTS, SOCIAL: See SOCIAL COSTS.

CREDIT: (1) granting the use or possession of goods and services; (2) granting the use or possession of goods and services without immediate payment (human services agencies may incidentally use credit, in this sense, to purchase incidentals, such as office supplies and food stuffs); (3) the right side of a ledger account. Generally, credit entries increase the balance of liabilities and equity accounts, and decrease the balance of asset, income, and expenditure accounts. Debit entries have the opposite effect.

CREDIT, LINES: See LINES OF CREDIT.

CRITICAL PATH ANALYSIS: A form of solution to a PERT (Program, Evaluation, and Review Technique) problem, in which the least costly sequence of project activities is located by plotting paths of sequential events and activities, and selecting the longest necessary completion path. Other sequences are then fitted to this critical path in a manner designed to minimize inactivity and reduce costs.

CURRENT GENERAL FUNDS: The net amount of unrestricted contributions, requests, grants or revenue remaining, and future expenditure. (Accepted definition, AICPA's *Audits.*)

CURRENT LIABILITIES: Those liabilities due and payable during the present period. In human service organizations, most liabilities are of this type. See also LONG-TERM LIABILITIES.

CURRENT RESTRICTED FUNDS: "Gifts and grants expendable only for purposes specified by donor or grantor. . . . Income from temporary investments of restricted funds, unless permitted by law to be used for general purposes . . . [and] income from funds, the principle of which is not expendable and the income of which is expendable for donor-specified purposes only" (AICPA's *Audits*).

DEBIT: The left side of a ledger account. The term has no other consistent meaning. A debit represents an increase or a decrease in the account, depending on its location. (See also CREDIT.)

DEBT MANAGEMENT: That aspect of FINANCIAL MANAGEMENT concerned with the tasks incidental to the processing or handling of an agency's DEBT.

DECISION-MAKING: Deliberate, intentional choice, particularly between a range of identified alternatives.

DECISION-MODELS OF BUDGET SYSTEMS: General or theoretical models of BUDGET SYSTEMS which focus primarily upon characteristic or critical decisions. (See INCREMENTAL BUDGET; PERFORMANCE BUDGET; PROGRAM BUDGET; PROGRAMMING-PLANNING-BUDGETING SYSTEMS; ZERO-BASED BUDGET.)

DEFICIT: A financial condition in which EXPENDITURES exceed INCOME during a FISCAL PERIOD. The ability of NON-PROFIT organizations to sustain deficits is very limited, and wholly dependent upon the extent of their RESERVES.

DEFICIT SPENDING: EXPENDITURES in excess of REVENUES.

DEPOSITS: (1) Money placed in a bank account, and constituting a claim upon the bank. (2) The act of entering money into a bank account.

DEPOSIT TICKET: A receipt customarily given by banks as evidence of a deposit. Such receipts should be kept as documentation of JOURNAL entries of bank deposits.

DEPRECIATION: A decrease in the value of an ASSET over time.

DIRECT COSTS: COSTS that vary directly with the output of an agency or program. Also known as variable costs.

DIRECT LABOR BUDGET: A SUB-FUND corrollary of the UNIT-COST BUDGET that projects personnel costs of service by identifying the "direct labor" content of producing a unit of service.

DONOR CONSTITUENCY: The aggregate of persons and organizations that demonstrate their support for a NON-PROFIT organization through financial contributions.

DOUBLE-ENTRY BOOKKEEPING: A system of financial record-keeping in which every transaction is recorded twice—once as a debit and once as a credit. Typically, the system of accounts in a double-entry set-up would include ASSETS, LIABILITIES, FUND-BALANCE (or surplus or capital), INCOME, and EXPENDITURES categories.

EARMARKINGS: A jargon term for the process of designating REVENUES for certain specific purposes. (The term itself is traceable to the practices of livestock sorting pens, in which animals are sorted into different groups and classes by dye marks on their ears.)

EARNINGS: Money payments to agency employees for work performed.

ECONOMIES OF SCALE: A term used to describe the tendency of certain costs of producing goods and services to increase less than proportionately with output. For example, an under-utilized therapist could increase his total caseload from ten to twenty—thus effectively doubling his production of service with no increase in cost.

EFFECTIVENESS: A measure of the achievement or attainment of goals basic to the determination of efficiency. To the extent that a program fails to accomplish its objectives, there is little, if any, basis for establishing its efficiency.

EFFICIENCY: A criterion of performance in the production of goods and services in which the solution or strategy chosen involves the least expenditure of resources necessary for goal attainment.

ENTITY: See BUDGET ENTITY.

EQUITY: (1) A principle in taxation—taxes should be levied so that the tax burden is distributed evenly or fairly among those being taxed. (2) In business, the residual value of assets after non-shareholder liabilities are satisfied. Since it is related to the investment and gains of stockholders (of which there ordinarily are none in human service agencies) the term has little application in this second sense to our concerns.

EVALUATION: After the fact, retrospective assessment and critical analysis of the worthwhileness of PROGRAM or service activities.

EXCEPTIONS, PRINCIPLE OF: See PRINCIPLE OF EXCEPTIONS.

EXPENDITURE: An OUTLAY or commitment of an organization's resources. Usually recorded in the ACCOUNTING system as a reduction of assets or as a LIABILITY.

EXPENDITURE CONTROL: One of a number of possible management control strategies, in which an effort is made to restrict or eliminate those activities that result in OUTLAYS beyond a determined level.

EXPENDITURE STATEMENT: A listing of the total expenditures in a given period, usually organized by a program, function, or other rational scheme. Also known as an expense statement for non-profit agencies, it may be combined with another statement into a single statement (sometimes mistakenly called a "budget.")

EXTERNAL AUDIT: An audit by an outside auditor, usually someone with professional accounting credentials (a CPA or LPA). Two types of external audits are of greatest interest in the human services—independent audits, required by many state not-for-profit legislation, and audits by a grantor or funding source.

FAIR-SHARE-OF-COST FEES: Charges to clients based upon a "fair" method of allocating all OUTLAYS proportionately to all who benefit.

FEASIBILITY STUDIES: Assessment of the opportunity costs of a proposed solution to a problem.

FEE BUDGET SYSTEM: One of the major types of BUDGET SYSTEM in which the primary concern is with an INTERNAL BUDGET that predicts the effects of fee income on program actions.

FEEDBACK, PRINCIPLE OF: See PRINCIPLE OF FEEDBACK.

FEES: Money payments collected from clients, significant others and "third party" payees. (See also PARTICIPATION FEES; FLAT RATE FEES; SLIDING SCALE FEES; FAIR-SHARE-OF-COST FEES; THIRD-PARTY FEES.)

F.I.F.O.: First In, First Out. A system of inventory in which items are circulated so that the "First In" are also the "First Out."

FINANCIAL INTERMEDIARIES: Also known as "fiscal intermediaries," or "third-party funding." Private organizations such as Blue Cross–Blue Shield, for example, act as fiscal intermediaries in the medicaid program.

FINANCIAL MANAGEMENT: In NON-PROFIT human service agencies, the control and intentional use of money and other scarce resources to further organizational goals consistent with law, ethics, and community standards.

FINANCIAL PLANNING: Preparing a set of financial decisions for action in the future that are directed at achieving program goals with special attention to financial means.

FINANCIAL RATIOS: Specific standardized statements of the relationship between two variables or factors that are useful for analytic or decision-making purposes.

FISCAL CONTROL: A system of rules, criteria, understandings, and contracts, designed to exercise control over the handling of the ASSETS of a FUND.

FIXED ASSETS: Those assets, such as land or buildings, that are not ordinarily susceptible to sudden or drastic fluctuations in either quantity or value.

FIXED CHARGES: A standard or universal fee assessed clients or users of a service, regardless of other criteria, such as age, sex, "need," or ability to pay.

FIXED COST: A cost that does not vary, in the short run, with variations in output. Fixed costs are ordinarily those that will be borne by an agency even when it will not bear outputs.

FLAT RATE FEES: Charges to clients established at a fixed rate that is assessed to all who receive similar services.

FLEXIBILITY, PRINCIPLE OF: See PRINCIPLE OF FLEXIBILITY.

FLEXIBLE BUDGET: A budget based on different levels of anticipated activity, e.g., a plan of agency activity with and without a major demonstration grant.

FLOATING DEBT: A short-term (or non-funded) debt, as opposed to a funded debt, which is secured by bonds or other securities.

FRONT MONEY: See SEED MONEY.

FUNCTIONAL BUDGET: Expenditure items are categorized by "functional" categories such as personnel, supplies, or travel.

FUND: A fund is an asset or group of assets, together with associated account-abilities (liabilities and equities), that are related to an activity or purpose and maintained as an accounting entity (AICPA definition).

FUND ACCOUNTING: The system of accrual accounting in which acounting records are maintained by funds. Most governments use this system. Multi-funded agencies in the human services often maintain a separate fund for each major grant or funding source.

FUND BUDGETS: Budget documents formulated to guide or assist in FUND DECISIONS.

FUND DECISIONS: Budgetary decisions affecting a FUND as a whole.

FUND DRIVES: See CAMPAIGNS.

FUNDED DEBT: Long-term debt secured by bonds or other securities. Generally, for long-term borrowing—to construct a new building, etc. A secured or funded debt carries lower interest and is less expensive than a floating debt.

FUND-RAISING: Administrative process of identifying, soliciting, and obtaining needed income or revenue through GRANTS, FEES, or other means.

FUND-RAISING AGENT: A staff member or representative of a non-profit organization whose responsibility is to engage in fund-raising activities, especially GRANTSMANSHIP, appeals to large donors, or BUDGET-MAKING.

GRANTOR AUDIT: The solicitor general, the office of management and budget, and some grantor departments in the federal government may conduct periodic audits of agencies. Also, other grantors may conduct audits of the financial records of recipients.

GRANTS: Unilateral transfer payments from one government, foundation, or agency to another agency or program, usually in support of service delivery or some other activity. Two principle types of grants are found in the human services: categorical and non-categorical. See also CONTRACTS.

GRANTSMANSHIP: A jargon term for the skills involved in locating money and obtaining it from sources in the form of GRANTS. A type of FUND-RAISING activity.

HUMAN CAPITAL: A term used to designate the skills and abilities possessed by persons that permit them to earn an income.

HUMAN SERVICES: Services and programs directed at contributions to the socialization and development of persons; social care for those incapable of full autonomy; counseling and guidance; support of self-help and mutual-aid activities; and the planning, organizing, financing, evaluation, and dissemination of information about such activities.

INCOME: Generally, income is the flow of money or goods to an individual, firm or agency. It is distinguishable from REVENUE, which is only the money portion of income. However, in most non-profit human service usages, the two terms are usually interchangeable.

INCOME STATEMENT: A basic financial statement designed to list the basic sources of income (or revenue) of an agency. Depending on the purposes of the statement, its audience, etc., listings may be by program, type of income (e.g., fees and grants), and so forth. Since 1974, the AICPA's *Audit* has endorsed the incorporation of income, or operating statements, into a single generic "statement of support, revenue and expenses, and changes in fund balances." In all likelihood, many agencies will continue to use separate income statements for some time, despite the AICPA position. This new format appears to be a significant technical advance in program budgeting.

INCREMENTAL BUDGETING: An historical method of BUDGET MAKING in which a BASE of funding established previously is assumed, and decisions are addressed to the size of an increment or increase. (Same as MARGINAL BUDGET.)

INDEPENDENT AUDIT: An audit made by an accountant or accounting firm specializing in such investigations. Usually a third party. The audit report of an independent audit may be legally required to be available to the public.

INDIVIDUALITY, PRINCIPLE OF: See PRINCIPLE OF INDIVIDUALITY.

INPUT-OUTPUT ANALYSIS: A type of inductive, empirical economics created by Wassily Leontief, in which the final outputs of goods and services to consumers are related to the intermediary and initial inputs.

INSURANCE: A procedure for pooling risks. The most common form is a contract to pay premiums to a company in exchange for the promise of compensation in the event of specified circumstances. Social Security is intended to be a type of social insurance.

INTERNAL AUDIT: An audit made by members of an agency's accounting staff. Often, a kind of self-study. The work of the public welfare quality control staff is an example.

INTERNAL BUDGETS: BUDGET FORMATS developed by an organization or department for internal management use only.

INVENTORY: Stocks or stores of goods used as raw materials in production, and of work in progress and finished goods. In the human services, inventories are ordinarily of two types: (1) office supplies and materials, and (2) food, clothing, linen, and other supplies incidental to feeding or clothing clients, or operating residential programs.

INVENTORY ANALYSIS: A set of techniques designed to determine optimum levels of inventories.

INVENTORY CONTROL: Procedures and rules established to maintain adequate management control over items in inventory.

INVESTMENT: (1) A sacrifice of resource in the present followed by subsequent benefits or gains. (2) An expenditure with the explicit expectation of benefit or gain.

JOURNAL: A book of original entries. In journals, every transaction is recorded when it is completed, if the agency uses accrual accounting, and when it is paid for or money is received, if the system is cash based.

LEDGER: A book of accounts. Each account in a ledger is recorded on a separate page, and summarizes a large number of journal entries. Ledger pages are ordinarily divided in half, the left recording the debits and the right the credits.

L.I.F.O.: Last In, First Out. An inventory circulation method in which the items received last go out first.

LINE-ITEM BUDGET: A budget format in which program, agency, or fund entities are summarized as a single entry or "line item." See FUND DECISIONS.

LINES OF CREDIT: Management determined EXPENDITURE guidelines or "credit limits" assigned to subordinates as part of implementation of a budget program.

MANAGEMENT: Administration. Some sources distinguish administration from management, usually suggesting that management is the narrower, more technical aspect of administration. The distinction is, however, a logical rather than an empirical difference, and is of questionable value.

MARGINAL BUDGET: See INCREMENTAL BUDGET.

MARGINAL COSTS: The change in the total costs of production resulting from an increase (or decrease) of one unit produced.

MICRO-ECONOMICS: That part of economics concerned with the study of individual decision units—consumers, households, and firms. The central concept of micro-economics is the market.

MULTI-FUNDED AGENCY: Literally, an AGENCY with more than one FUND. An AGENCY with a number of different revenue sources.

NON-CATEGORICAL GRANTS: Transfer payments, usually between levels of government, for no specific objective or use. Revenue-sharing is such a grant.

NON-PROFIT CORPORATION: Legal entity created by the state, under control of a board of directors, and forbidden by law to distribute its ASSETS as profits, gains or dividends.

OLD YEAR / NEW YEAR TABLES: Any financial report showing current items with comparable items from the preceding fiscal period for comparison.

OPERATIONS RESEARCH: An interdisciplinary field in which optimal solutions to management problems are sought. Critical path analysis, inventory analysis, linear programming, and program planning and budgeting are among the most widely known "o.r." techniques. The general model of operations research is systems analysis.

OPPORTUNITY COSTS: An approach to measuring "cost" in which value is measured in terms of the value of alternatives that must be foregone in order to achieve an objective.

OUTLAYS: An approach to measuring cost in which the cost of a commodity is defined as the expenditure of resources necessary to obtain it.

OUTPUT BUDGETING: Another term for PPBS (Program-Planning-Budgeting Systems).

PARTICIPATION FEES: Charges to clients based solely upon the fact of their participation in a service or activity.

P.A.Y.E.: "Pay As You Earn." Taxes collected by regular, periodic payroll deductions.

PAYROLL TAXES: A tax levied upon employers' wage payments. The state-federal unemployment compensation system is built upon such a tax.

PERFORMANCE BUDGET: A BUDGET FORMAT and system in which past accomplishments form the basis for decisions about future resources.

PERFORMANCE CONTRACT: An agreement between two or more parties than one or more of them will provide a service or perform some other activity in exchange for some payment or reward from the other(s).

PERSONNEL: The employees of an organization.

PERSONNEL ADMINISTRATION: The subfield of administrative science devoted to the personnel or manpower requirements of an administered organization. It is concerned with topics such as job analysis, work-load analysis, recruitment and selection of employees, career advancement and planning, and related issues. Affirmative action is largely a personnel issue.

PERT: Program Evaluation and Review Technique. A "time-budgeting" method useful in programming and project scheduling and involving many interdependent tasks.

PETTY CASH: A fixed-limit amount of cash fund available to staff members for small, non-routine, or emergency purchases. All disbursements from such a fund should be supported by petty cash vouchers and / or receipts. When the petty cash fund is exhausted the totals should be posted in the appropriate journals (with the vouchers as documentation and a check for the amount of the vouchers drawn to replenish the fund). Such a fund saves a large number of small checks and journal entries.

PHASE OUT: Controlled and sequential termination of defunded programs.

PLANNED FISCAL REORGANIZATION: Planned and intentional realignment of FUND ENTITIES.

PLANT FUNDS: Unexpended grants and appropriations held as cash or temporary investments for future purchases of plant or equipment, or the amount of equipment, buildings, and other tangible fixed assets held for use in the organization's operations.

POLICIES AND PROCEDURES REVIEW: An INTERNAL AUDIT of existing policies and procedures conducted after budget decisions have been made to assure conformity between agreements reached and existing practices.

POST BUDGET CONFERENCES: Meetings to follow up or implement budget decisions. A major feature of post-budget programming.

POSTING: A bookkeeping term to describe the process of (1) notation, or ot recording financial transactions in appropriate journals, and (2) summarizing, or recording, journal-column totals in appropriate ledger accounts.

PPBS: See PROGRAMMING-PLANNING-BUDGETING SYSTEMS.

PRINCIPLE OF EFFICIENCY: One of the principles of fiscal control in NON-PROFIT organizations, in which costs of rule-breaking are compared to costs of control necessary to eliminate rule-breaking.

PRINCIPLE OF ENFORCEMENT: A principle of fiscal control in NON-PROFIT agencies that says that rules must be enforcable.

PRINCIPLE OF EXCEPTIONS: The concept of MANAGEMENT BY EXCEPTIONS applied to the context of fiscal control.

PRINCIPLE OF FEEDBACK: A principle of fiscal control that says that systems of rules should be subject to change, based on information about their impact.

PRINCIPLE OF INDIVIDUALITY: A principle of fiscal control in NON-PROFIT organizations that says that rules of control must be tailored to the individual circumstances of the organization.

PRINCIPLE OF MEANING: A principle of fiscal control that states that rules must be meaningful to those who are expected to comply.

PRINCIPLE OF PRODUCTIVITY: A principle of fiscal control that states that the goals of service delivery should supercede the goals of fiscal control, all other things being equal.

PRINCIPLE OF REPORTABILITY: A principle of fiscal control concerned with specification of procedures for reporting or discerning rule violations.

PROBLEM-FREE INTERVAL: Period when a client is not troubled by a problem for which assistance is sought.

PRODUCTION BUDGET: A BUDGET FORMAT in which sales of goods during a period are combined with beginning and ending inventories to determine necessary production levels.

PRODUCTIVITY: The measure of the "productiveness" of a factor of production. Operationally, the ratio of the amount of input required to produce a given amount of output.

PRODUCTIVITY, PRINCIPLE OF: See PRINCIPLE OF PRODUCTIVITY.

PROFESSIONAL AND PARAPROFESSIONAL SERVICES BUDGET: A BUDGET FORMAT listing total costs of program personnel.

PROGRAM: An interrelated set of activities for the production of services.

PROGRAMMING: Process in which agency and program administrators seek to translate program goals and budget guidelines into meaningful work routines that will result in the production of services.

PROGRAM BUDGET: BUDGET FORMAT that assumes convergence of a program of activities with a FUND.

PROGRAM BUDGETING: A BUDGET SYSTEM in which decisions are based upon performance or expectations of integrated PROGRAMS of activities.

PROGRAMMING-PLANNING-BUDGETING SYSTEMS: A particular model of program budgeting in which decisions are ZERO SUM and based on program units that transcend organizational boundaries.

PROGRAM MATRIX BUDGET: A BUDGET FORMAT in which items are displayed in rows and columns by program and some other dimension (most typically, common functional expenditure classifications).

PROJECT BUDGET: A PROGRAM BUDGET for a fixed-time program of activities.

PROJECT SCHEDULING: The process of sequencing the activities of a project. Techniques useful in such scheduling include Gantt, PERT and PERT-Cost.

PUBLIC DEBT: The total excess of public liabilities over assets. The largest share of public debt in the United States has been accumulated by the federal government. Most public debt is funded.

PUBLIC EXPENDITURE: Outlays by public agencies for goods and services, subsidies and grants, and debt service.

PUBLIC FINANCE: A branch of economics concerned with governmental financial policies and actions, and their impact. Public finance is concerned with taxation as the most important governmental revenue source, and assessment of the fiscal impact of public policy. Social welfare finance consists of elements of public finance, together with voluntary, or non-profit, finance as these apply to the human services.

PUBLIC SECTOR: That portion of the national economy (or local economies) consisting of governmental production and consumption.

PURCHASE ORDER: A standardized form (or facsimile) identifying a purchase and its source, prices, quantities, and other pertinent information. May be the same as a purchase requisition.

PURCHASE REQUISITION: A request for approval to make a purchase. Includes the information on the purchase order, as well as the reason a purchase is necessary, when it is needed, etc. When forms are used, a requisition signed by an authorized official becomes a purchase order. Many human service organizations use memos for both purposes.

RATIO ANALYSIS: The analytic protocol for identifying key decision points in administrative systems, and the identification of a system of quantitative ratios to monitor changes at those points.

RESERVES: Liquid or fixed ASSETS in a FUND not committed to PROGRAM during the current fiscal period.

RESOURCE ALLOCATION: Decision or choice processes in which the administration determines what resources are available, and to what production and distribution processes they will be devoted. Budgeting is an important resource allocation process for most human service agencies.

RESOURCES: The agents or factors of production used to produce and distribute goods and services. The term also has a somewhat broader usage in the new political economy (Ilchman & Uphoff), where it signifies the agents that produce outputs, or results.

REVENUE: See INCOME.

RISK: A condition in which particular decision or action strategies carry a range of possible outcomes (including possible negative or undesirable consequences), none of which can be determined in advance. Operations research has devised a series of techniques and procedures for estimating and handling risk.

RISK CAPITAL: Long-term funds invested in activities subject to risk. Also sometimes known as SEED MONEY.

SEED MONEY: Contributions or other REVENUES contributed prior to the start of a program, especially to finance the initial costs before regular funding is in place. (Also called FRONT MONEY.)

SLIDING SCALE FEES: Charges to clients which fluctuate by some meaningful criterion, such as "ability to pay."

SOCIAL COSTS: Cost of an activity, output, or PROGRAM that are borne by society as a whole. The term is used both technically and euphemistically as a synonym for the social consequences of economic actions, e.g., the forced leisure of unemployed ghetto youths as a "social cost" of automation.

SOURCES OF REVENUE BUDGET: A listing of dollar and percentage of total revenue figures by major sources of revenue.

SPECIAL EVENT: A set of activities intended to promote PROGRAMS, causes, or ideas in order to improve relations with the DONOR CONSTITUENCY, or in other ways improve or expand COMMUNITY ACCOUNTABILITY, or increase support.

SPECIAL STUDIES: Cost analyses, evaluations, and other "one time" analyses conducted to resolve specific management problems.

STANDARDS: Criteria used in EVALUATION of performance.

SUB-FUND DECISIONS: Decisions affecting only a portion of the assets in a FUND.

SUPERVISION: A key aspect of fiscal control in NON-PROFIT human service systems.

SUPPLIES BUDGET: A BUDGET FORMAT detailing expenditures in the supplies classification.

SUPRA-FUND DECISIONS: Decisions affecting the ASSETS in more than one FUND, typically the whole agency.

TAX: A mandatory charge required by a government of some element of its economic environment. Intended to be used as revenue by that government.

THIRD-PARTY FEES: Charges to clients for services rendered that are paid by a "third party" (someone other than the client or the agency rendering the service).

THIRD-PARTY FUNDING: FEES or GRANTS or PERFORMANCE CONTRACTS that provide for support of a program by someone other than those receiving the service.

UNIT-COST BUDGET: Anticipated expenditures are projected in this BUDGET FORMAT by a formula of units of service produced multiplied by the standard cost per unit.

VARIABLE COSTS: Costs that vary directly with changes in the level of output. Also known as "direct cost." The opposite of FIXED COST.

VOLUNTARY FEDERATED DISTRIBUTIONS: A BUDGET SYSTEM in which agencies that are members of a common FUND-RAISING group receive proportionate shares of the FUNDS raised.

ZERO-BASED BUDGETING: A budget system in which decisions are made on "decision packages" that must be justified programatically.

ZERO-SUM BUDGET: Budget FORMATS in which no presumption of a BASE is allowed.

ADDITIONAL
REFERENCES

CHAPTER 1

Advisory Commission on Intergovernmental Relations. *The Gap Between Federal Aid Authorizations and Appropriations: FY 1966-1970.* (Washington, D.C.: The Commission in Cooperation with Council of State Governments, 1970.

Forder, Anthony. "Needs." *Concepts in Social Administration: A Framework for Analysis.* London: Routledge, Kegan Paul, 1974.

Gavin, Donald P. *The National Conference of Catholic Charities, 1910-1960.* Milwaukee: Bruce Press, 1962.

Gruber, Murray. "Total Administration." *Social Work* 19 (1974): 625-37.

Heath, Anthony. *Rational Choice and Social Exchange.* Cambridge, England: Cambridge University Press, 1976.

Ilchman, Warren, and Norman Uphoff. *The Political Economy of Change.* Berkeley: University of California Press, 1969.

Merriam, Ida. "Financing Social Welfare: Expenditures." *Encyclopedia of Social Work*, 16th ed., ed. Robert Morris, pp. 416-25. New York: National Association of Social Workers, 1970.

Merriam, Ida C., and Alfred M. Skolnik. *Social Welfare Expenditures Under Public Programs in the United States, 1929-1966*, Research Report No. 25. Washington, D.C.: G.P.O., 1968.

Mogulof, Melvin B. "Special Revenue Sharing and the Social Services." *Social Work* 18 (1973): 9-15.

301

National Institute of Mental Health. *Financial Administration and Mental Health Services*. Washington, D.C.: The Institute, 1968.

Pifer, Alan. *The Quasi-Governmental Organization*. New York: Carnegie Corp., 1967.

Rice, Dorothy P., and Barbara S. Cooper. "National Health Expenditures, 1929-1968." *Social Security Bulletin* 34, no. 1 (1970): 3-20.

Shuckett, Donald H., and Edward J. Mock. *Decision Strategies in Financial Management*. New York: American Management Association, 1973.

Solomon, Ezra. *The Theory of Financial Management*. New York: Columbia University Press, 1963.

CHAPTER 2

Briar, Scott. "The Age of Accountability." *Social Work* 18 (1973): 2.

Cruthirds, C. Thomas, "Management Should Be Accountable Too." *Social Work* 21 (1976): 179-80.

Demont, B. C., and P. A. Demont. "Practical Approach to Accountability." *Educational Technology* 13 (1973): 40.

Goldberg, S. P. "Accounting in Social Welfare." *Encyclopedia of Social Work*, 16th ed., ed. Robert Morris, pp. 2-8. New York: National Association of Social Workers, 1970.

Ishizaki, D. M., D. G. Thurman, and B. M. Ecker. "Research Service Partnership: Implications for Social Work Practice Accountability." *Gerontologist* 13 (1973): 105.

Kravitz, Sanford. "Dilemmas of Accountability." *Journal of Voluntary Action* 3 (1973): 105.

Newman, Edward, and Jerry Turem. "The Crisis of Accountability." *Social Work* 19 (1974): 5-16.

Rogers, I. L. "Emerging Patterns of Administrative Accountability." *Peabody Journal of Education* 50 (1973): 3-19.

Rosenberg, Marvin L., and Ralph Brody. "The Threat of Challenge of Accountability." *Social Work* 19 (1974): 344-50.

Simon, Herbert, "A Behavioral Model of Rational Choice." *Quarterly Journal of Economics* 69 (1955): 99-118.

Smith, Bruce L. R. "Accountability and Independence in the Contract State." *The Dilemma of Accountability in Modern Government: Independence Versus Control*, ed. B. L. R. Smith and D. C. Hague, pp. 31-69. New York: St. Martin's Press, 1971.

Turem, Jerry. "The Call for a Management Stance. *Social Work* 19 (1974): 615-24.

United Community Funds and Councils of America, Inc. *Accounting for Community Chests and United Funds: Principles and Methods*. Rev. ed. New York: The Funds, 1956.

Vasey, Wayne. *Government and Social Welfare: Roles of Federal, State, and Local Governments in Administering Welfare Services*. New York: Henry Holt, 1958.

Vatter, William J. *The Fund Theory of Accounting and Its Implications for Financial Reports*. Chicago: University of Chicago Press, 1947.

Wade, L. L., and R. L. Curry. *A Logic of Public Policy: Aspects of Political Economy*. Belmont, Calif.: Wadsworth, 1970.

CHAPTER 3

Advisory Commission on Intergovernmental Relations. *The Role of Equalization in Federal Grants*. Washington, D.C.: The Commission, 1964.

Andrews, F. Emerson. *Philanthropic Foundations*. New York: Russell Sage, 1956.

Boulding, Kenneth E., and Martin Pfaff, eds. *Redistribution to the Rich and the Poor: The Grants Economics of Income Distribution*. Belmont, Calif.: Wadsworth, 1972.

Boulding, Kenneth E., Martin Pfaff, and Anita Pfaff. *Transfer in an Urbanized Economy: Theory and Effects of the Grants Economy*. Belmont, Calif.: Wadsworth, 1973.

Cohen, Jacob, and Morton Grodzins. "How Much Economic Sharing in American Federalism?" *American Political Science Review* 57 (1963): 5-23.

Conrad, P. R. "Do's and Don'ts of Grantsmanship." *Child Welfare* 52 (1973): 4-47.

Hardcastle, David A. "General Revenue Sharing and Social Work." *Social Work* 18, no. 5 (1973): 3-9.

Hill, William G. "Voluntary and Governmental Financial Transactions." *Social Casework* 52 (1971): 356-61.

Hoshino, George. "Social Services: The Problem of Accountability." *Social Service Review* 47 (1973): 373-83.

Terrell, Paul. "Citizen Participation and General Revenue Sharing." *Social Work* 20 (1975): 429-35.

"The Big OEO/MC/Annual Arrangement/Planned Variation/IGS PNRS/Allied Services/MRS/BCA/Revenue Sharing Power Trip." *Restructuring the Federal System: Approaches to Accountability in Post-Categorical Programs*, ed. Joseph D. Sneed and Steven A. Waldhorn. New York; Crane Russak, 1975.

CHAPTER 5

Adams, Dwight. "Fund Executives and Social Change." *Social Work* 17 (1972): 68-75.

Cutlip, Scott M. *Fundraising in the United States: Its Role in America's Philanthropy*. New Brunswick. Rutgers University Press, 1965. See p. 535.

Ford, L. S. "Federated Financing." *Encyclopedia of Social Work*, 15th ed., ed. Fidele Fauri, pp. 327-32. New York: National Association of Social Works, 1965.

Katz, Harvey. *Give! Who Gets Your Charity Dollar?* Garden City, N.Y.: Anchor Press, 1974.

Levin, Herman. "The Essential Voluntary Agency." *Social Work* 11 (1966): 98–106.

Lewis, Marianna O., ed. *The Foundation Directory.* 3rd ed. New York: Russell Sage Foundation, 1967.

Loewenberg, Frank M., ed. *Professional Components in Education for Fundraising.* New York: Council on Social Work Education, 1975.

Seeley, John R. et al. *Community Chest: A Case Study in Philanthropy.* Toronto: University of Toronto Press, 1957.

Sills, David A. "Raising Funds." *The Volunteers: Means and Ends in a National Organization.* Glencoe, Ill. Free Press, 1957. pp. 149–73.

Voluntary Health and Welfare Agencies in the United States: An Exploratory Study by an Ad Hoc Committee. New York: Schoolmasters Press, 1961.

Zander, Alvin, and Theodore Newcomb, Jr. "Group Levels of Aspiration in United Fund Campaign." *Journal of Personality and Social Psychology* 6, no. 2 (1967): 157–62.

CHAPTER 6

Advisory Commission on Intergovernmental Relations. *Federal Approaches to Aid State and Local Capital Financing.* Washington, D.C.: The Commission, 1970.

Anton, Thomas J. *The Politics of State Expenditure in Illinois.* Champagne-Urbana, Ill.: University of Illinois Press, 1966.

Burkhead, Jesse. *Government Budgeting.* New York: Wiley, 1956.

Fenno, Richard. *The Power of the Purse: Appropriations Politics in Congress.* Boston: Little, Brown, 1966.

Fox, H. W. "Humanizing Budgetary Systems for Administrative Reinforcement." *Personnel Journal* 52 (1973): 52.

Goodman, Nathaniel. "The Catch in Functional Budgeting: To What End?" *Social Work* 14 (1969): 40–48.

Howard, S. Kenneth. *Changing State Budgeting.* Lexington, Ky.: Council of State Governments, 1973.

Lee, Robert D., and Johnson, Ronald. *Public Budgeting Systems.* 2nd ed. Baltimore: University Park Press, 1977.

March, Michael, and Edward Newman. "Financing Social Welfare: Government Allocation Procedures." *Encyclopedia of Social Work*, 16th ed., ed. Robert Morris, pp. 426–43. New York: National Association of Social Workers.

Milhouse, A. M. *State Capital Budgeting.* Chicago: Council of State Governments, 1963.

Minmeir, George S. *An Evaluation of the Zero-Base Budgeting System in Governmental Institutions.* Research Monograph no. 68. Atlanta: Georgia State University, 1975.

National Association of State Budgetary Officials, Institute on Welfare. *Budgeting for Public Assistance.* Lexington, Ky.: University of Kentucky, 1969.

Niskanen, William A. "Improving U.S. Budget Choices." *Tax Foundation Tax Review*, vol. 32, no. 11 (1971).

Rautenstrauch, Walter, and Raymond Villers. *Budgetary Control.* New York: Funk and Wagnalls, 1957.

Samuels, Warren J. *Pareto on Policy.* New York: Elsevier, 1974.

Sharkansky, Ira. "Budget Innovation in the States." *American Political Science Review* 67 (1973): 1,029.

Simon, Herbert A. "A Behavioral Model of Rational Choice." *Quarterly Journal of Economics* 69 (1955): 99–118.

Swieringa, Robert J., and Robert H. Moncur. *Some Effects of Participative Budgeting on Managerial Behavior.* New York: National Association of Accountants, 1975.

United Nations, Economic and Social Council. *Report of the Secretary to the 16th Session of the Social Commission: Methods of Determining Social Allocation* (March 31, 1965).

Wildavsky, Aaron. "Annual Expenditure Increment: Or How Congress Can Regain Control of the Budget." *Public Interest* 7 (1973): 84–102.

CHAPTER 7

Anshen, Melvin. "The Federal Budget as an Instrument for Management and Analysis." *Program Budgeting*, ed. David Novick, pp. 3–23. Santa Monica: Rand Corp., 1965.

CHAPTER 8

Holcombe, Newton. "Operational Information for Effective Management." *Child Welfare* 38 (1959): 28–33.

CHAPTER 9

Goodman, Nathaniel. "Salaries, Costs, and Workloads." *Social Work* 4 (1959): 49–57.

Hill, John G. "Cost Analysis in Social Work Service." *Social Work Research*, ed. Norman Polansky, pp. 223–46. Chicago: University of Chicago Press, 1960.

Raider, Melvyn C. "An Evaluation of Management by Objectives." *Social Casework* 56, no. 2. (1975): 79–83.

CHAPTER 10

American Public Welfare Association. *Standard Classification of Public Assistance Costs.* Chicago: The Association, 1942.

Borus, Michael E., John P. Brennan, and Sidney Rosen. "A Benefit-Cost Analysis of the Neighborhood Youth Corps." *Human Service Organizations*, ed. Yeheskel Hasenfeld and Richard English, pp. 660–79. Ann Arbor: University of Michigan Press.

Bureau of the Budget. "Measuring Productivity of Federal Government Organizations." *Public Administration*, ed. Robert Golembrewski, et al., pp. 66–73. Chicago: Rand McNally, 1966.

Department of Health, Education and Welfare. Health Services and Mental Health Administration. *Financial Planning Manual*. Health Maintenance Organization Technical Assistance Publication. Washington, D.C.: G.P.O., 1972.

Dorfman, Robert. *Measuring Benefits of Government Investments*. Washington, D.C.: Brookings Institution, 1965.

Due, John F. *Government Finance: An Economic Analysis*. 3rd ed. Homewood, Ill.: Richard Irwin, 1963.

Elkin, Robert. "Framework for Decision-making: Applying PPBS to Public Welfare Program Structure." *Public Welfare* 29 (1969): 157–66.

Fuchs, Victor R., ed. *Production and Productivity in the Service Industries*. Washington, D.C.: National Bureau of Economic Research, 1969.

Fuchs, Victor R., and Jean Alexander Wilburn. *Productivity Differences Within the Service Sector*. Washington, D.C.: National Bureau of Economic Research, 1967.

Gorham, William. "Allocating Federal Resources Among Competing Social Needs." *HEW Indicators*. Washington, D.C.: G.P.O., Aug. 1966.

Greenberg, Leon. *A Practical Guide to Productivity Measurement*. Washington, D.C.: Bureau of National Affairs, 1973.

Harberger, Arnold C., Robert Haneman, Julius Margolis, William Niskanen, Ralph Turvey, and Richard Zeckhauser. *Benefit Cost Analysis, 1971*. Chicago: Aldine, 1972.

Hill, John G., and Ralph Ormsby. *Cost Analysis Method for Casework Agencies*. Philadelphia: Family Service of Philadelphia, 1953.

Hill, John G., Ralph Ormsby, and William McCurdy. *Time Study Manual*. New York: Family Service Association of America. 1962.

Levin, Richard, and Charles Kirkpatrick. *Planning and Control with PERT*. New York: McGraw-Hill, 1966.

Levine, A. S. "Cost-Benefit Analysis and Social Welfare." *Welfare in Review* 3 (Feb. 1966): 1–11.

Lohmann, Roger. "Break-Even Analysis: A Tool for Effective Budget Planning." *Social Work* 21, (1976): 300–07.

Lohmann, Roger. "Matrix Analysis and Social Planning." Mimeographed, n.d.

Marshall, A. W. *Cost/Benefit Analysis in Health*. Santa Monica: Rand Corp., (1965). See pp. 32–75.

Morris, Milton D. *The Federal A-95 Review Process: Making It Work for Minority Groups*. Washington, D.C.: Joint Center for Political Studies, 1975.

Musgrave, Richard A. *Essays in Fiscal Federalism*. Washington, D.C.: Brookings Institution, 1965.

Mushkin, Selma J. *An Operative PPB System: A Collaborative Undertaking in the States*. Washington, D.C.: George Washington University, 1968.

Niskanen, William A., Arnold C. Harberger, Robert Haneman, Ralph Turvey, and Richard Zechauser, eds. *Benefit-Cost and Policy Analysis, 1972: An Aldine Annual on Forecasting, Decision Making, and Evaluation.* Chicago: Aldine, 1973.

Novick, David. *Program Budgeting.* Cambridge, Mass.: Harvard University Press, 1965.

Office of Economic Opportunity. Systems and Analysis Division, Community Action Program. *PERT for CAA Planning: A Programmed Course of Instruction in PERT.* Vol. 1: OEO Training Manual 6321-1. Washington, D.C.: G.P.O., 1969.

Prest, A. R., and R. Turvy. "Cost-Benefit Analysis: A Survey." *The Economic Journal* 75 (1965): 683–731.

Smithies, Arthur. "Conceptual Framework for the Program Budget." *Program Budgeting,* ed. David Novick, pp. 24–60. Santa Monica: Rand Corp., 1965.

Spindler, Arthur. "PPBS and Social and Rehabilitation Services." *Welfare in Review* 6 (1969): 22–28.

Steffy, Wilbert, Thomas Zearley, and Jack Strunk. *Financial Ratio Analysis: An Effective Management Tool.* Ann Arbor: University of Michigan, 1974.

Thorelli, Hans. "The Tantalizing Concept of Productivity." *American Behavioral Scientist* 4, no. 3. (1960): 6–11.

Troupp, Emanuel. "Expectation, Performance, and Accountability." *Social Work* 19 (1974): 139–48.

CHAPTER 11

Chase, Samuel B., Jr., ed. *Problems in Public Expenditure Analysis.* Washington, D.C.: Brookings Institution 1968.

Tax Foundation, Inc. *Tax Burdens and Benefits of Government Expenditure by Income Classes, 1961 and 1965.* New York: The Foundation, 1967.

Thorow, Lester C. *The Impact of Taxes on the American Economy.* New York: Praeger, 1971.

Titmus, Richard. "The Role of Redistribution in Social Policy." *Commitment to Welfare.* New York: Pantheon, 1968, pp. 188–99.

INDEX

Accountability, 120-21, 206, 237; and administrative cost, 42; of administrators, 60; breaking even, 20-21; and Charity Organization Societies, 26, 27; and entity, 39; movement, 237; in non-profit agencies, 10; and performance contracts, 63; and transactions, 32-33; trend to, 13-14; types of, 26-28; see also Community accountability; Fiscal accountability; Internal accountability

Accountants, 20-21, 27

Accounting, 24; accuracy in, 44; accrual basis, 40-41; basic concepts, 37-39; and budgeting, 122; cash basis, 40; closing, 32; conservatism, 43; consistency, 43; cycle and financial statements, 44; data, 23; and fiscal control, 24-25; flexibility, 133; full disclosure, 44; functional basis, 41; fund, 38; information system, 23, 26, 29; IRS requirements, 26; and management, 48; and management technology, 27; materiality, 44; modified accrual basis, 41; posting, 32; principal responsibilities of, 28-37; and programming, 25; simplicity, 44; standardized reporting

forms, 33; as technology, 24; see also Fund accounting

Accounts payable: budget, 160, 161-62; and cash flow, 131; management, 232-34

Accounts receivable: aging of, 231, 233; billing records, 88-89; budget, 159-61; collecting, 42-43; entries, 32; and fee collections, 88-89, 230-31; and flat rate fees, 84; journal, 28; management, 230-32

Administrative expense, 42

Affirmative action budget, 172

A fortiori analysis, 246

Allocation: and cost measurement, 13; decisions and planning, 128-29; in financial management, 10; internal, 205, 265

American Association of Fund-Raising Counsel, 109

American Cancer Society, 132

American Heart Association, 132

American Institute of Certified Public Accountants (AICPA), 38, 41, 42, 47, 50, 112, 113, 114, 159, 173

Annual fund drives, 101; meetings, 110; reports, 49-50; review of employees, 203

Appropriations, 126

Assets, 38; distribution, 9; expenditure and income effects, 40; liquid, 228

Audits, 35-37; dissemination of, 37; exceptions, 36; internal, 184-85; procedures in fund-raising, 112; reports, 37; statements, 35

Authorizations, 127

Balance: in budget documents, 121, 149; fund, 40

Balance sheet, 34-35

Base: in budget-making, 126; and breaking even, 226; in fund-raising, 66

Benefit-Cost. *See* Cost-benefit analysis

Benefits, 244-45

Black United Funds, 132

Block purchases, 88

Board of directors, 9, 185; and costs of social problems, 218; and debt, 221

Bookkeeping, double-entry, 25-26

Break-even analysis, 226-27

Break-even motive, 15-21

Breaking even, 11-14; and accountability, 20-21; and base, 226; and budget, 121; as central fiscal process, 18-19; and cost principle, 19; as criterion, 19; double-edged nature, 18; and effectiveness, 20; and efficiency, 20; in fee systems, 134; in fiscal control, 20; and fund-raising, 19, 109; as link of fiscal and program objectives, 19-20; and planning, 19-20; and productivity, 20; and program/project

Budget, 119-23; administrative cost, 159-60; affirmative action, 172; analysis, 122; arenas, 123; balanced, 121; and breaking even, 121; brevity in, 149; categories, 150; committee, 98; complexity, 73; consolidated summary, 124, 173, 174-77; as continuous management concern, 125, 129-30; cost of debt, 168-69; cycle, 125; deadlines, 125; decision-making, 135; decisions and analysis, 123, 129; decision systems, 135-46; departmental, 173, 181, 265; direct labor, 165-66; documents, 149; entity, 120; federal deficits, 121; formats, 150-52; functional, 120; fund, 151; fund-raising, 167; guidelines, 125;

headings, 150; hearing, 125; implementation, 125; increment, 66, 73, 126, 136-40; information systems, 149; line item, 127; overhead cost, 95; preliminary proposal, 125; production, 166; program, 120; project, 120, 155; request, 125; revenue-expenditure, 154; review, 125; special purpose, 157-72; statements of operations, 122; strategies, 69-70; supplies, 168; sub-fund, 151; supra-fund, 152; systems, 124; unit cost, 162-65; zero sum, 145-46

Budget-making, 122-23; analogy with accounting, 122; base in, 126; constituencies, 128; and fee systems, 133-34; and formal organization, 127; and informal organization, 128; irony of, 116; numerical imagination in, 146; public distribution, 129-31; strategies, 128; technology, 116; zero-base budgeting, 145

Campaigns: capital, 101; committees, 98; *see also* Fund-raising

Capital budgeting, 161, 162, 168, 219-221; and programming, 184

Capital equipment, 168

Capital expenditures, 208; and fees, 94-95

Capital improvements budget, 161, 162

Case statements, 75; as proposals, 76

Cash flow, 228; and borrowing, 221; management of, 228-30; monthly, 229

Categorical grants, 60

Certified Public Accountant, 27; *see also* American Institute of Certified Public Accountants

Citizen participation, 14

Client populations, 13, 70; and fund-raising, 54; participation, 14

Closing process, 32

Communications, lack of, ix; skill in fund-raising, 78

Community accountability, 27; *see also* Accountability

Community Chests, 102

Community confidence, 72-73

Community profile and sliding scale fees, 85

Constituencies, 70; and advisory groups, 71; in budget-making, 128; donor, 41; pressure from, 72; and programming, 178

Consultants, and reprogramming, 185

Contingency analysis, 246

Contingency funds, 134

Continuity in budget decisions, 129–30

Contracts: and fees, 82; and fiscal control, 113

Control: and fees, 82; and fiscal control, 113

Control, fiscal. *See* Fiscal control

Cost, 245; benefit ratio, 220; and breaking even, 19; fair share of, 86; and fees, 82; fund-raising, 113–14; net, 216; industry standard, 49; opportunity, 216; in performance budgeting, 140; of social problems, 218; and third-party payment, 88

Cost accounting, 46–47; and financial management, 14; and goals, 46; techniques, 46–47; and unit-cost budgets, 162, 164; and UWASIS, 47

Cost analysis, 216; and service mix, 218–19; and special events, 112; studies, 47

Cost-benefit analysis, 242–48; a fortiori approach, 246; contingency approach, 246; and exchange principle, 242–43; fixed benefit approach, 246; fixed cost approach, 246; fixed utility approach, 246; sensitivity approach, 246; synthesis of new alternatives, 247

Cost centers, 164

Cost control, 196; and cost elimination, 211; and monitoring, 204; policies and procedures, 210–11; standards of, 212; *see also* Control; Fiscal control

Cost elimination, 211

Cost of collecting receivables, 42–43

Cost of debt, 168–69

Costing out social problems, 17, 218–19; unit cost approach, 218, 250

Cost measurement, 13, 17

Criteria in fiscal control, 200; of sliding scales, 85

Current community effort, 99

Debt management, 221–22; and board, 221; and capital purchases, 168

Decision packages in zero-based budgeting, 145–46

Decision points, 249

Decision systems, 135–46

Deficit financing, 168, 227

Departmental budgets, 157, 173, 181, 265

Desk-top budget reference, 173, 174–77

Developmental Disabilities Act, 99

Direct fund-raising, 110

Direct labor budgets, 165–66

Disbursement. *See* Expenditure

Donor constituency, 41

Dual-track organizations, 180

Dual-class structure, 81

Effectiveness, 241; and breaking even, 20

Efficiency, 241; and breaking even, 20; and fiscal control, 201–2; in public distributions, 131

Elitist view of fund-raising, 103

Enforcement in fiscal control, 201

Entity: and accountability, 39; budget, 74, 120; and financial reports, 38; fiscal, 37; practical significance, 39

Evaluation, 245; in financial management, 10, 109; in zero-based budgeting, 145

Exceptions and fiscal control, 201; *see also* Management by exceptions

Executor role in agencies, 234

Existing programs, 183–88

Expenditure: control, 10; fund-raising, 42; items in budget documents, 150; matching income, 18; and output, 17; personnel, 203; program, 41–42; public, 12; as transactions, 28

Experience in fund-raising, 109; in marginal analysis, 140

Feasibility: and financing, 217–18; in new agency or program, 218; and opportunity cost, 216

Federated funding, characteristics, 99–100; and distributions, 133; and planning, 132; termination of, 234; and uncertain future, 132

Feedback in fund-raising, 113; deficits, 121; federal budget, 126; fiscal role, 59–60; social mandates, 59–60

Fees, 80–81, 83; abuses in sliding scales, 85–86; and accounts receivable, 84; and billing, 88–89; and breaking even, 134; and capitalization, 94–95; and choice, 82; and client contracts, 82; collections, 230–31; collections journal, 28; and contingency funds, 134; and control, 88–90; and cost allocation, 82; and crisis, 82; disadvantages, 82–83; and dual class, 81; and fairness, 96; and feedback, 89; and fund-raising ethics, 110; fixed, 84; flat rates and income projection, 84; and free goods, 96; indifference approach to predicting, 93; and internal subsidies, 87; and needs, 95–96; participation, 231–32; planning issues, 90–94; and population traits, 84; predicting, 92; range approach to revenues from, 92; receivable, 88–89; recording and collecting, 88–89; and risk, 134; sliding scale, 85; structures, 95–96; systems and budget-making, 133–34; third party, 87–88; and two-class structure, 96; types, 83–87; and unpredictability of income, 82; user, 87; user types, 87; and voluntary services, 81–82; waivers, 96

FIFO, 209

Financial management, 5–8; allocation, 10; and breaking even, 18–19; and computers, 14; and cost accounting, 14; evaluation in, 10, 109; and expenditure control, 10; fund-raising, 10; and general integration of knowledge, xii; management, 7–8; state of the art, 11–12

Financial manager and audits, 36; and training, 14

Financial planning, 215

Financial ratios in business, 252; in human services, 253

Financial statements, 44–46, 121

Fiscal accountability, 27, 131, 206

Fiscal control, 199–203; and accounting, 24–25; and amendment, 201; and breaking even, 20; and contracts, 200; and cost control, 196; criteria, 200; and efficiency, 201; and enforcement, 201; and fairness, 196; and feedback, 202; fixed expenses, 229; in fund-raising campaigns, 106–7; incentives, 199–200; and internal budgets, 205–6; and management by exception, 196–97, 201; and meaning, 202; and morale, 213; and motivation, 200; and productivity, 202; and social control, 200; and supervision, 203–5

Fiscal flow model, 253–4

Fiscal impact, 239

Fiscal and program objectives, 39; in cost accounting, 46

Fiscal structure of agency, 249; observation points, 249; working model, 250–51

Fixed budget analysis, 246

Fixed utility analysis, 246

Flexibility, 44

Formal organization, 217

Foundations, 133

Free goods, 96

Fringe benefits checklist, 267

Full disclosure, 44

Functional basis, 41

Functional budget, 120

Fund, 38; accounting, 3, 38; balance, 40; decisions, and budget formats, 151

Fund-raising, 51–55, 100; agencies, 54; agent, 66–79, 108–9; askers, 75; audit procedures, 112; base, 66; and breaking even, 19, 109; budget, 167; campaigns, 100, 101; chairman, 75; clients, 54; communication, 78; confidence in, 73; control in, 77, 106–7; costs, 113–14; counsel, 110; direct, 110; elitist view, 103; and emotion, 105; expenditures, 42; experience in, 109; feedback, 113; and fees, 83; and financial management, 10; formal proposals, 68–69, 75; and honesty, 75; and human behavior, 104; and influence, 74, 79; and information 73, 77, 107; knowledge in, 78, 104; and leadership, 75, 102; and management by exceptions, 108; and management of collections, 112–13; and management decisions, 67; management fund raiser. 78–79; mass solicitations, 74; and motivation, 102–6; in multi-funded agencies, 53; mutual respect in, 73; needs-goals philosophy of, 76; negotiations in, 73; in non-profit agencies, 10;

organized, 74–76; organizing, 106–8; as occupation, 108; planning, 74, 78, 107–8; private grants, 74; professional services, 170; program, 155; responsibility, 52; strategies, 67, 76; taxes, 54–55; and technological skill, 78; two-tier approach, 75; typology, 54; and volunteer organizations, 106; and volunteers, 104

Gantt chart, 189, 222, 223, 224
General financing problems of human services, 17–20
General journal, 28
Givers, 54
Goal matrix, 142
Grants: and budget, 129; as redistribution, 58–59; see also Categorical grant; Limited categorical grant; Performance contracts; Program grant; Revenue sharing
Grantsman role, 64
Grantsmanship, 63–64, 65
Guidelines, 125

Hierarchial balance of salary structure, 198
Hiring in non-profit agency, 10
Human service, 8–9; administrators, xiii; ratios for, 253

Implementation. See Programming
Incentives and fiscal control, 199–200; and programming, 184
Income, and assets, 40; as transaction, 28; unpredictable, 82
Incorporation checklist, 267
Increment, budget, 126; in fund-raising, 66
Incremental budgeting, 136–40
Incrementalism, 73; in zero-based budgeting, 145
Indifference curves, 93
Individuality and fiscal control, 200–201
Industry standard costs, 49
Influence in fund-raising, 74, 79
Informal organization, 128
Information systems, 172; see also Accounting information system; Budget information system
Information, control, 206–7; and fees, 89
Information in fund-raising, 107, 73, 77

In-kind contributions, 43
Integration of accounting and management, 48–49
Integrity, organizational in program budgeting, 142
Interest and discount, 220
Intergovernmental cash transfers, 59
Internal accountability, 26–27
Internal allocation processes, 265
Internal audits, 184–85
Internal budgets, 205–6
Internal subsidy, 87
Inventory control, 209–10

Journal, 28; accounts receivable, 28; fee collection, 28; general, 28; payroll, 28, 30; travel, 31

Labor markets and salaries, 199
Land and debt, 168
Land grants, 58–59
Legal authority, 235
Legal checklist, 267
Liabilities, 38, 40; and phase-out, 188
Licensed Public Accountant, 27
LIFO, 209
Limited categorical grants, 62
Line-item budget, 120, 127, 155; entries, 153; and program matrix, 156
Lines of credit, 182, 265; and special events, 112
Linking decisions and implementation, 143
Logic of budget documents, 149

Mail contributions, 112–13
Management by exceptions, 23–24, 201; and fiscal control, 196–97; and fund-raising, 108; and programming, 183
Management by objectives, 14
Management Information System, 248–49; accounts payable, 232–34; accounts receivable, 230–32; cash flow, 228–30; of collections, 112–13; of debt, 221–22; fund raiser, 78–79; knowledge and skill, 13; science techniques, 13, 27; and special events, 110; and supervision, 13; surveys, 184–85

Managerial revolution in human services, 3, 52
Marginal analysis, 136–40; and conflict, 139; experience in, 140; situational assessment, 139; time in, 138
Matching income and expenditures, 18–19. *See* Breaking even
Medicaid and Medicare, 87
Methods of financing, 217–18
Model cities, 99
Money as measure, 15–16
Motivation and fiscal control, 200; and fund-raising, 102–6
Multi-funded agency, 45, 99; and budgets, 173; and fund-raising, 53; preparation of reports in, 33

Names, in budget documents, 150; in fund-raising, 108
National center for non-profit human service finance, 114, 262
National service delivery systems, 12
National Social Welfare Assembly, 112
Needs, and fees, 95–96; and goals in fund-raising, 76
Net present value, 220
New programs and programming, 180–81; and feasibility, 218
Non-profit agencies, accounting systems, 26; characteristics of, 9–10; distribution of assets, 9; executor role, 234; fiscal structure, 249; fund-raising, 10; personnel in, 10

Observation points in fiscal structure, 249
Office setup checklist, 266
Older Americans Act, 99
Old year/new year tables, 170–71
Open awareness, 207
Organizational: change, 234; death, 234; research, 14
Output, and expenditures, 17; measurement and quality, 141; and performance budgets, 86; as productivity, 141; and unit cost budgets, 164
Outside fund raiser, 108–9

Participation fees, 83–84, 231–32; and supervision, 84

Past data in budgets, 155–56
Past and future in marginal analysis, 138
Payback method, 220
Payroll journal, 28, 30
Performance budgets, 140–42; and cost, 140; and output assessment, 140
Performance monitoring, 204
Performance objectives, 23, 63; statement, 34–35
Personal: liability checklist, 267; services and human services, 8
Personnel, 203; selection, ix
Persuasion and fund-raising, 79
PERT, 14, 189, 222–26
Petty cash fund, 207
Philadelphia cost studies, 47
Planning: and accounting, 25; administrative, 215; and allocations decisions, 19–20, 128–29; and breaking even, 19; and fees, 90–94; in financial management, 10, 122; and fiscal reorganization, 234–35; and fund-raising, 74, 77, 107–8; and income projection, 84; and internal budget, 205; and programming, 178; social, 214–15; and special events, 111; systems, 14
Policy: cost control, 210–11; feasibility of change, 217; guidelines, 182–83; manuals, 184; and procedures review, 187–88; and programming checklist, 265
Political action and non-profit agencies, 10
Political sophistication, 78
Post-audit actions, 36–37
Post budget conferences, 185–87, 265
Posted ledger entries, 33
Posting, 32
PPBS, 14, 123, 144–45
Practical problems, 15–21
Practice theory, xi
Predicting: costs, 86; fee revenues, 90–94
Preparation of reports, 33–35
Price, 217, 245
Private grants, 74
Problem-free interval, 239–41
Production budget, 166–67
Productivity, 241–42; and breaking even, 20; and fiscal control, 202; as output, 141
Professional and para-professional services budget, 169–70

Profit, 15; motive, 1-2

Program: and breaking even, 19; budgets, 142-43, 155; developer, 189-90; expenditures, 41-42, 142; grants, 61-62; matrix, 156; objectives, 39

Programming, 178-79; and accounting, 25; benchmarks, 179; in campaigns, 184; and constituencies, 178; in dual tract organizations, 180; in existing programs, 183-88; and incentives, 184; and management by exceptions, 183; new programs, 180-81; and phase out, 188-89; and planning, 178; and policy guidelines, 182-83; policy manuals, 184; and precedents, 183; and sunset laws, 184; three-stage model, 177; and time, 179

Project budgets, 153, 155; goal matrix, 142; and special events, 111-12

Project scheduling, 222-26

Proliferation of services, 13

Proposal writing, 68-69, 77

Public distribution budgeting, 129-31

Public expenditures, 12

Purposive accounting, 48

Purchasing, 207; advance approval, 208; control, 207-9; discretionary, 211

Quality control and budget decisions, 130

Quantities in unit-cost budget, 164

Quarterly Administrative Cost Budget, 160; cash flow projection, 230

Range approach, 92

Ratio analysis, 248-54; trend analysis in, 250

Rational control, 199-200

Reallocation, 197

Reconciliation of checking accounts, 32

Recording: transactions, 28-32; fee payments, 88-89

Recordkeeping in fund-raising campaigns, 113

Recruitment of volunteers, 107

Red Feather, 132

Reporting: checklist, 266; by fund, 45-46; and fiscal control, 201

Reprogramming, 184-85

Resource allocation, 52

Responsibility in fund-raising campaigns, 106

Retired couples budget, 85

Revenue: expenditure budget, 154; and income, 40; items in budget documents, 150; sharing, 62-63, 131; see also Income

Risk, capital, 134; and fair share of cost, 86; and public distributions, 130-31

Rules in fiscal control, 200

Sacrificial giving, 75; guidelines for, 103

Salaries, 197-99

Satisficing, 137

Scheduling checklist, 266

Seed money, 94-95

Sensitivity analysis, 246

Self-study in reprogramming, 184-85

Service delivery, 13

Service mix, 218-19

Signed reports, 113

Simplicity, 44

Situational assessment, 139

Sliding scale fees, 85-86

Social: planning, 214-15; policy planning, 215; control, 200; workers, stereotypes, 20-21; services, 8

Sources of Revenue Table, 158

Special events, 101; annual meetings, 110; and cost analysis, 112; and direct fund-raising, 110; lines of credit, 112; and management decisions, 110-12; planning, 111; and project budgets, 111-12

Special studies, 206; of feasibility, 215-18

Special purpose budgets, 157-72

Speculative borrowing, 221-22

Staff fund raiser, 108-9

Standardization, 164-65

Standardized report forms, 33

Strategy, in budget-making, 69-70, 128; with constituencies, 71; in fund-raising, 67, 76

Statements: of performance, 34-35, 45, 122; of conditions, 34-35, 45, 122

Sub-fund budgets, 151

Summarizing transactions, 32-33

Sunset laws, 131; and programming, 184

Supervision: of bookkeeping, 29; checklist, 266; and management, 13; in fiscal control, 203-5; and participation, 84

Supplies budget, 167–68
Supply and demand of staff, 199
Support services, 41
Supra-fund budgets, 152
Surplus, 227
Survey Research Center, 85
Synthesis of new alternatives, 247

Technical skill, 78
Techniques: cost accounting, 46–47; fund accounting, 3
Terminations: of mail service, 234; of memberships, 234
Theft, 209–10
Theory, grants, 58–63
Third-party payments: block purchases, 88; and fees, 87; real costs, 88; and vendor payments, 88
Time: frames, 179; horizons, 179; lines, 222–23; sense, 179; sequences, 179; units, 164
Title XX, 87, 99
Toeholds, 138
Top-flight leadership, 102
Transactions, 28, 32–33, 39–41
Transcending control, 48
Transfer of assets, 235
Transfer payments, 58
Travel journal, 31
Trend analysis, 250
Trial balance, 33, 34
Trust, 73
Two-class service system, 96
Two-tier fund-raising, 75
Types of fees, 83–87; from user's perspective, 87–88

Uncollected fees, 231
Understanding, 200
United Way, 41, 47, 50, 100, 116, 123, 132; and cost accounting, 47; as public utility, 132
Unit comparison, 250
Unit cost: budget, 162–65; centers, 164; and cost accounting, 162; information, 250; and output units, 164; and social problems, and standardization, 164, 165; time units, 164
United Way of American Service Information System (UWASIS), 250; and PPBS, 145
Unpaid fees receivable, 89
Urban Workers Family Budget, 85
User fees, 87

Vagueness of issues, 77–78
Vendor payments, 88
Voluntary organizations, 106; and fair share of cost, 86; and fees, 81–82
Volunteers in fund-raising, 104; reports from, 113

War chests, 101
War on Poverty, 99
Working models of fiscal structure, 250–51
Work load review, 204
Write-offs of uncollected fees, 231

Zero-based budgeting (ZBB), 123, 145–46
Zero-sum budget systems, 126, 131